ALLENDE'S
CHILE

An Inside View

ALLENDE'S CHILE

by Edward Boorstein

INTERNATIONAL PUBLISHERS, New York

© 1977 by International Publishers Co., Inc.
All rights reserved
Fifth Printing, 1987
Manufactured in the United States of America

Library of Congress Cataloging in Publication Data

Boorstein, Edward, 1915–
    Allende's Chile.

    Includes bibliographical references and index.
        1. Chile—Politics and government—1970–
    2. Allende Gossens, Salvador, 1908–1973. I. Title.
    F3100.B66   320.9'83'064   77-4894
    ISBN 0-7178-0494-1
    ISBN 0-7178-0488-7 pbk

To Jaime Barrios

Who fought in the Presidential Palace till the end
And was murdered in cold blood the next day
By the soldiers of the fascist junta
And to Nancy
For her bravery

Acknowledgements

People in many parts of the United States, and also in Canada, Mexico, Cuba, and Europe kindly made available to me materials on Chile. The Louis M. Rabinowitz Foundation gave me a generous grant to write this book. My wife Reggie, Victor Perlo, and Louis Diskin made criticisms and suggestions which have greatly improved it. To all, I am deeply grateful.

Contents

To understand a revolution and its actors, it is necessary to observe from very close and to judge from very far: extremes which are hard to bring together.

Bolivar

The basic question of every revolution is that of state power.

Lenin

Preface

Nothing impresses some people as much as failure, and the temporary failure of the Chilean Revolution has tended to obscure the achievement of the Chilean revolutionaries. Through years—decades—of patient, day-to-day struggle, often while suffering brutal repression, the Communist and Socialist parties built up strong mass backing. Against a historical heritage of differences, they forged an essential unity, eventually welding together the Popular Unity coalition of six parties. How difficult it is to achieve such unity, and how vital, can best be gaged by considering the experience of the fractured Left in many other countries. During the Popular Unity (UP) government, the Chilean revolutionaries struggled with flawless courage and often great skill and flexibility against powerful enemies—the experienced Chilean oligarchy and the rich, cunning U.S. imperialists who stood behind it. To defeat the UP government, the imperialists were forced to make an enormous and painstaking effort, to deploy a wide range of weapons, including their ultimate one—fascism. Even while going down in defeat, the UP government made an enduring contribution to the process of revolution in Chile, leaving the workers and their allies—in Spanish, *el pueblo,* the ordinary people—with the memory of a government that was *theirs,* that worked for them, not for the foreign and domestic monopolies and the rich. "Its thousand days were the brightest in the history of the Chilean people . . ."[1] All this is a heritage that will tell in the struggle ahead.

I offer this book in the hope that it will shed light on the revolutionary process that unfolded under the UP government, clarify some of the lessons for my fellow Americans and others. For this book to be fully useful, I have to also write about mistakes. The Chilean revolutionaries themselves would not have it otherwise. Volodia Teitelboim of the Political Commission of the Communist Party of Chile can serve as example: "The Chilean events raise many problems that go far beyond our country and have evoked unabating interest throughout the world. . . . Analysis of Chile's problems is not the monopoly of the Chileans. It is the right of all revolutionary parties, of everyone who is not indifferent to the fate of other nations, and everyone is free to pass judgment. We do not intend to hide behind a wall of so-called ideological nationalism, maintaining that we alone are entitled to speak of our mistakes. . . . Friendly . . . criticism . . . only helps us."[2]

Still one must be careful in talking about mistakes. Many of the "mistakes" attributed to the Chilean revolutionaries were not mistakes at all. Some writers have accused the Chilean leaders of the most outlandish things—failure to understand the elementals of Marxism-Leninism, the problem of the state, the need to arm the people, etc. Such criticisms are worse than useless; they sow confusion. They tell a great deal about the lack of understanding of those who make them and nothing about the Chilean leaders. These leaders were Marxists, people tested in long years of practical political struggle. They knew the elementals and far more. If the problems had been half as simple as some of the critical writers describe them, these leaders would have solved them ten times over. Mistakes were made, but on an altogether different level. To truly understand the mistakes, one must first understand the difficulties—why the easy, formulalike solutions presented by some critics were not possible.

As a matter of general perspective, one should keep in mind what a revolutionary struggle is like—many-sided, complex, full of uncertainties, dangerous—and that it is, of course, much easier to write books than to manage revolutionary reality.

1

A Personal Introduction

In early 1971 my Chilean friend Jaime Barrios, with whom I had worked in Cuba during the early years of the Cuban Revolution, invited me to work with the Popular Unity government in Chile. I was unable for personal reasons to move to Chile immediately, so Jaime arranged for me to be advisor to Javier Urrutia, president of the Chile Trading Corporation in New York and coordinator of all other Chilean state agencies in that city. I worked at Chile Trading from March 1971 till September 1972, and then left for Chile to work as assistant to Jaime who was at first general manager of the Central Bank and then economic advisor to President Allende.

Jaime and I felt keenly our experience in Cuba. We had seen there the fierceness of the imperialist resistance to the revolution. Almost constantly for many months we had lived in the expectation that the imperialists would intervene militarily—send in the marines, attack with mercenaries, do something. We felt that the struggle in Chile was also one of life or death. We hardly ever met without discussing the problem of coup d'etat.

We were also struck by the fact that, along with underlying similarities, there were important differences between Cuba and Chile. Chile's political traditions were different; democracy and constitutionalism had a longer history and were more deeply-rooted; much of revolutionary strategy and many specific tactics had to be different.

In the midst of the struggle in Chile, you developed a sense of how varied yet basically fierce it was. You saw and heard it every time you read a newspaper or turned on the radio; the hammering away for and against the government was constant and relentless to a degree going far beyond ordinary politics. You followed it in countless forms—elections for Congress; efforts by Congress to stymie the president by rejecting the laws he proposed or impeaching one minister after another; elections to determine whether UP or opposition people would head the University of Chile, or lead a student federation, or the union at the Chuquicamata copper mine; legal proceedings to determine who would control the Channel 9 television station; court actions against Chile by the Kennecott Copper Corporation in New York, Paris, Amsterdam, and Stockholm; street demonstrations; political statements or newspaper editorials aimed at winning the armed forces; strikes to weaken the economy and soften the government in preparation for its overthrow.

Part of the dynamics of a revolutionary struggle is that it sharpens and limits available choices, cutting the ground from intermediate possibilities. What would the overthrow of the UP government mean? Fidel Castro, on December 2, 1971, in the farewell speech of a twenty-five day visit spoke clearly:

"We have seen fascism in action. . . .

What do the exploiters do when their institutions no longer guarantee their domination? How do they react when the mechanisms historically depended upon to maintain their domination fail them? They simply go ahead and destroy them."[1]

The coup, when it came, struck with shocking ferocity. The morning of the first day, my wife and I, listening to the radio, heard orders by the military to the UP-controlled radio stations to go off the air immediately or they would be "attacked by both land and air." Later a voice announced: "The women have five minutes to leave the Moneda (presidential palace) before the bombing begins." Soon the planes screamed by. In the afternoon, an announcement declared that all those fighting against the junta

after 3:30 P.M. would upon capture be shot immediately—
"resistance is futile; you have seen what we can do by what we
did at the Moneda."

One night the members of the junta made statements on
television. Gustavo Leigh, head of the air force, declared that the
junta would "extirpate the cancer of Marxism" from Chile.
Augusto Pinochet, head of the army and president of the junta,
announced that the Congress was suspended "until further
notice." Soon the junta banned the UP political parties, "re-
cessed" the other parties, and abolished The Central Workers
Confederation. It also took over the universities and began a
massive purge of "leftist extremists" among faculty and students.

Jaime and his wife, Nancy, entered the Moneda early on the
morning of the coup. Nancy left with the other women shortly
before noon when President Allende ordered them to do so. After
a long afternoon of flight through the fighting in the center of
town, she found asylum in the Mexican Embassy. Jaime fought in
the Moneda to the end.

Edicts ordering UP political figures and government officials to
turn themselves in began to be read on the first day of the coup.
My wife and I listened intently to the lists and soon heard the
names of friends and people I had worked with. Frequent
warnings about "thousands of foreign extremists in Chile" followed during the next few days. We picked up a leaflet on the
street which said: "There will be no mercy toward foreign
extremists who have come to Chile to kill Chileans. Citizens, stay
alert to discover and denounce them to the nearest authority."

We decided that it was only a question of time before the junta
got around to arresting me and that we ought to get out of its
reach as quickly as possible. With the help of Nancy we obtained
asylum in the Mexican Embassy six days after the coup. Our
decision to act quickly turned out to be right. On October 5, the
junta published an order for my arrest, but by this time we were
in Mexico City.

At the Mexican Embassy, we eagerly asked Nancy for news of
Jaime. There was no firm news, only contradictory rumors.
Neither Nancy, his children, nor their friends could find out what
had happened to him. Months later the news came. Jaime had

been murdered in cold blood, shot within hours after having been captured at the Moneda and taken to the Tacna regiment of Santiago.

Why did the junta kill so many people—two thousand according to *The New York Times,* and fifteen thousand according to Harald Edelstam, the former Swedish Ambassador to Chile, who does not have the interests of U.S. imperialism to defend? Because the junta, as well as the Chilean bourgeoisie, and the U.S. imperialists who stand behind them, needed this terror to be able to rule.

Revolutions teach. A revolutionary struggle makes clear interests which ordinarily are hidden, brings out forces which ordinarily are latent, moves the different classes to resort to weapons which ordinarily are held in reserve. Not just successful revolutions, but also unsuccessful revolutionary struggles contain lessons. (The Paris Commune was studied carefully by Marx and Lenin and yielded some of the most important principles of socialist revolution.)[2]

Through its very failure, the Chilean Revolution illustrates a number of Marxist-Leninist principles. It shows the masses of Chile and other countries, through experience, that there is no such animal as armed forces which are simply "professional"— above classes, loyal to constitution and law above all else. It confirms that without winning state power and eliminating the bourgeois state, you cannot construct socialism.

But besides confirming basic principle, the Chilean experience also adds to our knowledge of revolution because it is in certain respects unique, a first—a revolutionary process started on the basis of an election victory. In all previous socialist revolutions, armed struggle came before the revolutionaries took over the government. Only when they had won state power did they have to assume the responsibilities of government. In the Chilean Revolution, the election victory gave the Unidad Popular the responsibilities of government, but only a beachhead of state power.

The Chilean Revolution is the first testing ground of many things—the strategy and tactics of imperialism and the local oligarchy to meet the threat of a democratically elected socialist government; the strategy and tactics of elected revolutionaries to win full state power and establish socialism; the problems of governing a country and running its economy in the midst of—as part of—the struggle for power.

2

Bits of Background

The Orthodox Chilean histories honor Pedro de Valdivia—the Spaniard who led an expedition of *conquistadores* into Chile from Peru, founded Santiago and several other Chilean cities, and was the first colonial governor—as the founder of Chile. A massive statue of Valdivia stands in Santiago's historic square. the Plaza de Armas. A city and countless avenues and streets are named after him.

But to Pablo Neruda, whose *Canto General* flashes with the pithy insights of a great poet into Latin American history, Valdivia was an "executioner" who divided up Chile among thieves as though it were a dead jackass, returned Indian prisoners with their noses and ears cut off, and left the country full of death, solitude, and scars. To Neruda, Lautaro, the young chief who led bands of Araucanian Indians in guerrilla warfare against the Spanish intruders and defeated Valdivia in a battle in which the hated Spaniard's head was cut off and passed around on a pike, was "our father." No statue of Lautaro stands in Santiago, no Chilean city bears his name.

Chileans have been taught to see their origins in Valdivia and the Spaniards, but the Chilean people are not simply Spanish. They are mainly *mestizo*—a mixture of Spanish and Indian. Only

7

the upper classes are mostly Spanish, and they too contain an admixture of Indian.

Valdivia's expedition into Chile included one hundred and fifty Spanish men, but only one Spanish woman. The union of these men and Indian women began the formation of what is today the bulk of the Chilean people. After the conquest, far more Spanish men than women migrated to Chile. The men were mostly soldiers who came to make their fortune by fighting; families would have been hindrances to them. The fusion between Spanish and Indian took place rapidly. Before fifty years had gone by, the *mestizos* were much more numerous than the Spanish.

The conquest of Chile was resisted by the Araucanians in a war which lasted over three hundred years. So fierce was this war that "Be careful or they'll send you to Chile" became a watchword among soldiers in Spain.[1] The Araucanians at first tried to meet the Spaniards in open combat, but were overwhelmed by the use of horses and superior equipment. Then they learned to use horses themselves, replaced their bows and arrows with maces and clubs, and stopped launching themselves in masses against the enemy. Everyone who writes about this war has high praise for the military qualities of the Araucanians. They developed tactics remarkably similar to those of modern guerrilla warfare.

Alejandro Lipschutz, the distinguished Chilean anthropologist, explains the indomitable resistance of the Araucanians by the nature of their society—it was classless. "*Por rey jamás regido*— never ruled by a king"—says Ercilla, a Spanish soldier and poet who fought against the Araucanians and was so impressed that he sang their praises in *La Araucana,* which became Chile's national epic. Unlike the lower classes in the stratified societies of the Incas and Aztecs, the Araucanians had never had rulers and simply could not swallow the idea of having Spanish overlords. They were defending *their* land, *their* people, *their* way of life.

A three hundred year war is bound to have great effects on the societies waging it. Eventually, it ended up destroying the old Araucanian society, leaving several hundred thousand Araucanians—in their own language *Mapuches*—who now live in the south of Chile, robbed of their land, deprived of their culture and still referring to ordinary Chileans as "foreigners." The effects on the other side are described by Luis Galdames in *A*

History of Chile: "Such a prolonged and dreadful struggle had ended by imprinting very special characteristics on the political and social life of the country. During the frequent periods of warfare in the sixteenth and seventeenth centuries, people lived amidst the most despairing apprehensions, and under a strictly military regime. . . . The colony was impoverished and depopulated, the government was hated, life was uncertain, and domestic customs were impaired by the rigidity of camp life."[2]

The first Spaniards in Chile were soldiers, conquerors, unused to work and knowing little about tilling the soil, breeding animals, and working mines. So the Indians were forced to do the work. A conqueror would receive an *encomienda,* which means that the Indians of a certain area were "commended" to him, and he made them work. The Indians built the first houses, public buildings, churches. They did the farm work. They worked the placer mines, spending the greater part of the day with their legs in water. In military campaigns they served as beasts of burden. No one—neither the aged, the young, nor the women—was exempt. "It was the general belief among the Spaniards," says Galdames, "that the Indians did not belong to the human race, that they were not worth more than a horse or a dog."[3]

Great numbers of Indians died following the Spanish Conquest. Many were killed in the fighting. *Encomenderos* sometimes did away with "unruly" Indians. The cruel working conditions caused many deaths. Deadly epidemics of smallpox, measles, and typhus occurred. At the same time the birth rate declined with the disruption of home life caused by the wars and the impressment of Indians into forced labor. Intermingling with the Spaniards and *mestizos* also helped reduce the Indian population. By the end of the eighteenth century, the Indians outside the territory controlled by the Araucanians were almost completely exterminated. They had been replaced as a work force, both on the farms and in the cities, by the *mestizos.*

In the nineteenth and twentieth centuries many non-Spanish immigrants came to Chile. British merchants also arrived. After 1848 large numbers of Germans settled in the south where to this day, in many cities and towns and large stretches of the countryside, the people speak German as well as Spanish. French, Italians, Yugoslavs, Jews, and Lebanese also arrived, and today in Santiago there is an *Estadio Francés,* an *Estadio Italiano,* an *Estadio Israelita,* and an *Estadio Sirio*—private parks with playing fields, swimming pools, tennis courts, restaurants—where the people of similar backgrounds get together among themselves.

By the second half of the nineteenth century, the non-Spanish immigrants, who tended to keep apart from the lower-class *mestizos,* had begun to break into the Chilean upper classes. So although Chile's older aristocracy is mainly of Basque origin, some of Chile's "best families" bear British names like Edwards or Lyon or French names like Subercaseaux. The result of the new immigration has been to accentuate the difference between a *mestizo* lower class and a largely European upper and middle class.

You can see the division between *mestizo* and European by walking around Santiago. In Las Condes, La Reina, La Avenida Américo Vespucio, the rich sections, with their giant mansions and numerous two- and three-car garages, you see people who look European—in features, complexion, and stature. In La Granja, Barrancas, Conchalí, or one of the other *poblaciones marginales*—marginal communities—of the poor, with their wooden shacks, unpaved streets and barefoot children hauling water from far-away pumps, you see people who, with few exceptions, look *mestizo*—in eyes, skin, straight jet black hair, and short stature.

Most upper- and middle-class Chileans would deny that Chilean society is racist. We are not like you in the United States, a luncheon companion told me one day in the cafeteria of the Central Bank; we don't divide ourselves according to race. But in the Central Bank itself it was obvious that almost all the higher-ranking jobs were held by European types, while the charwomen were *mestizas.* A similar division holds throughout Chilean society.

Prejudice against Indian and *mestizo* continues among Chile's upper and middle classes till the present day. Often at our luncheon discussions, Chileans would tell me that Chilean workers needed a strong discipline because they are *flojos y borrachines*—lazy drunkards; they get it from the Indians. I would counter that Ercilla, who had firsthand experience with the

Araucanians, said in his epic that they were *duro en el trabajo*—
hard workers. I usually got nowhere.

It is not just some technicians at the bank who maintained such
prejudices. Francisco Encina, the leading Chilean bourgeois
historian of the last half century, writes: "In the *encomienda,* the
new Chilean race was created. . . . In its bosom the *mestizo*
realized the greatest of human conquests: the habit of work." For
Encina, the whip and the gun, which the Spaniards used to
enforce a murderous discipline in the *encomienda,* had their
value.

Encina also states that "certain endemic faults, like alcoholism,
go completely with the aboriginal influence."[4] Miserable living
conditions and the profits made by landholder and merchant from
the sale of liquor to the poor have nothing to do with it.

"Racist interpretations are commonplace in Chile . . ." writes
Professor Frederick B. Pike. "The anti-Indian literature is vast. A
random sampling illustrates the broad aspects of the prejudice
that is an important national characteristic. One writer asserted
that high infant mortality among the lower classes results from
the stupidity and proneness toward uncleanliness and drunken-
ness bequeathed by their Indian blood; another stated that the
mental inferiority of Araucanians is recognized by almost all
Chileans; while from still a different source came the pronouncement that the racial superiority of the white upper classes made
unavoidable the exploitation of the inferior, mixed-blood lower
classes."[5]

Once as my wife and I were watching a march of poor people
from the Barrancas slum down the *Alameda*—the main avenue of
central Santiago—a well-groomed lady turned to us and pointing
to the demonstrators, said: "*Miren los mugrientos, que quieren
ellos?* Look at the dirty ones, what do *they* want?"

VALDIVIA rewarded the *conquistadores* who accompanied him
not only with *encomiendas* of Indians, but also with grants of
land. This division of people and land began a process of great
importance in determining the nature of the future Chilean
society.

The original land grants to the *conquistadores* were immense.
Some received whole valleys stretching from the Andes to the

Pacific. Others received more moderate grants, but began immediately to enlarge them by taking over bordering land or the nearby hills from which their water came. Some *encomenderos* received only Indians without, theoretically, any rights to land, but since the Indians were of no use without land they simply took land over—either that on which the Indians lived or any other that was handy. This process went on until, in the words of George M. McBride, in his classic, *Chile: Land and Society,* "the large farm estates . . . became established as the dominant agricultural units in Chile. Almost all the best land . . . was included within the bounds of these large farms. . . . there was left little room for any other type of holding in the entire area occupied by whites."[6]

Originally, the labor force for these estates consisted of *encomendado* Indians. These Indians were forced to do whatever the master required—to provide him with wheat, corn, eggs, and other products, to do construction work, to perform personal service. "No household of Spaniards," writes McBride, "was without its retinue of native servants. . . ."[7]

At first, the Indians fled to the woods from their foreign masters whenever they could, but with time this changed. The breakup of the Indian communities and the monopolization of the land by the Spaniards made it progressively less possible for the Indians to sustain themselves outside the estates. And with each successive generation, more Indians were supplanted by *mestizos* who had never known a life outside them.

So long as the landowners faced problems in holding on to their labor force, the *encomienda* system was maintained, with the Indian remaining a ward of his master, legally obligated to render certain services to him. But as the laborers found themselves with no alternative to living and working on the estates, the system gradually changed. The laborers and their families performed services for the master in exchange for certain rights—the laborer might have to work 160 or more days per year for the master and was allowed to live in a hut on the estate, to pasture some animals on it, and to use a little land to plant crops for himself and his family.

From the old *encomiendas* and land grants had arisen a new unit—the hacienda; the old *encomendero* had become the *hacen-*

dado and the old "Indio" laborer had become the *inquilino*—tenant. The new freedom of the laborers, like that of the ex-slaves after the Civil War in the United States, was more formal than real. The laborers remained subject to the master, tied to his estate, obligated to spend their lives working for him.

What sort of agriculture can you expect from a system in which people and land were divided the way they were in Chile? A Chilean economist of the last century wrote: "With the lands granted according to favoritism and not work, and in quantities so exorbitant that they sometimes amounted to whole districts; with the lands placed under the superior direction of *encomenderos* who lacked all industrial skill, and worked by Indians subject to forced labor and lacking all interest in the process of cultivation, the territorial properties of Chile were during all the centuries of the colony nothing other than vast ranches in which only the natural and almost spontaneous product of the soil was obtained."[8]

The hacienda was not just an economic unit, but a whole society. Besides the manor house of the *hacendado* and the huts of the *inquilinos,* it contained work- and warehouses, stores for selling supplies and wine to the *inquilinos,* and a church. The landholder reigned as a little monarch on his estate. The *inquilinos* required his consent to get married, and he often was godfather to their children. When an *inquilino* died, it was the *hacendado* who distributed his goods among the heirs. The *hacendado* acted as judge in cases of disputes and crimes, and many haciendas had cells or dungeons in which to punish recalcitrant *inquilinos*.

By the end of the colonial period, the hacienda had become one of Chile's most important institutions. "It was," writes McBride, "the characteristic unit of population; more important by far than the few small cities that existed in Chile at that time. . . . Its separation of master and man gave cast to the entire social structure, with its sharply distinguished upper and lower classes, just as the relationship between these two individuals determined the type of governmental institutions that existed. . . ."[9]

HOW much, even in modern times, Chile's agriculture bears the marks of its origins can be seen from a couple of quotations from

Investment in Chile, published by the U.S. Department of Commerce. "There is a very great concentration of agricultural land in the hands of a very few owners in Chile while an excessive number of agricultural properties are too small for economic exploitation." In 1955, 2.8 percent of the properties accounted for 41 percent of the arable land, while, at the other end, 64 percent of the properties accounted for only 12 percent. "The hacienda, or as it is more commonly called in Chile, the *fundo,* is the typical form of rural holding. . . . It traces its origin and, in most cases, its legal title back to the *encomienda* and *estancia* granted by or under the authority of the Spanish crown after 1544."[10]

Concerning how agriculture was run, *Investment in Chile* said:

> All authorities agree that there is need for a great deal of improvement in land management practices and farming methods in Chile. . . . Perhaps the most serious problem of all is the underutilization of land. . . . Most Chilean sources, other than the large landholders themselves, tend to place the responsibility on the shoulders of the *hacendados.* The Ministry of Agriculture, for example, points out that on properties of 1,000 hectares and over, i.e., the so-called latifundium, land is only partially used, mechanization and modern techniques are insufficiently utilized, and irrigated lands are frequently kept in natural pasture. . . . [11]

Like their forbears, the modern Chilean landholders have been uninterested in working in agriculture. As Claude G. Bowers, the U.S. Ambassador to Chile from 1939 to 1953 describes it, they "live part of the year on their *fundos* and part in their town houses in Santiago. For the most part they are cosmopolitans, to be found, in season, on the Riviera, at Biarritz or in Switzerland."[12]

The class division forged in colonial days between landholder and *inquilino* has come down to modern times. Here are a few conditions laid down by a *fundo* owner for his *inquilinos* in 1965–66:

1) Each house will supply the *fundo* with the work of two *obligados.*
2) The use of the house and grounds will be considered part of the remuneration of both.
3) Each *obligado* will also receive: the use of a quarter of a *cuadra* of land [a *cuadra* is about an acre]; pasture for two animals; 3

hundred-weights of flour and 150 kilos of beans per year; wood for
personal use. . . .

4) Each *obligado* will receive a wage of 1.22 *escudos* [about 30 U.S.
cents] daily. . . . [13]

The class division showed itself strikingly on the haciendas in
the contrast between the hovels of the *inquilinos* and the mansions of the landholders. One Sunday my wife and I went to see
an estate called Peñalolén on the outskirts of Santiago. After
passing a long row of mud huts, we saw the giant manor house
inside extensive, parklike grounds. But at the gate we were told
we couldn't enter; the building had been "taken" by some of
Santiago's needy, and forty families were now living in it.

Another time we went through an estate in the nearby town of
San Felipe. The gate was larger and finer than those at Columbia
University; a tree-lined road led to the owner's residence, a
palace the size of a city block and two stories high; behind it was
a pool some hundred yards long, surrounded by trees clipped into
artificial shapes in the manner of Versailles. The building was
now being taken over by the University of San Felipe for use by
one of its faculties.

The *hacendado* dominated and used his *inquilinos* politically.
Here are some lines from Neruda's *Election In Chimbarongo,
1947:*

> In Chimbarongo, in Chile, some time ago
> I went to a senatorial election.
> I saw how they elect
> the pillars of the fatherland.
> At eleven in the morning
> the carts arrived from the country
> packed with *inquilinos*.
> It was winter; and wet,
> dirty, hungry, shoeless,
> the serfs of Chimbarongo
> got down from the carts.
> Grim, sun-burned, ragged,
> they were pressed together and led away
> with a ballot in their hand,
> watched and crowded

> they returned to receive the pay,
> and again they were led,
> lined up like horses,
> to the carts.
> Afterward
> they were thrown
> meat and wine,
> leaving them bestially
> degraded and forgotten.
> I listened later to the speech
> of the senator elected in this way:
> "We, Christian patriots,
> we, defenders of order,
> we, children of the spirit."*

Traditionally, the landholders have exercised great political power in Chile. During the colonial period and early years of independence, they were the most powerful domestic political force. Later, they lost power to the urban bourgeoisie, but still remained strong. As a class they have never been just landholders, but also merchants, selling their products abroad and at home. For a long time now, the landholders and urban bourgeoisie have intermingled with one another through intermarriage and through landholder investment in urban enterprises and urban bourgeoisie investment in land. Yet there remains a partly distinct group of landholders whose interests consist more heavily of land than those of the rest of the bourgeoisie. There remains also the landholder heritage in the outlook of the whole bourgeoisie and in the working of many Chilean institutions.

The pervasive, enduring stamp the landholders have placed on Chile can be illustrated by its inflation. Chile has had one of the world's highest rates of inflation—one that has now been running a century and in which annual increases in the price level of 25 to 75 percent have been common. The inflation began in 1879 when Chile, having to finance a war against Peru and Bolivia, turned to the direct issue of treasury notes and bills, in effect, the printing of money. But this type of financing was continued even after the war ended. The landholders had discovered how greatly they

* Author's translation.

could profit from a depreciating peso: They could export their wheat and other products for gold and then pay their debts in depreciated paper currency; to the extent that the government could finance itself by printing money, they could avoid taxes. Chilean writers are fond of quoting Professor Frank Fetter's *Monetary Inflation in Chile:*

> There is something of a paradox in the fact that a country ruled in the past by a conservative aristocracy, with so stable a political history and so excellent a public credit record, should have had so checkered a monetary experience. The explanation is to be found principally in the heavy indebtedness of the landed gentry, and their dominance in governmental affairs.[14]

The landholders have traditionally viewed Chile as a big hacienda to be run for their benefit. They have always used their power ruthlessly to eliminate any threat to their interests. They detested Bernardo O' Higgins—the leader of the war of independence and first ruler of independent Chile—because he taxed them to fight the war against Spain, because he moved to abolish titles of nobility, because he wanted to eliminate the primogeniture inheritance system which prevented the large estates from being divided and thus preserved the power of the landholder class. So they overthrew the George Washington of Chile by a coup d'etat. Several times later in Chilean history, they overthrew or helped overthrow governments they didn't like. Less powerful in recent years, they still constituted a force, which, concentrating in Chile's most reactionary parties, looked balefully at all attempts at progress even through moderate bourgeois reforms.

IMPERIALISM, in various forms, has imposed itself on Chile from the country's beginnings.

First there were the Spaniards who made themselves the rulers of Chile and incorporated it into the mercantile system under which Spain monopolized the trade of its colonies and restricted them to the production of those goods it could not itself produce. As one historian put it, the colonies were allowed to manufacture neither a nail nor a horseshoe. Chile was made dependent not only on Spain, but also on Peru. The viceroys of Peru, says Encina, regarded Chile "as a simple appendix of the vice-royalty;

a granary destined to supply the vice-royalty's need for wheat and tallow; a market to nourish the prosperity of Lima's commerce. . . . They only considered the interests of the Peruvian consumer or merchant, without taking into account the effects of their measures on Chilean economic development."[15]

Both Britain and the newly formed United States favored the independence of Latin America from Spain, so that they could gain access to its raw materials and markets. During the early years of the wars of independence, Britain was allied to Spain against Napoleon and therefore limited in what it could do to help the insurgents. But after Napoleon fell, it maneuvered to prevent other European countries from giving Spain armed support to put down the rebellion; its merchants sold arms to, and its subjects enrolled in the Latin American forces. A Scot, Lord Cochrane, led the first Chilean naval squadron in actions to drive Spain from Peru. And the United States sent agents to the new national governments who encouraged and advised them.

The wars of independence saw the beginning of a century of business rivalry between Britain and the United States in Latin America. Since Britain was the leading economic power at that time, the advantages lay with her. Both countries started to penetrate Chile, but within a few years Britain had far outdistanced the United States, and converted Chile into her economic satellite.

By 1875, 58 percent of Chile's exports went to Britain and 41 percent of her imports came from there.[16] The pattern of trade was that between mother country and colony. Chile became the world's leading copper producer, supplying 66 percent of Britain's imports in 1870; she was also one of her leading suppliers of wheat. Britain was the main source of the manufactured goods consumed in Chile.

Britain dominated much more than Chile's foreign trade. British commercial agents controlled Chile's copper industry, even without being significant producers; they gave credits to the producers in return for commitments to sell them the output; and there were many complaints that a few refiners in Swansea, Wales could move the price up and down as it suited them. British businessmen, through their hold on foreign trade and their wholesale houses, also controlled a large part of Chile's internal trade. British commercial houses engaged not only in buying and selling, but also in banking. Between 1822 and 1879 the Chilean government obtained ten foreign loans—all from Britain.[17]

Britain used her political power to support her economic domination. When Chile, to encourage the refining of copper within the country, imposed a tax on the export of the raw material, the British Foreign Office instructed its Santiago representative to ask the Chilean government to annul the tax. When Chile increased the import duty on coal to protect domestic production, the foreign office also objected. Britain exerted pressure on Chile to adopt a policy of free trade. Enjoying a virtual monopoly of industrialization, Britain could undersell all competitors and required free access to the world's markets. Chile's situation was the opposite of Britain's, but in the 1850s she adopted a policy of free trade.

Modern imperialism in Lenin's sense of monopoly capital came to Chile in the 1880s. Through the war of 1879–83 with Peru and Bolivia, Chile obtained the rich nitrate lands in what are now its northern provinces of Tarapacá and Antofagasta. But the chief beneficiaries of the war were British speculators like John Thomas North. Peru had expropriated the nitrate properties in 1875, issuing bonds to their former owners. During the war the value of these bonds plummeted, and North, using capital obtained from banks in Chile, bought up as many as he could. When Chile, after the war, decided to turn over the properties to the holders of the bonds, North had a strong foothold in the nitrate industry. Then, following the same monopoly logic as John D. Rockefeller, North moved to get his hands on all the other industries on which the nitrate industry depended. He acquired control of the water supply essential to the desert region, the railroad, the public lighting company, the company which monopolized supplies to the mines, and the steamship line which monopolized the transport of the nitrate to the consuming countries. In 1888 he founded the Bank of Tarapacá and London, Ltd. Before long, North and a few allies had turned Chile's northern provinces into their private fiefdom.

British domination of the Chilean economy grew even greater than before. Before 1880 six of the eight million pounds of British investment in Chile consisted of loans. Now, direct investment—the hallmark of modern imperialism, signifying control of property inside the country and therefore greater penetration—soared from two million pounds in 1880 to eighteen million in 1890.[18] Britain's control of the nitrate industry meant control of Chile's key economic activity on which everything else depended. Nitrate sales soared in the 1880s to become Chile's leading export. And the export tax on nitrate became the largest single source of government revenues, accounting for 45 percent in 1891. Indirectly, nitrate accounted for a large additional percentage through import duties on goods mostly purchased with nitrate earnings.

With economic domination went political influence. The British had powerful allies in the classes that did business with them—the landholders who sold them wheat, the mine owners who sold them copper, and the importers who bought from them. North had on his payroll a number of lawyers important in Chilean politics, for example Enrique MacIver, a leader of the Radical Party and Carlos Walker Martinez, a leader of the Conservative Party. The Nitrate Railway Company had a political slush fund of 100,000 pounds, revealed when British stockholders sued the company to find out how company money was being used.

Chile's ruling classes enjoyed a fiesta with the nitrate bonanza. They increased their travel abroad, boosted their import of foreign luxuries, and dismantled the few direct taxes that were falling on them, leaving themselves virtually free of any tax burden.

But as British imperialism penetrated, the inevitable happened: a movement of "Chile for Chileans" arose. Chileans called for the recovery of their riches, for the exploitation of these riches for the benefit of Chileans, not foreigners. A class of industrial bourgeoisie was taking shape and its spokesmen called for "protecting national industry and by this means opening the great sources of riches possessed by the country."[19]

In 1886 a man who was not only anti-imperialist, but who also had a clear vision of the need for economic development—José Manuel Balmaceda—became president of Chile. Balmaceda worked out a comprehensive policy. He proposed state-ownership of the railroads. He spoke of breaking the nitrate monopoly of the British capitalists, and of forming national nitrate companies whose stock would not be transferable to foreigners. He argued that "we should invest" the extraordinary receipts from nitrates "in productive works so that when nitrates lose their importance because of natural discoveries or the progress of science, we will have formed with national industry and the state railroads, the base of new income. . . ."[20] He also wanted to give tariff protection to Chilean industry so it could develop. Chile's mines, he argued, should not just have to supply raw materials to the external market, but they could be the base of a powerful national metallurgical industry.

Balmaceda began to carry out a vast public works program. His government proceeded to double the railroad network, and build new roads, telegraph lines, bridges, docks, water supply systems, hospitals, and schools.

Inevitably, Balmaceda's policies called forth fierce opposition. The British could not of course stomach the threat to their interests. Chile's upper classes were disgusted by Balmaceda's public works program; it was wasting money on schools and roads which could better be used to insure their freedom from taxes. The landholders protested that it was causing a scarcity of agricultural labor and a rise in wages.

North voyaged from London to Chile to see what he could do. His lawyers led the opposition to Balmaceda in Congress which worked to block Balmaceda in everything. They refused to vote taxes. They used a measure that was to be resurrected eighty years later against Allende—the impeachment of one minister after another—forcing Balmaceda repeatedly into setting up new Cabinets. Despite everything, Balmaceda stood firm. In January 1891 the opposition took to insurrection.

The revolt was led by the navy—British-oriented since Lord Cochrane's day. According to a memorandum of the American minister in Chile to the State Department: "It is known that many English firms have made liberal contributions to the revolutionary fund. It is openly recognized by the leaders of the civil war that, among others, John Thomas North has contributed 100,000 pounds sterling."[21] British ships helped by transporting opposition leaders, coal, and foodstuffs to Iquique in the nitrate country which the insurrectionaries captured and made their headquarters.

In August 1891 the insurrectionaries triumphed. The British minister reported to the foreign office that "We, the British, are in great favor among all classes."[22]

But now a new threat to British imperialism emerged—the competition of rival imperialisms, German and U.S. The growing economic strength of Germany and the United States compared to Britain was making itself felt. German investments in Chile grew rapidly in the 1890s, and soon predominated in the electric power industry and the urban trolley car system. U.S. investment began to grow after 1900. In 1905 the Braden Copper Company, later to become a subsidiary of the Kennecott Copper Corporation, was formed to exploit the copper of El Teniente; in 1911 the Chile Exploration Corporation, later to become a subsidiary of the Anaconda Corporation, was formed to exploit Chuquicamata copper; and in 1913 the Bethlehem Steel Corporation acquired the iron mines of El Tofo. German and U.S. trade with Chile shot up. The Chilean investment and trade of the United States and Germany were fast catching up with those of Britain. Chile was now the scene of ferocious imperialist rivalry.

The first world war settled the rivalry. Germany was all but eliminated. Britain, coming out of the war weakened, a debtor nation, had to cede ever more ground. The United States emerged supreme, with an empire in Latin America, of which Chile was a part.

After the war, U.S. imperialism completed its control of the key positions in the Chilean economy. U.S. corporations already held the large copper mines—all important now because copper was replacing nitrate as Chile's key export. Balmaceda's worries about the future of Chile's nitrate had been justified—it was losing its markets to the synthetic nitrate invented during the war. Still, there were some profits left in the old industry, and in the twenties the Guggenheims got control of the British-owned Anglo-Chilean Nitrate and Railway Co. and the Chilean-controlled Lautaro Nitrate Co. In 1927 ITT acquired most of the stock of the British-controlled Chili Telephone Co., and between 1929 and 1931 the South American Power Co. bought the properties of the British-controlled Chilean Electric Tramway and Light Co.

At the same time, the U.S. government wrested dominant

influence in Chile from the British. From the beginning, the U.S. government exerted its power to preserve an imperialist-dominated society. In 1932 a coup d'etat overthrew the government. Among the coup leaders were such left-wingers with socialist aspirations as Marmaduke Grove and they proposed a program to eliminate imperialism from Chile. U.S. businessmen, the U.S. Embassy, and the State Department, all became alarmed. The U.S. Ambassador, William Culbertson, established contact with Carlos Dávila, a right-wing leader of the governing junta and heard his view that "foreign interests should not be molested." Culbertson gave his support to Dávila, who mounted a new coup, established himself as provisional president, and exiled the left-wing members of the junta to Easter Island.[23]

The depression of the 1930s caused a shift in one aspect of the relationship between imperialism and Chile. By shrinking Chile's export earnings, it brought a severe balance of payments crisis which forced her to slash imports. She raised customs duties and prohibited some imports altogether, abandoning the free trade policy maintained since the 1850s. A slow process of industrialization began as manufacturing developed to produce substitutes for goods that had formerly been imported. World War II, by cutting off foreign supplies, reinforced this process.

In 1939 a popular front government created a Development Corporation (CORFO) to establish or strengthen industries important for economic development. Besides expanding Chile's electric power industry, this institution was eventually to provide Chile with steel, oil, and a number of other industries.

But the imperialists continued to suck riches out of Chile. Enormous company earnings were only one way of doing this. During World War II, the Allied Metals Board fixed the price of copper at the super-low level of 11 3/4 cents a pound; the price during World War I had been 22 to 27 cents. Eduardo Novoa, in his book *La Batalla Por El Cobre,* calculates the loss to his country at $500 to $600 million.[24] During the Korean War, the United States again used its imperialist domination of Chile to get copper dirt-cheap.

3

From González Videla to Allende

After World War II, the United States used its power to integrate Chile into the anti-Communist system it tried to establish throughout the "free world." In 1946 Gabriel González Videla was elected president with the support of the Communist vote. The United States was working wherever it could to have Communists removed from positions of importance. The then U.S. Ambassador to Chile, Claude G. Bowers, writes: "In two interviews with González Videla . . . he said that since the Communists had given him his plurality he would be obliged to place three Communists in his ministry. I got the impression he did not think they would stay long."[1] In 1947 Chile signed the Rio Treaty for the "security" of the Western Hemisphere and in 1948 it joined the Organization of American States (OAS), both tailored to the anti-Communist policies of the United States.

The United States then initiated in Chile, and throughout Latin America, a systematic program to gain influence among officers of the armed forces. Under the Mutual Security Act of 1951 and the Mutual Defense Agreement signed with Chile in 1952, it began to provide military "aid," to send military instructors and advisors, and to train Chilean officers in the United States and the Canal Zone. Edwin Lieuwen, in a book published for the quasi-official Council On Foreign Relations, comments that "the mission program . . . serves no important military purpose, [but] is nevertheless most useful in providing opportunities for cementing political as well as professional relationships between the sending and the recipient government. Also, the practice of training Latin American officers in the United States helps to secure their political sympathies."[2]

The CIA also got under way at this time what was eventually to be a massive penetration of all strategic sectors of Chilean society. By "the early 1950s," it had already started, according to the Senate Intelligence Committee report, *Covert Action in Chile, 1963–1973,* a "media" project which "operated wire services."[3]

The process of industrialization through import substitution made progress for some time. Chile's import of industrial goods was 35 percent less in 1945–49 than in 1925–29, while industrial output was 125 percent higher. By the 1950s Chile was producing a variety of industrial goods, including textiles, wood and metal products, fats and oils, and leather goods. Most of the factories were small and backward, and many of the goods were poorly made as compared to those from developed countries; but Chile did have a national industry. She produced a much larger variety of industrial goods than Cuba did before its revolution.

Toward 1955, however, difficulties arose. The number of imports that could easily be substituted dwindled. New industries required a more difficult technology and far larger amounts of capital than the Chileans had. The foreign monopolies saw their opportunity and began to move in, either by establishing new enterprises or by buying out or joining existing ones. In the late 1950s and during the 1960s a wave of direct foreign investment swept over Chile.

What sort of industries did the foreign corporations bring? General Motors, Ford, Chrysler, Fiat, Leyland, and Citroen established plants for the assembly of Novas, Falcons, Dodge Darts, Simcas, etc. Several foreign companies set up plants for the production of tires from imported materials. The General Telephone and Electronics Company set up a plant to assemble TV sets out of components from its Sylvania subsidiary in Puerto Rico. And Remington Rand set up a plant for the assembly of metal office furniture from imported components.

Over 85 percent of Chile's people needed more and better food, adequate clothing, good mass transit, and decent housing. Chile needed investments deliberately planned to solve its problems. What she got were investments designed to make money for foreign corporations geared to producing for rich, developed capitalist countries—plants to produce fancy-type industrial goods from imported materials and parts. Between the need to import materials and parts, and to remit profits, royalties, and interest abroad, the new plants added a heavy, continuous burden to Chile's already weak balance of payments. The investment in automobile manufacturing was especially pernicious. It brought with it a train of other wasteful investments and expenditures— new highways leading to the swanky Santiago district of Vitacura or to the skiing resort of Potrillos, as well as the foreign exchange cost of the oil required to run the cars.

Soon the foreign corporations dominated a strategic part of Chile's industry. In 1968–69 these corporations participated in the ownership of 25 percent of Chile's industrial corporations; these 25 percent being among the largest—often the leaders in their field—represented 60 percent of Chile's industry.[4]

With penetration into manufacturing went further penetration into finance. The National City Bank, which had first entered Chile in 1916, set up a new company—Financiera Nacional—to handle medium and long term financing. The Bank of America set up a subsidiary with eight branches. The International Basic Economy Corporation (IBEC), a Rockefeller family company, set up Fondo Crecinco, the largest mutual fund in Chile.

Foreign loans flowed. Chile's foreign indebtedness soared from $600 million in 1960 to $3 billion in 1970. The servicing of this debt placed an enormous burden on the balance of payments. Three hundred million dollars in payments for debt service were scheduled to fall due in 1971 and $400 million in each of the years 1972 and 1973. Depending on the price of copper, $400 million would represent 35 to 40 percent of the total value of Chile's annual exports. Chile was hooked and increasingly had to borrow large sums just to pay the interest and amortization on the old debt.

Cultural penetration helped economic penetration along. Already in 1911 Encina was analyzing the effects of what today we would call cultural imperialism: "In the weak economy penetrated by the superior one, there develops a great capacity for consumption without a corresponding increase in the capacity for production. . . . The desires to consume are communicated by imitation with much greater rapidity than the corresponding desires to produce. Because of this, the contact of an advanced and inferior civilization brings a profound disturbance to the development of the latter, with the most grave economic and moral repercussions. . . . From this [contact] derives our truly enormous consumption, given our economic strength, of luxury goods. . . . The value of our [exports] . . . goes in large part to Europe to pay for clothing, coaches, jewels, furniture, voyages, etc."[5] This was written before Chile had been penetrated by modern communications and advertising. U.S. movies, television programs, and magazines like *Reader's Digest* and *Time* helped create in Chile's upper and middle classes a desire to live in the style they think Americans do—without of course giving up the cheap servants which Chile's underdeveloped economy provided them.

The comprehensive foreign penetration multiplied the ties between the imperialists and Chile's bourgeoisie. In Balmaceda's day, the foreign corporations were associated mainly with Chile's commercial, financial, and mining bourgeoisie; the industrial bourgeoisie, seeking protection against foreign competition, had interests that conflicted with those of the imperialists. Now, strong, growing ties united the imperialists with the cream of Chile's industrial bourgeoisie. Moreover, the different types of Chilean bourgeoisie were becoming increasingly merged with one another and associated with the imperialists. A striking example is the Edwards family, long an influential member of the Chilean oligarchy: It owned a chain of newspapers (including Chile's leading paper—*El Mercurio*), a bank, and a number of industrial, mining and landholding companies, besides being associated with the Rockefeller IBEC in the Fondo Crecinco mutual fund, possessing a 20 percent interest in the Chilean subsidiary of Ralston Purina, and holding a large amount of stock in Pepsi-Cola.[6]

For U.S. imperialism, Chile was important not just because of the corporate interests there, but also for broader political and strategic reasons. Chile was part of the U.S. empire. When the United States decided to wage economic and political warfare against revolutionary Cuba, Chile, despite domestic opposition, went along with a series of anti-Cuban actions by the OAS and broke relations with Cuba in 1964. When the imperialists, in response to the threat that the Cuban Revolution would serve as an example to other countries, decided that Latin America ought to have an Alliance for Progress that would ward off revolution by promoting reform, Chile was a country on which they counted for showcase results.

In the 1964 presidential election in Chile, the United States backed Eduardo Frei, a Christian Democrat whose political line was similar to that of the Alliance. The U.S. Embassy in Santiago maneuvered behind the scenes to get the Conservative and Liberal parties to withdraw from the "Democratic Front," of which they were a part, and support Frei, thereby uniting the Right and the bulk of the Center against the left-wing candidate.[7]

"A group of U.S. businessmen in Chile offered," according to the Senate committee's report, "to provide one and one half million dollars to be . . . disbursed covertly by the U.S. government," but this offer was rejected; "however, CIA money represented as private money was passed to the Christian Democrats through a private businessman."[8]

The CIA intervened massively in the campaign. Here are some details, taken from the Senate committee report:

> The Central Intelligence Agency spent more than $2.6 million in support of the election of the Christian Democratic candidate. . . More than half of the Christian Democratic candidate's campaign was financed by the United States. . . . In addition to support for political parties, the CIA mounted a massive anti-Communist propaganda campaign. Extensive use was made of the press, radio, films, pamphlets, posters, leaflets, direct mailings, paper streamers, and wall painting. It was a "scare campaign" which relied heavily on images of Soviet tanks and Cuban firing squads and was directed especially to women. Hundreds of thousands of copies of the anti-Communist pastoral letter of Pope Pius XI were distributed by Christian Democratic organizations. . . . "Disinformation" and "black propaganda"—material which purported to originate from another source, such as the Chilean Communist Party—were used. . . . During the first

week of intensive propaganda activity . . . a CIA-funded propaganda group produced twenty radio spots per day in Santiago and on 44 provincial stations; twelve minute news broadcasts five time[s] daily on three Santiago stations and 24 provincial outlets; thousands of cartoons, and much paid press advertising. . . . The propaganda campaign was conducted internationally as well. The CIA ran political action operations independent of the Christian Democrats' campaign in a number of important voter blocks, including slum dwellers, peasants, organized labor, and dissident Socialists.[9]

Frei won the election with 56.1 percent of the votes to Allende's 38.9 percent. "A CIA study concludes," says the *Covert Action* report, "that U.S. intervention enabled Eduardo Frei to win a clear majority in the 1964 election, instead of merely a plurality."[10] Without U.S. intervention, the election would have been far closer, perhaps very close. The election illustrates—though only imperfectly—the degree of penetration attained by the imperialist network.

This network kept growing during the Frei years. U.S. investments mushroomed and each new American enterprise was a focus of power, able to collect intelligence, provide cover for CIA agents, and supply money to political candidates and parties. Every year new contingents of Chilean military and police officers were trained at American schools and bases. During this time, the United States maintained an average of 48 military advisers in Chile[11] who were able to extend their professional and personal relationships with the elite of the Chilean military. Under programs of the American Institute for Free Labor Development (AIFLD), an organization founded in 1962 as part of the Alliance for Progress, thousands of Chilean trade unionists were being indoctrinated at short seminars in Chile, and a number of selected labor leaders—for example, ex-heads of leftist unions—were being sent for long courses to the United States.[12] The CIA was perfecting its "assets," preparing for future contingencies.

The CIA kept very busy after Frei's victory. The Senate committee's report states that "During the years between the election of . . . Frei . . . and the presidential election campaign of 1970, the CIA . . . spent . . . almost $2 million on covert action in Chile . . . conduct[ing] twenty covert action projects. . . ."[13]

Agents financed by one project "placed CIA-inspired editorials almost daily in *El Mercurio* . . . and, after 1968, exerted substantial control over the content of that paper's international news section."[14]

Other CIA "projects were directed toward:

Wresting control of Chilean university student organizations from the communists;

Supporting a women's group active in Chilean political and intellectual life;

Combating the communist-dominated *Central Unica de Trabajadores Chilenos* (CUTCH) [Central Workers' Confederation] and supporting democratic labor groups; and

Exploiting a civic action front group to combat communist influence within cultural and intellectual circles."[15]

No possibility for increasing imperialist power in Chile was overlooked.

FREI and the Christian Democratic Party were well-suited to the needs of the imperialists. The core of Frei's strategy was to use reform to avert revolution. Even his rhetorical technique of invoking revolution was similar to that used by the imperialists in promoting the Alliance for Progress. President Kennedy announced, "We propose to complete the revolution of the Americas." Frei called for a "Revolution in Liberty."

The ideology of the Christian Democratic Party was "communitarianism," a fuzzy doctrine interpreted somewhat differently by different members of the party. Communitarianism distinguishes itself from both liberal capitalism and Marxist socialism, holding that liberalism produces injustice and "isolation of the individual from his social surroundings while Marxism merely substitutes the oppression of the state for that of the capitalists."[16] The way out of the dilemma is to organize society into communities. Each enterprise would become a community, with workers participating in the ownership and management of the enterprises in which they work, while state ownership and intervention would be limited. Private ownership and distinct classes would continue to exist, but there would be—in the words of Frei—an end to "the profound class conflict inherent in our present social organization."[17] How communitarianism was to be brought about is not clear, except that it was not to be imposed by state decree. Behind the moralistic, philosophical language in which communitarianism was presented lay key elements of the Christian Democratic political strategy—to break up the class solidarity of the lower classes by giving their members a capitalist-type interest in their individual enterprises; to scare people with the specter of the evil socialist state.

In line with its ideology of ending class conflict, the Christian Democratic Party was a multi-class party. Some members were industrialists, bankers, and businessmen, belonging to the modern, liberal, reformist sector of the bourgeoisie, the one most closely tied to foreign interests. The bulk of its members were middle class—professionals, technicians, government employees, students, small businessmen, and medium farmers. But there were also members from the lower classes—copper workers, service workers, *inquilinos.*

Reflecting the heterogeneous composition of its membership, the leadership of the party represented a wide range of interests and political points of view. At the right stood Edmundo Pérez Zujovic, owner of a large construction company associated with Bethlehem Steel's Chilean subsidiary and interested in the labor peace he thought necessary to attract foreign investment. At the left stood Jacques Chonchol, a young agronomist who had worked with the Food and Agriculture Organization (FAO) in Cuba during the early years of the revolution and wanted to see Chile carry out a thoroughgoing land reform. Also to the Left, though not as radical as Chonchol, was Radomiro Tomic, a leader of the party since its earliest days. Frei tried to stand above the different wings but was closely associated with Pérez Zujovic.

In outlining his program, Frei stated that Chile had been suffering for several generations from a crisis—mentioning unequal distribution of income, economic stagnation, and control of power by a minority. The crisis, said Frei, had to be resolved. A "rapid transformation of the inadequate and unjust forms and structures" must take place. The people must be allowed to participate in all forms of power, political, economic, and cultural. "Otherwise, there will inevitably flourish an irresistible tendency toward takeover by the state. . . ."[18]

Frei proposed to: "Chileanize" the large mining enterprises and utilities controlled by foreigners; carry out a "profound" land reform; "radically transform the tax system, placing emphasis on progressive taxes on personal income;" control the inflation in four years; increase the annual rate of production growth from 1.5 to 3.2 percent per capita per year; carry out an extensive program of "Popular Promotion" which would cover the country with a network of community organizations through which "marginal sectors," such as shantytown dwellers, could be incorporated into the life of the "national community" and the people in general could participate in the exercise of power.[19]

When "Chileanization" came about, it was based on a proposal by Kennecott.[20] The company had a simple, yet ingenious way to meet the problem of rising sentiment in Chile that copper should be nationalized. Chile would be given majority ownership and apparent control of the El Teniente mine—for a compensation, of course; but to protect Kennecott's interest, control of operations would remain with it.

Under the 1967 agreement which "Chileanized" El Teniente, Chile, through the Copper Corporation (CODELCO), acquired 51 percent of the shares in a new mixed company owning the mine. For this 51 percent, it had to pay Kennecott's subsidiary, Braden Copper, $80 million, even though the book value of the company as a whole was only $67 million. Braden claimed that the book value was unrealistically low, but if this was so, it was because Braden had been allowed in the past to depreciate assets at a favorable rate, and to pay lower taxes. Braden was thus allowed to enjoy one set of values for tax purposes and another for sale.[21]

Anaconda did not at first accept any change in arrangements for its Chuquicamata and El Salvador mines. But when copper prices and Anaconda's profits soared with the Vietnam War, Chilean congressmen, including Christian Democrats, talked more and more of nationalization. Anaconda relented, agreeing in 1969 to arrangements similar to those previously made with Kennecott, but now called "contracted nationalization."[22]

Kennecott and Anaconda continued to manage the copper industry with practically as much power as they had enjoyed before; they had made sure of this through contracts on administration and on sales which they insisted be signed before they would accept the new arrangements. Kennecott's Braden Copper was empowered to run El Teniente—to handle operations and labor relations, acquire materials and equipment, make investments, contracts and pay debts. Anaconda subsidiaries were empowered to direct officials of its mixed companies on organization, administration, operation, accounting, and geological investigation. The copper produced would be sold as before through Kennecott and Anaconda sales subsidiaries, which would have full control of sales policy. Although Chile was now formally the majority owner, it still did not have control of its copper.[23]

"IN the land reform . . . ," said Frei, "we shall not pursue the aim of stealing property, but rather of perfecting it."[24] The strategy of his land reform for "perfecting" property was severalfold—to reduce revolutionary pressure in the countryside by eliminating the most blatantly large estates and satisfying some of the *campesinos'* aspirations; to give property, and thus a stake in the capitalist system, to a broad group of *campesinos;* to keep the *campesinos* from forming one large revolutionary force by creating divisions among them; to promote a modern agriculture by increasing investment and getting rid of pre-capitalist remnants in the countryside.

The land reform law of 1967 permitted the expropriation of estates of over 80 "basic hectares" and of "abandoned" and "poorly exploited" estates.*[25] The 80 basic hectare limit was high; during the debate on the land reform bill, the leftist parties and many Christian Democrats had argued for a limit of 40.

The law provided for compensation, partly in cash and partly in 25-year bonds. It also gave the landholder certain rights. If his estate was being expropriated because of its size—the usual case—he could keep a "reserve" of 80 basic hectares. Within certain guidelines, the landholder had the right to select the land for the reserve, and it could include "the warehouses, silos, installations, and other improvements" to the estate. The landholder could also keep all "animals, machinery not fixed to the ground, tools, equipment and other movable goods. . . ."[26] The

---

* A hectare equals 2.47 acres. A "basic hectare" is a measure of land of different quality and is equivalent to one hectare of good, irrigated land near Santiago; 80 basic hectares may equal 500 hectares of dry arable land in the South or several thousand hectares of hill pastures.

new farm units formed on the expropriated land would have to buy such items from the landholder or be stocked from scratch.

Although the land reform began to reduce the number of estates of over 80 basic hectares, it strengthened the hold on Chilean agriculture of the next size estates, those with 40 to 80 hectares. The number of such estates began to increase even before the 1967 law was passed, for many landholders divided their estates to escape the coming reform, one piece going to the wife, another to a son, etc. As the 1967 law was put into effect and expropriated landholders established their reserves, this size group grew further. These new units were economically strong, since the landholders reserved the best land and kept their cattle, equipment, and supplies.

The basic farm unit set up on the expropriated land was the *asentamiento*, a form of cooperative run jointly by its members and the government's Agrarian Reform Corporation (CORA); but members were allowed plots of land for their private use as they had been on the old estates. After three to five years, the members could decide to dissolve the *asentamiento* and divide the land among themselves. Ordinarily, one *asentamiento* was set up on each estate, but because of the reserve, it covered a smaller area. Many *asentamientos* were too small for efficient exploitation, but could not be combined with others because of the reserves and unexpropriated estates separating them.

Membership in the *asentamientos* was restricted. Preference was given to those who had been living and working permanently on the estate at the time of expropriation; workers who moved from farm to farm, known as *afuerinos*—outsiders—were excluded. Women were not given membership and no provision was made for granting it to the children of members as they reached adulthood. The restriction of membership divided the *campesinos* into groups with conflicting interests.

Those who already enjoyed membership did not want to admit new members, worried that this would mean lower profits per member while the *asentamiento* lasted and less land per member when the land was divided. When the *asentamientos* needed extra workers they took them on as wage laborers. Over a third of the work force on the *asentamientos* were hired nonmembers. Conflicts often arose between members and hired workers over wages and working conditions. Some *afuerinos* opposed the land reform, feeling that they had enjoyed higher incomes and greater security against unemployment under the old system.

Besides the *afuerinos,* the *minifundistas,* those who work very small farms, did not receive any land under the reform. Together the *afuerinos* and *minifundistas* made up more than two thirds of all *campesinos.*

The reform did nothing to meet the special problems of the *Mapuches,* concentrated in several southern provinces such as Cautín and Arauco. The *Mapuches* suffered acutely from having to work tiny plots, and from rural unemployment. Apart from handicraft products and an occasional animal, few *Mapuche* families produced anything beyond what they required for their own subsistence. They lacked credit, equipment, technique— everything. When they did have something to sell, they were at the mercy of the merchants. Because the estates in the provinces in which the *Mapuches* were concentrated ran smaller than those in central Chile, the 80 basic hectare limit left these provinces with a low percentage of expropriable land, though the need for such land was greater than elsewhere.

As the land reform proceeded, the *asentamiento* members came to constitute a new rural middle class. The large landholders tried to form an alliance with them against a more radical reform that would benefit those remaining in need of land.

The restriction of *asentamiento* membership was not the only way the Christian Democrats fostered division among the *campesinos.* They also used the power of the government to split the *campesino* union movement, and placed a large part of it under their control. They put through a law that removed the obstacles to *campesino* unionization created by previous laws and then used the Institute for Agricultural Development (INDAP), which had credit and other favors to dispense, to promote the formation of a new confederation of *campesino* unions—Triunfo Campesino—though two older confederations, one Christian Democrat-oriented, already existed. By 1970 Triunfo Campesino contained 45 percent of the total *campesino* union membership and, together with the other Christian Democratic-led union, the total was 66 percent.[27]

The landholders resisted the land reform, often with violence. Landholders formed armed groups. A zonal official of CORA who went out to take possession of an expropriated estate was clubbed to death by a hireling of the landholder.

Faced with landholder opposition, Frei's government proceeded gingerly with the expropriations. By the end of its term it had expropriated 1,408 estates—a third of the total eligible. In 1964 the Christian Democrats had proclaimed a goal of settling one hundred thousand families on *asentamientos;* by 1970 they had actually settled thirty-two thousand.

FREI's promise to "radically transform the tax system, placing emphasis on progressive taxes on personal income" turned out to be Alliance for Progress-type rhetoric. No radical transformation was even begun. The proportion of revenues coming from direct taxes on income and property—the progressive taxes—actually declined from 27 percent in 1964 to 23 percent in 1970. Indirect taxes (sales, turnover, stamp), falling heavily on those with low incomes, continued to be the chief sources of revenues.[28]

Also unfulfilled was Frei's promise to control inflation in four years. The increase in the consumer price index in 1964 was 38 percent. It dropped to 17 percent in 1966, then climbed to 35 percent in 1970.

Despite favorable copper prices, Frei did not succeed in bringing the rate of economic growth to anywhere near a satisfactory level. The price of copper rose by 45 percent in the London market and 81 percent in the New York market between 1964 and 1970. Here are the figures for the annual increase in gross product per capita during those years:[29]

Year	Percent Increase
1964	1.6
1965	2.4
1966	4.6
1967	0.0
1968	0.6
1969	1.0
1970	0.7

During the first two years of Frei's term, the growth rate rose from the low rate of 1964. During the last four years, the economy stagnated, with growth rates far below the 1.5 percent which Frei had disdainfully dismissed as inadequate.

Finally, Popular Promotion—the creation of a network of Neighborhood Committees, Mothers' Centers, etc.—was mainly a political device to increase the grassroots strength of the Christian Democrats. The CIA shared the Christian Democrat view of the importance of building up grassroots strength; the *Covert Action* report states that "CIA assistance enabled the Christian Democratic Party to establish an extensive organization at the neighborhood and village level."[30] The community organizations were cleverly conceived politically, and could sometimes do useful work; if a community could use a playground, the Neighborhood Committee could try to solve the problem. But such committees could not integrate the people of the shantytowns into the rest of the community, anymore than a liberal mayor of New York could solve the problems of the people of the ghettos by setting up store-front neighborhood organizations. Integrating the shantytowns required the solution of problems bigger than organizing Neighborhood Committees. Nor could these committees do more than give people an illusion of participation in power.

Several times during the Frei regime, true power, as opposed to sham power, revealed itself. On March 11, 1966, soldiers opened fire against striking workers of Anaconda's El Salvador mine. The workers, accompanied by women and children, had refused an order to clear out of a union hall in which they were meeting. The shooting left six men and two women dead and thirty-seven wounded.[31] On March 9, 1969, police of the Mobile Group—a special shock force and favorite of the United States Office of Public Safety Assistance—were trying to dislodge squatters who had erected a shantytown at Pampa Irigoin near the city of Puerto Montt; they launched tear gas and, when the squatters answered with rocks, opened fire. Pérez Zujovic, minister of interior, had given instructions to be "tough." The results: eight dead, twenty-six wounded.[32]

After Frei had been in office a while, the Christian Democratic Party began to suffer from internal dissension. Some members became aware that the "Revolution in Liberty" was not a revolution. Many were troubled by the massacre of the miners at El Salvador. When economic stagnation set in in 1967 frictions worsened.

Leftists in the party tried to switch it to a more radical course. In 1966 leftist groups began to argue for a "non-capitalist road to development." A year later, Chonchol, who as radical head of the Institute for Agricultural Development (INDAP) was earning the hatred of the Chilean Right, presided over a commission of the party which prepared a "Political Technical Report" proposing the adoption of the "non-capitalist road." Frei rejected the proposal, and in 1968 Chonchol was forced out of his position as head of INDAP.

Some leftist Christian Democrats proposed that the party form a "Popular Unity" with the Marxist parties to carry out the revolutionary changes that Chile required. The party's national committee rejected this proposal. Soon after, in 1969, Chonchol and several other Left leaders bolted the party and founded the United Popular Action Movement (MAPU), which later formed part of the Popular Unity coalition headed by Allende.

Frei's administration was to some extent successful in achieving its political goals. By getting in its own land reform before that of a truly revolutionary government, it was able to sow division among the lower classes of the countryside, to reduce the chances of a powerful revolutionary upsurge by a unified mass of *campesinos*. The Christian Democrats gained strong positions in the *campesino* unions, made advances in other unions, and formed politically useful Neighborhood Committees.

Yet the Frei administration also unwittingly caused stirrings among the people of Chile. By talking about the need for structural change, it helped make the idea that it was necessary a commonplace. The rhetoric of "Chileanization" and the perception that it was a fraud helped spread the desire to see copper truly nationalized and eventually this desire was shared by the overwhelming majority of Chileans. The land reform awakened expectations among the *campesinos*. In one place after another—impatient at the slowness of the reform—they began to seize land themselves. In May 1970 the *campesino* unions held a nationwide strike to demand an end to armed landholder resistance, and a speeding of the reform. In the cities, also, there were strikes, student demonstrations, hunger marches, and seizures of land by people seeking a place to put up their shantytowns.

Recognizing the unrest, the Christian Democratic Party nominated one of its more leftist leaders—Radomiro Tomic—as its candidate for president in the election of 1970. Tomic's campaign had a leftist tone. His campaign program called for "nationalizing immediately and completely the principal copper producing enterprises."[38] He spoke of a war against underdevelopment, and of the failure of capitalism. This was not enough to prevent the victory of Allende.

4

Constitutionality—Myth and Reality

In early 1971 I happened to voice an opinion to a colleague at the Chile Trading Corporation in New York that Chile would soon be facing disorder and violence. "No," he said, "that is not the way we Chileans settle things; you have to understand 'the Chilean idiosyncrasy'; our tradition is to settle things peacefully, according to law." Later in Chile, as my wife and I were talking politics with the wife of a friend, we referred to the possibility of a coup. "No," came the reply, "we are not one of those tropical countries."

Like the people of other countries, Chileans have myths about themselves. One of the most prevalent is that in Chile everything is always done peacefully, according to constitution and law.

To call this a myth is not to deny that for long stretches Chile has enjoyed bourgeois democracy, and that this fact is of great political importance. But to understand both Chile's history and its attempt at socialist revolution it is essential to measure carefully—to attribute to bourgeois democracy in Chile neither more nor less significance and strength than it had, to understand why bourgeois democracy prevailed during certain periods, while at times open force came into play.

The following table summarizes civil wars, coups, and near-coups in Chile from its declaration of independence in 1818 to 1970:

1823   Aristocracy revolts against B. O' Higgins, first ruler of independent Chile, and forces his resignation.

1827   Military coup overthrows President Agustin Eyzaguirre, replacing him with General Francisco Antonio Pinto.

1829   Pinto, unable to settle differences between groups moving toward civil war, resigns and is replaced by Francisco Ramón Vicuña, who is overthrown in civil war which lasts six months.

1850   Under influence of revolutions of 1848 in Europe, an uprising against the government breaks out, but is quickly put down.

1851   Uprising in April 1851 is quickly put down.

1852   Civil war breaks out in September 1851 and lasts till January 1852.

1859   Civil war breaks out in January and lasts till April.

1877   Minor army mutiny breaks out in city of Punta Arenas.

1891   In January navy starts civil war against Balmaceda which ends with his overthrow in August.

1924   In September 1924 military coup forces President Arturo Alessandri out of office, replacing him with a military junta.

1925   In January 1925 a second coup, led by younger officers, overthrows junta and recalls Alessandri.
        In October 1925 a third coup, led by Colonel Carlos Ibáñez, then serving as minister of war, forces Alessandri out again. Emiliano Figueroa Larraín becomes president, but the real power is Ibáñez.

1927   Ibáñez becomes president through an election in which he is the sole candidate. He rules as dictator till 1931.

1931   Strikes and riots, due to economic crisis, force Ibáñez to resign. Juan Esteban Montero is elected president.

        Uprising by crews of several naval vessels breaks out, but is quickly put down.

1932   Coup led by Marmaduke Grove, chief of the air force, and two civilians, Eugenio Matte and Carlos Dávila, overthrows the

Montero government, forms a governing junta, and proclaims the "Socialist Republic of Chile."

Twelve days later, Carlos Dávila overthrows the junta and becomes provisional president.

Three months later, a new coup forces Dávila out. Elections are held and Alessandri becomes president again.

1938　Gonzales von Marees, leader of Chilean Nazis, organizes an attempt at coup in which several hundred of his followers occupy a building across from the presidential palace. *Carabineros* massacre sixty of them after their surrender.

1939　Carlos Ibáñez attempts a coup which is quickly crushed.

1969　On October 21 General Roberto Viaux, forced into retirement for voicing officers' grievances and building a personal following among them, illegally takes command of the Tacna Regiment, which goes on alert for possible action. The government alerts loyal units and the political parties mobilize worker and public support against a coup. Viaux gives up command, but his demands—increased military pay and resignation of minister of defense and the commander of army—are met.

In the 150 years from independence to 1970, Chile has had four civil wars, one of which overthrew the existing government; some ten coups which toppled the existing governments; and a number of unsuccessful coups, uprisings, and mutinies. The armed forces participated in the overthrow of several early rulers and, later, of Presidents Balmaceda in 1891 and Alessandri in 1924 and 1925.

Against this background, many statements—often learned ones—about Chile's armed forces are ludicrous. Edwin Lieuwen in a section of his book headed "Countries in which the Armed Forces are Nonpolitical," writes:

> In . . . Chile and Colombia, the armed forces occupy a unique position. They are autonomous bodies, dominated and controlled by devoted professional officers. The latter do not openly espouse the cause of any class nor do they express any social or political philosophy. In both countries, the armed forces have traditionally kept aloof from politics—in Chile since the early nineteenth century. . . . Only in grave national crises (in Chile in 1925 . . .) have they

intervened. Their failure . . . taught them a lesson. Having burned their fingers in attempts at extramilitary functions, they soon withdrew from politics and resumed their traditional professional orientation.[1]

"Devoted professional officers." Devoted to whom and to what? The Chilean armed forces "withdrew from politics," says Lieuwen. Actually, they have withdrawn from politics as many times as some people have "given up" smoking.

"The state," wrote Lenin, "is a product and a manifestation of the *irreconcilability* of class antagonisms . . . an organ of class *rule,* an organ for the *oppression* of one class by another. . . . A standing army and police are the chief instruments of state power."[2]

The armed forces of Chile spring from its class society. They are instruments of coercion and force created by the ruling class to maintain its rule. Everything about them—the system of command, the social origin of the officers, the education and training of the officers and men—reflects the purposes of the ruling class. Chilean history tells us that the idea that Chile's armed forces are simply professional, above classes and their conflicts, servants of the whole of society, and obedient only to constitution and law is nonsense.

Yet it is also true that compared to most other Latin American countries Chile has had long stretches of constitutional, bourgeois democratic government. From Prieto in 1831 till Balmaceda in 1891, all of Chile's presidents finished the term of office for which they were elected; the same holds for the period from 1891 till the overthrow of Alessandri in 1924; and again for the period 1932 to 1970.

The comparative stability and democracy of Chile were not accidental. As early as 1815 Bolivar was saying, "If any [republic] endures for a long time in America, I am inclined to think it will be the Chilean. . . . Chile can be free." Among the reasons that Bolivar gave was that Chile would "preserve its unity of political and religious views."[3] The basic reason for the comparative stability and democracy of Chile was the unity and strength of its ruling class.

Chile at the time of independence was a small, compact country, concentrated in what is today its central valley; some regionalism existed, but not enough to create the ruling class divisions it did in other Latin American countries, such as Argentina. Chile's population was homogeneous compared to that of Peru, for example. The Araucanian Indians had their own territory in the south, and their long fight against the Chilean advance helped unify the rest of the country. Chile did have a sharp class division, but the lower classes were kept in such darkness that they offered little threat to upper-class rule. Finally, Chile's mining and merchant bourgeoisie were fused with its landed aristocracy, and this reduced the likelihood of conflicts among the upper classes themselves.

Chile produced, shortly after independence, an exceptionally able, conservative leader who realized that stable, constitutional government would be advantageous for the ruling class, and who was able to lay a strong foundation for it. Diego Portales came to power in 1830 as the leader of a revolution by conservative aristocrats against the *liberales* who had dominated the government since shortly after the fall of O' Higgins in 1823. The conservatives saw only "anarchy" in the period of liberal rule. Different military leaders vied for power. One head of government followed another, each change resulting in the reorganization of the government. The disorder was costly, draining the national treasury so low that often there were not enough funds to cover the government and army payrolls. On top of all this, the liberals were carrying out dangerous political measures— broadening the participation of the people in government.

Portales's aim—in the words of an admirer, the historian Alberto Edwards—was to create a "strong and enduring power, superior to the prestige of a *caudillo,* or the power of a faction;" to create respect for "authority in the abstract," for the law. For the interests of the ruling class as a whole, such a system was better than one in which different leaders and factions fought by any means possible to win power, and then ruled arbitrarily. Because of Chile's favorable conditions and his own skill, Portales was able to establish his system, extinguishing at the same time the movement toward the increasing participation of the people.

Portales's concept of a government superior to factions left its mark on all governmental institutions. In line with this concept, the armed forces could not be allowed to consist of cliques engaged in factional politics, but had to be tightly integrated organizations, obedient to the civilian government. A tradition of unity, of anti-factionalism, developed and has come down to the present day, playing a role in the politics within the armed forces that led up to the coup against the Allende government. In the army, the tradition of obedience and discipline was accentuated by the Prussian regimen introduced by Emilio Körner, a German army officer. Körner was contracted in the 1880s to organize and train the Chilean army.

The system established by Portales was constitutional, but far from democratic. As a Spanish historian put it, the Portales constitution made the president "the delegate of the dominant oligarchy." It "guaranteed the authority of a few dozen landholding families."[4] The participation of the people in governing was prevented in many ways: Only those with a minimum of property or income had the right to vote, the Senate was elected indirectly, etc. Many conquests have been won by the Chilean people since Portales, but Chilean democracy remained limited. Professor Pike wrote in 1963: "What we have praised as democracy in Chile since 1920 has amounted to little more than a system in which a small privileged class has been gentlemanly in determining through very limited electoral processes, which of its members would rule the country."[5]

Just as the birth of constitutional democracy in Chile depended on certain conditions, so too did its continuance require them. Limited factional quarrels could not easily cause breaks in constitutional democracy. But serious conflicts could—conflicts between important sectors of the upper class or between classes, and certainly conflicts which threatened the rule of the bourgeoisie as a whole. With Balmaceda, a rising industrial bourgeoisie was in conflict with the traditional oligarchy and the imperialists, and this accounts for the uprising against him. The struggle of the lower classes, the threat from them, helps explain the coups of 1931 and 1932. Because constitutional democracy has advantages and the people back it, Chile's ruling class did not lightly suspend it. But when it had to, it did not hesitate to do so. Chile's armed forces have not been used to intervene openly in politics except when necessary, but when necessary, there has been no compunction.

Yet even flawed, periodically interrupted, bourgeois democracy is vastly different from open dictatorship, and puts deep marks on a country. The Chilean people were less subject to arbitrary oppression than those of most other Latin American countries. A tradition developed that the right way to do things was constitutionally. Most Chileans were proud of their country's tradition of stability and democracy; they felt that democracy was their right and they supported it and worked to improve it.

CHILE's trade union and socialist movement developed in the setting of bourgeois democracy. The trade union movement was among the earliest to get started in Latin America. By the late 1880s, workers in the northern nitrate provinces and in many cities throughout Chile were organizing and striking. Newspapers with names like *The People, The Oppressed,* and *Echoes of the Workshop* appeared. The unrest led to the formation in 1887 of the Democratic Party—the first people's party in Chile—composed of professionals and shopkeepers, artisans, and proletarians—which stated as its aim the "political, social, and economic emancipation of the people."[6] By 1894 this party had elected its first representative to the Chamber of Deputies.

The Democratic Party was itself reformist, but within it there was a ferment of socialist ideas, and from it emerged several revolutionary working-class leaders, including the great Luis Emilio Recabarren. A typographer by trade, Recabarren progressed rapidly from democratic reformism to revolutionary socialism, using the knowledge he had learned at his trade to found and edit working-class newspapers. In 1903 he accepted an invitation to become the editor of *El Trabajo (Work),* a newspaper published by the Mutual Aid Society of the workers of the northern nitrate port of Tocopilla. Then he travelled throughout the nitrate country—a desert without grass, trees, or birds—going from one forsaken mining settlement to another, telling the workers to join hands, unite their voices, and fight. He worked to turn the mutual aid societies, concerned with providing help with medicines and funeral expenses, into organizations for struggle.

He taught socialism, telling the workers that they themselves must destroy the exploitation and misery from which they suffered.

The authorities reacted. The police descended on Recabarren's presses, burning them, and scattering the type. He bought new presses but was arrested and imprisoned. He spent his time in jail writing leaflets, articles, pamphlets.

In 1906, running as a member of the Democratic Party, Recabarren was elected deputy to the Chilean Congress. Using various pretexts, the Chamber of Deputies refused to accept him. As one member said, it was "not tolerable that the idea of social dissolution held by Mr. Recabarren should be represented in the Chamber."[7]

Recabarren founded the Workers Socialist Party in 1912. When World War I broke out, he took a strong stand against it; "the war," he said, "should be followed by revolution." Under Recabarren's influence, a grouping of mutual aid societies of railroad workers was developed into Chile's first great trade union central—the Workers Federation of Chile (FOCH)—whose aim was to include all the country's wage workers. Recabarren then led FOCH into joining the Red Trade Union International, with headquarters in Moscow.

The Workers Socialist Party ran Recabarren for president in 1920. He won few votes, but the action meant the opening up of a new front of struggle, the use of electoral activity to help educate and mobilize the masses and to win positions that could help advance the revolutionary movement. The party also participated in the parliamentary elections of 1921, winning two seats in the Chamber of Deputies, one for Recabarren. This was the first time that legitimate representatives of the Chilean working class succeeded in entering the Chilean Congress. Recabarren also led the way in the transformation, in 1922, of the Workers Socialist Party into the Communist Party.

In 1925 the Communist Party, seeing a threat to democracy in the forced resignation of President Arturo Alessandri, and the presentation by a reactionary coalition of bourgeois parties of a single presidential candidate, Emiliano Figueroa Larraín, took the initiative in forming a National Committee of Wage Earners—a sort of popular front, the precursor of several others to be formed in the future. Running on a liberal-democratic platform, José Santos Salas, the committee's candidate, won 80,000 votes to Figueroa's 180,000. A little over a year later, Colonel Carlos Ibañez forced Figueroa out and established a dictatorship. Besides outlawing the Communist Party, closing its offices and its press, Ibañez banished to remote areas, exiled and/or imprisoned many of its leaders and members. Ibañez also worked to destroy FOCH and other trade union organizations. He persecuted progressives, democrats, and opponents of all types, such as former President Alessandri and two former ministers of foreign affairs.

The Communist Party—inexperienced and caught before it had a chance to put into effect its planned reorganization for illegal work—was hit hard by the Ibañez dictatorship. Its youth organization almost disappeared; its contacts with the masses were weakened. Still the Party worked heroically; its Central Committee met in secret; and it put out many issues of illegal newspapers. Even while outlawed, it reorganized itself, and by the time the Ibañez dictatorship fell in 1931, the framework of a new organization had been formed.[8]

The Socialist Party was founded in the turmoil of the early 1930s. In the aftermath of the overthrow of Ibañez in 1931 and the twelve-day Socialist Republic of Chile set up by Grove and Matte in 1932, a number of new socialist political groups arose—the New Public Action, the Revolutionary Socialist Action, the Socialist Order, the Socialist Marxist Party, and the Unified Socialist Party. In 1933 these groups joined together to form the Socialist Party. The new party published a Declaration of Principles accepting "Marxism as a method for interpreting reality;" the "class struggle"; the need to transform capitalism into socialism; the "dictatorship of the workers;" . . . and "internationalism and anti-imperialism."[9] The government of Alessandri—theoretically democratic—persecuted the Socialist Party, from time to time deporting or imprisoning its leaders, often forcing the party to work in clandestinity.[10]

Despite harassment and persecution, the Marxist parties grew, participated in elections, and gained electoral strength. The trade union movement recuperated from the damage inflicted during the Ibañez dictatorship. And in 1936 a new Confederation of Chilean Workers (CTCH) was formed. By this year, the Marxist parties and the trade union movement were strong enough for the Radical Party to be willing to join in a Popular Front against the reactionary parties, and an agreement forming such a front was signed by the Radical, Socialist, and Communist parties.

The Popular Front was a progressive, not a socialist movement. It "aroused great enthusiasm among the masses," says one writer; the masses liked the idea of unity.[11] In 1938 the Popular Front's candidate—Pedro Aguirre Cerda, a Radical—was elected president. The Socialist Party had three Ministers in the Popular Front government, among them the future president, Salvador Allende. The success in getting the Popular Front elected had an effect on people's political thinking; many felt it showed that a coalition of parties dedicated to a socialist program could win the government through election.

In 1948 the Communist Party was again outlawed; under pressure from the United States moving into its cold war, the González Videla government put through a "Law for the Permanent Defense of Democracy" which made the Party illegal. Again Communists were imprisoned, banished, and exiled; Pablo Neruda was forced to flee across the mountains to Argentina into exile. And the names of the 25,000 Communist voters were wiped off the election rolls.[12] As usual the persecution extended to non-Communist trade union leaders, politicians, and others critical of the regime.

But the Communist Party was now experienced, better prepared to work under illegality. After a while, Communist newspapers reappeared. In 1952 one of the offshoots of the Socialist Party, which had split, ran the first Marxist candidate for president of Chile, Salvador Allende; the Communist Party supported him. Communists played a key part in forming the new Central Workers' Confederation (CUT) in 1953. In 1956 the Communist Party joined with the Socialists, shortly to be reunited into one party, to form the Popular Action Front (FRAP). The Law for the Permanent Defense of Democracy was abrogated in 1958; within a month the Party was participating in the presidential election.

The FRAP candidate, Allende, came within 35,000 votes of winning in 1958. FRAP ran Allende again in 1964, but this time he was running against a united opposition and the massive intervention of the United States; he lost to Frei, but he received 39 percent of the vote as compared to 29 percent in 1958.

By this time Socialist-Communist unity was strong. The road to unity had been difficult and long. Historically, there had been a number of differences between the two parties, and also between different factions of the Socialist Party, some dating back to the early 1930s—differences over policy toward the Soviet Union, over the kinds of alliances appropriate for a working-class party to make, and over immediate goals. One wing of the Socialist Party had felt at the time FRAP was being formed that it should be a workers front, composed only of workers parties and the trade union confederation, CUT. Another wing and the Communist Party had wanted FRAP to be a broad alliance, a national liberation front, in which bourgeois parties, like the Radical Party, supported by the middle classes, could participate. Some differences had been worn away by time, others remained. But both parties had learned from the experience of years that they could work together in the CUT, in strikes, and in elections. At the Thirteenth Congress of the Communist Party in 1965, Luis Corvalán, Secretary General of the Communist Party, listed the things that united the two parties—anti-imperialism, friendship with the Cuban Revolution, agreement on the need to fight together with the socialist and non-aligned countries for world peace, and the same general appreciation of the transformations necessary for Chile. Other speakers stressed that "what unites us is much stronger than our differences." And speaking as a guest, Aniceto Rodríguez, Secretary General of the Socialist Party, said, "Life itself has taught us the need for unity and counsels us to persevere in it."[13]

For the 1970 presidential election, a left-wing coalition was again formed, called the Popular Unity, consisting of the Communist, Socialist, Radical, MAPU, and two very small parties—the Social Democrats and the Popular Independent Action. *The Program of the Popular Unity* called for the "replacement of the present economic structure, doing away with the ꜱower of foreign and national monopoly capital and the *latifundia* in order to initiate the construction of socialism."[14]

The Popular Unity movement was not something that had been dreamed up one day in someone's head. It flowed logically from Chile's history.

5

Between Election and Inauguration

As in every important Chilean election since 1963, the imperialists intervened in the 1970 presidential election. According to the *Covert Action* report: "The CIA spent from $800,000 to $1,000,000. . . . The large-scale propaganda campaign which was undertaken by the U.S. was similar to that of 1964: an Allende victory was equated with violence and repression." The United States effort concentrated on " 'spoiling operations' against the Popular Unity coalition. . . ." It tried to splinter the Radical Party; it used 'black propaganda' . . . to sow dissent between Communists and Socialists, and between the national labor confederation and the Chilean Communist Party."[1]

The U.S. corporations participated. "During the period prior to the September election, ITT representatives met frequently with CIA representatives both in Chile and in the United States and the CIA advised ITT as to ways in which it might safely channel funds both to the Alessandri campaign and to the National Party. The CIA was kept informed of the extent and the mechanism of the funding. Eventually at least $350,000 was passed by ITT to this campaign. A roughly equal amount was passed by other U.S. companies. . . ."[2] In their book, *The CIA and the Cult of Intelligence,* Victor Marchetti and John Marks identify Anaconda

Copper as another of the companies that spent a large sum to prevent Allende's election.[3]

The vote in the election was as follows:[4]

	Votes	Percent
Salvador Allende, Popular Unity	1,070,334	36.6
Jorge Alessandri, National Party	1,031,159	35.3
Radomiro Tomic, Christian Democratic Party	821,801	28.1

The newly elected president was to be inaugurated on November 3, 1970. In the sixty days between election and inauguration an overture was played out which introduced the main themes of the impending revolutionary process. The central question was whether Allende would even be allowed to take office without an armed struggle.

The day after the election, *El Mercurio,* a leading strategist in the fight against the UP, carried the headline, "Narrow Triumph of Allende." But in an editorial it stated that the result was not final: it was "far from an absolute majority and will have to receive the ratification of Congress within 50 days." Chile's constitution did state that if no candidate received an absolute majority, Congress would, within 50 days, choose from the two candidates with the highest vote. But Chile was a multi-party country in which victory by an absolute majority in a presidential election was rare, and by custom, the candidate with a plurality had been automatically ratified. The same editorial also argued that it was the responsibility of the leaders of the "democratic sectors of Chile . . . to maintain these sectors disciplined and united so that the country is not delivered to a policy which will soon profoundly change the Chilean way of life."

The next day, the head of Alessandri's election headquarters read a communique calling on "the democratic forces and their representatives . . . to unite and defend, within order and respect for the law, the right which the Constitution grants them to designate the President of the Nation. . . . The citizenry is conscious that the electoral process has not terminated."[5]

On September 10 *El Mercurio* carried more editorials designed to mobilize the "democratic forces" against a Marxist government. "Many voters are asking themselves about their chances of liberty and work in a socialist regime like that which is drawing close." Socialism would mean scarcities, rationing, the loss of freedom over how to educate one's children, the replacement of professional judges by class judges. The same day, a statement by Alessandri appeared which showed where the argument that the electoral process had not terminated was intended to lead. "In case I am elected by the Congress, I will resign, which will mean a new election."

Part of the means for mobilizing the "democratic forces," for creating agitation and dread at the prospect of an Allende government, was economic sabotage. The day after the election, a campaign of telephone calls began, urging people to withdraw their bank deposits to protect themselves against the coming insolvency of the banking system. The next business day, long lines of depositors awaited the opening of the banks, and by noon these had closed their doors, saying that they had run out of cash. The right-wing press carried headlines and stories about the run on the banks, including pictures of the lines.

A flight of dollars out of Chile developed. Under the regulations of the Central Bank, Chileans can only acquire dollars for certain approved purposes, among them travel. Now black-market speculators encouraged people to apply for dollars to travel. These people could then sell the dollars at enormous profits to the speculators who would in turn sell them to those who wished to transfer funds abroad. The amount of dollars sold by the Central Bank for "travel abroad" zoomed.

Many enterprises suspended their purchases and suddenly insisted on immediate payment in cash from their customers. Some companies began to lay-off people, while others cut down hours of work.

Every few days *El Mercurio* carried headlines, stories, and editorials about a "Grave Economic Moment," a "Decrease in Commercial Sales," and a "Decline in Stock Market Values." On September 11 it said in an editorial:

> The possibility of numerous expropriations in the fields of industrial and agricultural production as well as distribution, transportation, and commerce menaces not only the proprietors of the affected enterprises, but also those who work in them, since no one can

foresee the orientation that the expropriating State will give to these production units. Also affected would be the suppliers who in large measure depend on orders placed by the present management of these enterprises. . . . Thus there are hundreds of thousands of working people who have resolved to prepare themselves for whatever may come by the simple expedient of not making any avoidable expenditures or investments. Lamentably, no solution can be foreseen for the decline in sales so long as the uncertainty exists.

On September 23 under the headline, "Pronounced Industrial and Commercial Decline," *El Mercurio* carried a report by the Society for the Development of Manufacturing which stated that, comparing the second week of September with the same week of August, industrial production had gone down by 9 percent and sales by 61 percent. On September 25 it spoke in an editorial of "a panic that had destroyed a prosperity which seemed to be advancing firmly. . . ."

Andrés Zaldívar, Frei's minister of finance, instead of trying to calm people's fears about the banks, and limit the outflow of dollars, issued a statement on September 8 that "the present situation is difficult to deal with."[6] On September 23 he gave a talk on radio and television. Ordinarily, ministers of finance trying to dampen a crisis do not stress the worst facts and figures, but Zaldívar revelled in them. "Between September 7 and 17, withdrawals from the Savings and Loan System were almost 340 million escudos." Zaldívar neglected to mention that by the time of his talk the rate of withdrawals was declining sharply.

Some industries have proceeded to suspend their expansion plans and even paralyze those already under way. . . . The sales of durable household goods, such as television sets, radios, and furniture have declined by 50 to 80 percent. . . . The case of automobiles is even more critical. . . . This industry is especially important because of the chain effect it produces on the suppliers of parts who together with the assembly industry employ 15,000 persons. . . . The construction of housing has been seriously affected. . . . The monetary system is being forced to emit money in an amount so great that it menaces the very bases of economy.[7]

Under the guise of presenting an "objective" report, Zaldívar was trying to spread panic. Such actions by the UP's enemies were the kind that showed in the open. Behind the scenes much more was happening.

On September 7 an ITT official in Chile reported to the home office:

> The Alessandri faction has not surrendered. . . . In a very confidential and private session on Sunday afternoon with Dr. Arturo Matte, Alessandri's brother-in-law and his closest advisor, I was briefed on their strategy: They are somehow expecting the electoral tribunal to show that the official vote recount favored Alessandri, not Allende, and that President Frei will support this decision. The armed forces, most of whose leaders are pro-Alessandri, would be expected to support Frei. The mechanics of just how this would be achieved were merely hinted and I inferred it would require some money and influential pressures, perhaps from Washington. Mr. Matte said that with Frei and the armed forces support, a larger segment of the Christian Democratic bloc would be persuaded to vote for Alessandri. Once elected by Congress, Dr. Alessandri would . . . resign the presidency. This would result in new elections in which Frei would be eligible for another Presidential term. Frei's stature is such, most Chileans believe he would defeat any opposition candidate.

The memorandum pointed out that "the Alessandri camp is fully aware of the consequences of such a maneuver—a bloodbath. . . . Dr. Matte, acknowledging this, said this was necessary to prevent communism from taking over the country."[8]

On September 9 the ITT Board of Directors met for its monthly meeting in New York City. ITT Chairman Harold S. Geneen and John A. McCone, a director who had formerly headed the CIA, had a conversation about the political situation in Chile. "What he told me . . . ," McCone testified afterward,

> was that he was prepared to put as much as a million dollars in support of any plan that was adopted by the government for the purpose of bringing about a coalition of the opposition to Allende so that . . . this coalition would be united [in the Congressional run-off] and deprive Allende of his position. . . . He said that this idea had been transmitted to Mr. Kissinger's office, and he asked me if I would support it, and I did. I came to Washington a few days later and I met with Mr. [Richard] Helms [head of the CIA] and I told him of this availability of these funds, and I also met with Mr. Kissinger and I told him, if he had a plan—now, Mr. Kissinger thanked me very much

and said I would hear from him. I did not hear from him again. . . . [9]

Though Kissinger did not get in touch with McCone, he too was aghast at the prospect of an Allende government. At an off-the-record press briefing (September 16), he said:

> I have yet to meet somebody who firmly believes that if Allende wins there is likely to be another free election in Chile. . . . Now, it is fairly easy for one to predict that if Allende wins, there is a good chance that he will establish over a period of years some sort of Communist government. In that case you would have . . . not an island off the coast which has not a traditional relationship and impact on Latin America, but in a major Latin American country, you would have a Communist government, joining, for example, Argentina, which is already deeply divided, along a long frontier, joining Peru, which has already been heading in directions that have been difficult to deal with, and joining Bolivia, which has also gone in a more leftist, anti-U.S. direction, even without any of these developments. So I don't think we should delude ourselves that an Allende takeover in Chile would not present massive problems for us, and for democratic forces and for pro-U.S. forces in Latin America, and indeed to the whole Western Hemisphere. What would happen to the Western Hemisphere Defense Board, or to the Organization of American States, and so forth, is extremely problematical."[10]

President Nixon, described by one *New York Times* source as "extremely anxious," by another as "frantic," called a meeting at the White House (September 15), attended by himself, Kissinger, Helms, and Attorney General John Mitchell. Helms's notes at the meeting "reflect," according to the Senate Intelligence Committee, "both its tenor and the President's instructions."

"One in 10 chance perhaps, but save Chile!
worth spending
not concerned risks involved
no involvement of Embassy
$10,000,000 available, more if necessary
full time job—best men we have
game plan
make the economy scream
48 hours for plan of action."[11]

The committee sums up the instructions: "President Nixon informed CIA Director Richard Helms that an Allende regime in

Chile would not be acceptable to the United States and instructed the CIA to play a direct role in organizing a military *coup d'etat* in Chile to prevent Allende's accession to the Presidency."[12]

Just after the White House meeting, new instructions also went to the U.S. Embassy in Chile. "Late Tuesday night (September 15)," reports an ITT memorandum from Chile, "Ambassador Edward Korry finally received a message from State Department giving him the green light to move in the name of President Nixon. The message gave him maximum authority to do all possible—short of a Dominican Republic-type action—to keep Allende from taking power."[13]

Although the CIA and the U.S. Ambassador in Chile were both instructed to work for a coup, they were to pursue this goal—in U.S. government jargon—on different "tracks." The embassy and several other U.S. agencies, including the CIA, were to work on Track I; the CIA alone was to work on Track II. Those in both tracks were to try to get the Chilean military to move against Allende. But Track I was to work for a coup with the cooperation, or at least acquiescence, of Frei. On Track II the CIA was to promote a coup without Frei, and it was to work super-secretly, reporting only to the White House, not informing the U.S. Ambassador, the State Department, or even the top-level interdepartmental 40 Committee, responsible for authorizing covert operations.[14]

It quickly became clear that Track I was not prospering. Frei was vacillating. According to the ITT memorandum just quoted, he "stated privately to his closest associates, to Alessandri, and *to a State Department visitor last weekend* . . . that the country cannot be allowed to go Communist and that Allende must be prevented from taking office. Publicly, however, he is keeping out of the battle up to this point while feeling *steadily increasing pressure from the U.S.* and his own camp. Never known for displaying guts in a crunch, he is faced with a dilemma of not wanting to be charged with either turning Chile over to Communist rule or contributing to a possible civil war."[15]

Many in the armed forces who might go along with a constitutional-appearing coup in which Frei cooperated, were also hesitant. The ITT memorandum quotes Matte as saying that *"the armed forces are agreed on the extreme danger to democracy that Allende's assumption of power involves. They agree he must be stopped.* However, the armed forces leadership and Frei prefer a constitutional way out (i.e., congressional election of Alessandri) that doesn't preclude violence—spontaneous or provoked."[16]

Finally, the CIA found out early that a U.S. plan to bribe Christian Democratic congressmen to vote against Allende in the congressional run-off election would not work. Too many Christian Democrats, especially those in the left- and Tomic-wings of the party, firmly intended to vote for Allende. Tomic himself had sent a card to Allende after the election saying, "Congratulations on your victory. . . ."

Work continued on Track I. But CIA headquarters in Washington, following Nixon's instructions to Helms, cabled the CIA Chief of Station in Santiago on September 21 that "parliamentary legerdemain has been discarded." The United States was placing its main hope on a "military solution" without Frei, if need be, without constitutional cover.[17]

Crucial for the U.S. strategy, for both Tracks, I and II, was "making the economy scream." On September 28 William Broe, head of the CIA's Clandestine Services for the Western Hemisphere, told Edward J. Gerrity, a senior vice-president of ITT, "that he was looking for additional help aimed at inducing economic collapse" in Chile and made the following "suggestions" on how this could be brought about:

1) Banks should not renew credits or should delay in doing so.
2) Companies should drag their feet in sending money, in making deliveries, in shipping spare parts, etc.
3) Savings and loan companies there are in trouble. If pressure were applied they would have to shut their doors, thereby creating stronger pressure.
4) We should withdraw all technical help and should not promise any technical assistance in the future. Companies in a position to do so should close their doors.

Broe provided a list of companies with the suggestion that ITT get them to cooperate in these measures.[18] How economic sabotage fitted into the strategy for blocking Allende is also made clear by the ITT papers:

It appears almost certain that marxist Salvador Allende will be confirmed by the Congress as Chile's next President. . . . There is only a thin tendril of hope of an upset based on a sharp and unlikely switch in voting sentiment among the Christian Democrats. . . . *A more realistic hope . . . is that a swiftly deteriorating economy (bank runs, plant bankruptcies etc.) will touch off a wave of violence resulting in a military coup.*[19]

Other things besides the economic crisis helped create a climate of abnormality and violence. Just as in Cuba in the months before the Bay of Pigs invasion, bombs exploded frequently. Allende commented: "We have seen how bombs are placed—bombs and more bombs. . . ." This seditious activity is "not spontaneous. There are foreign advisors here, people with a lot of experience, mercenaries trained to create this climate. . . . Official reports . . . inform us that, from July to September, 5,300 U.S. citizens entered the country. . . . Among these 5,300 must be a sizeable number of CIA agents. . . ."[20]

Pablo Rodriguez, the leader of the newly founded party, Fatherland and Liberty (Patria y Libertad), a fascist organization, complete with swastika-like symbol, declared at a public meeting: "If they want civil war, here we are, ready." The CIA helped found Patria y Libertad, providing it with $38,500 in 1970.[21]

CIA officials were pessimistic about the chances of carrying out Nixon's orders to prevent Allende's accession to power. Helms later testified: "My heart sank over this meeting, because . . . the possibility of bringing off something like this seemed to me at that time to be just as remote as anything could be. In practical terms, the Army was constitutionalist. . . . And when you look here at the time frame in which the man was suddenly asking you to accomplish something, it seemed really almost inconceivable. . . ." Deputy Director of the CIA Thomas Karamessines also testified: "There was much talk among Chilean officers about the possibility of some kind of coup . . . but this was not the kind of talk that was being backed by . . . serious organizational planning." The Senate Intelligence Committee summed up: "Although there was talk of a coup in Chilean military circles, there was little indication that it would actually take place without U.S. encouragement and support."[22]

The CIA did what it could. It set up a special task force under Karamessines to manage the promotion of a coup. It encouraged Chilean officers who were talking coup to act, assuring them—in the words of the Senate Intelligence Committee—"that the U.S. government would support a coup both before and after it took place."

A number of Chilean officers were involved. Karamessines testified "that a good dozen or more Chilean senior officers were privy to what was going on . . . they were all talking to one another exchanging views and trying to see how best to mount the kind of coup that they wanted to see take place."[23]

Among the Chilean plotters were the retired General Roberto Viaux, who had led the Tacnazo rebellion in 1969, and General Camilo Valenzuela, commander of the Santiago garrison. Details of how the plotting was carried forward on the Chilean side are available from two books, *Conversaciones Con Viaux,* a long interview with him, and *El Caso Schneider,*[24] which contains material from the court-martial of Viaux and his co-conspirators.

Viaux relates that after the September 4 election he entered into discussions with Valenzuela to see what could be done to keep Allende from taking office. Later, after making appropriate soundings, Viaux and Valenzuela held meetings with Admiral Hugo Tirado, second in command of the navy, General Joaquín García, second in command of the air force, and General Vicente Huerta, in command of the national police (Carabineros).

Viaux says that he and Valenzuela decided that they did not want to take action in such a way as to cause division in the armed forces, especially not in the army. So the idea "took form in our thinking that, as far as possible, it should be the very Commanders-in-chief and the Director of the uniformed police who, united and by common agreement, and even more than this, with the consent of the Government itself, should join together in a *coup d'etat.*"[25] This posed problems since, apart from the Carabineros, the plotters did not include the Commanders-in-chief. In the army, Valenzuela was only fifth in rank.

The Commander-in-chief of the Army, General René Schneider posed a special problem. He was a leader of the constitutionalist sector of the army and a key obstacle to a coup. Earlier in the year he had declared: "The Army is the guarantor of a normal election and that the Presidency of the Republic will be assumed by the one who is elected by the people through an absolute majority, or by the Congress as a whole in case none of the candidates obtains more than 50 percent of the vote."[26] This and related statements by him that the army's respect for the constitution was unalterable became known as the "Schneider Doctrine."

Besides plotting with other officers, Viaux was also in contact with high-ranking members of the Frei government. He learned that Minister of Defense Sergio Ossa, Minister of Economy Carlos Figueroa, and Minister of Finance Andrés Zaldívar, representing a sector of the Christian Democrats that did not want to "deliver the Government" to communism, were pressing Frei to do something. He was told beforehand of the talk on the economy Zaldívar intended to give on September 23 and what Zaldívar hoped it would lead to. After the talk, "four ministers would resign, which would bring in its train the resignation of the whole Cabinet. Faced with this situation, Mr. Frei would name a Cabinet of Administration formed of personal friends and officers on active service, among them General Schneider; thus [i.e., by removing Schneider from active command] the problem of command of the army would be solved and there would be freedom to act. In this way, also, constitutional appearances would be preserved. . . ." But the ministers did not resign and Frei did nothing after Zaldívar's speech.

Early in October, says Viaux, he received a message that Frei wanted him to make a coup, but that he should "do it well, with complete certainty of success, otherwise [Frei] would be forced to proceed against [him]."[27] Viaux took this message to his co-conspirators, but there remained the problem of getting the action to take place under the auspices of the Commanders-in-chief. This problem began to move toward solution when, even as Viaux and the others were conspiring, Tirado was promoted to Commander-in-chief of the Navy. Another part was solved when the conspirators learned that the Commander-in-chief of the Air Force, Carlos Guerraty, would join them once the action started.

This left the problem of the command of the army, which the conspirators decided to solve by kidnapping. They first thought of kidnapping the four highest-ranking officers, which would have left Valenzuela in command; later, they decided to kidnap the two highest; finally, only Schneider. Viaux says that the idea of kidnapping Schneider "was approved unanimously (that is, by all five, Tirado, Valenzuela, García, Huerta, and me)."[28] Viaux undertook to organize the kidnapping.

How did Allende meet the conspiracy to keep him from taking office? He spoke throughout the country, often to giant demonstrations, explaining the UP program, warning that a plot to keep him from taking office was afoot, stating what he would do if the conspirators resorted to force; and he maneuvered politically to weaken the backing for the conspiracy.

At a massive victory demonstration in Santiago on September 5 Allende stated:

> We are not under any circumstances going to back down from the Popular Unity Program that was the people's combat flag. I will not be just another president; I will be the first president of the first truly democratic, popular and revolutionary government in Chilean history. . . . We have won in order to overthrow imperialist exploitation once and for all, to put an end to the monopolies, to carry out a serious and profound agrarian reform, to control the export and import trade, and to nationalize credit. . . . The changes needed by the country can only be carried out if the Chilean people truly assume power and exercise it effectively. . . . by means of a new political constitution which will institutionalize the massive incorporation of the people into the control of the state.[29]

Allende spoke of the economic sabotage. The crisis was a maneuver of the imperialists, the monopolists, and the large landholders, probing for ways to get around the electoral victory of the people. It was artificial: Nothing basic in the economy justified it. Confusion was being sown deliberately: The nationalization of the banks did not mean that deposits would be confiscated. Sometimes Allende got tough. He told the workers at one factory: "Tell the owners that we want all the factories to work, but warn them in my name that if they paralyze them artificially, you are going to take them over and you are going to make them produce."[30]

Several times Allende warned the conspirators that if they tried to carry out their plans there would be a fight. To a mass demonstration in Santiago on September 13 he said: "The people will know how to defend its victory. . . . If [the conspirators] in their madness provoke a situation that we do not want they should know that the whole country will come to a stop, that no enterprise, factory, workshop, school, hospital, or farm will operate: This will be our first demonstration of force. . . . Let them know . . . that we have a sense of responsibility, but that we also know what a force a disciplined and organized people represents."[31] Sometimes Allende put it more tersely: "If the bourgeoisie wants to use force, we will reply with force."

Allende worked to prevent the conspirators from obtaining the moral and constitutional justification many of them felt they needed. Even while warning of conspiracies, he urged his followers to remain calm and disciplined, to avoid disorder and violence. At the victory demonstration he told the people: "You will all retire to your homes without provoking anyone and without being provoked."

At every opportunity Allende explained that the only ones who had anything to fear from a UP government were the imperialists, the monopolists, and the large landholders. Not everything would be nationalized. Besides the social area composed of nationalized enterprises, there would be an area of mixed capital—government and private together—and an area of private capital. Allende tried to reassure Chile's many thousands of small entrepreneurs: "Private industries—production and trade—may continue as they do now with the difference that the state will give them help, especially credits and commitments to buy their products."[32]

The UP program, Allende stated, would be carried out within the law. Democratic rights would be guaranteed under the new constitution. "Regarding voting, our program is specific: There will be elections with guarantees for all, including our opponents. The vote will be universal and secret."

Allende appealed to the constitutionalism and patriotism of the armed forces. "There is no dispute between the Armed Forces and the people of Chile. I believe that the Chilean Armed Forces have proven during their years of existence that they respect the Constitution, the law, and the people's will, and will continue to do so."[33] Economic development, said Allende, must be of interest to the armed forces, since an underdeveloped country cannot really defend itself.

Allende met with groups of officers to discuss their problems and explain UP plans. Many officers were worried about their personal futures under a Marxist government. Allende reassured them: There would be a bigger role for them in the future than they'd had in the past; their administrative and technical skills would be used in the task of economic development. Allende discussed the problems of military pay and promotion with the officers. According to an ITT memorandum, he "promised various officers that he [would] not change the military organizational structure."[34]

Finally, Allende was conciliatory toward the Christian Democrats, holding out his hand to the more progressive elements and the CD congressmen who had decided not to back the "Alessandri formula" and to those who were wavering. He spoke warmly of the CD youth who, on the night of the election, had joined the UP youth to celebrate a victory over the Right. He praised the honesty of his "friend" Radomiro Tomic for his recognition of the UP victory. He said that there was an opening for a dialogue between Christian Democracy and Popular Unity.

Even while some CD leaders, like Zaldívar, were pressing for action to keep Allende from taking office, or like Frei, were probing the possibility of doing so, others felt either that it was right that Allende be allowed to become president or that there was no acceptable way of blocking him. Many Christian Democrats began to explore an alternative to blocking Allende—letting him take office, but only on condition that he agree to a list of "constitutional guarantees."

As early as September 9 *El Mercurio* stated that "there has been speculation concerning the assurances that the Popular Unity would give for the maintenance of some constitutional guarantees, such as the system of periodic elections, the democratic selection of authorities, the liberty of the press. . . ." *El Mercurio* expressed skepticism about the value of such guarantees. But many CD congressmen seemed willing to vote for Allende if he agreed to them.

Negotiations between the Christian Democrats and the Popular Unity got under way and agreement was reached on a constitutional reform bill embodying the guarantees. The text, made public on October 9, revealed the main purpose of those Christian Democrats who determined what guarantees to insist on: They were trying to prepare the most favorable conditions for the struggle for power they knew was coming.

The Christian Democrats wanted to avoid the arming of the people, the creation of a people's militia; they wanted a monopoly of armed power to remain with the traditional armed forces; and they wanted to prevent the president from being able to increase his control of the armed forces by incorporating outside personnel. The pertinent article of the guarantees reads:

> The public force is constituted only and exclusively by the Armed Forces and the Carabinero Corps, institutions essentially professional, hierarchical, disciplined, obedient, and non-deliberating. Only by virtue of a law can the complement of these institutions be fixed.
>
> The incorporation of new personnel into the Armed Forces and Carabineros can only be effected through their own specialized schools, except for personnel dedicated to exclusively civilian functions.[35]

Almost as though they had read Lenin on the subject, the Christian Democrats wanted to avoid the creation of any kind of people's power—based on the "direct initiative of the people from below, and *not on a law*."[36] One guarantee provided that "in no case can [popular organizations] arrogate to themselves the right to speak in the name of the people or attempt to exercise powers which belong to the authority of the state."[37]

Yet certain popular organizations might be controlled by the Christian Democrats, or at least by the combined opposition to the UP, and it was desirable to protect them; they might later be useful to mobilize mass opposition to the UP government. The guarantee read: "Neighborhood Committees, Mothers' Centers, Trade Unions, and other social organizations through which the People participate in the solution of their problems . . . are granted independence and liberty to carry out the functions assigned to them by law."[38]

With the agreement on guarantees, the last thin hope of a coup with constitutional cover died. Now the chances of blocking Allende depended on a straight military coup.

Viaux and his co-conspirators moved ahead with preparations for kidnapping Schneider. Valenzuela suggested a plan. On October 19 several generals were giving a dinner for Schneider in a house on President Errázuriz Street. He, Valenzuela, would keep the other generals engaged in conversation after the dinner, making sure that Schneider left alone, thus providing an opportunity for kidnapping him. The CIA helped supply the kidnappers with weapons, delivering the first installment—tear gas grenades—on October 18. A kidnapping attempt got under way on October 19, but failed to materialize when Schneider unexpectedly went to his private rather than his official car, and the kidnappers lost him from sight. On October 20 a second attempt, as Schneider was being driven home from his office, failed. At 2:00 AM on October 22 a U.S. military attache, serving as go-between for the CIA, passed three submachine guns with ammunition to a Chilean officer who was connected with the plotters. A few hours later came the final attempt: Several cars suddenly surrounded the Mercedes in which Schneider was being driven to his office, forcing it to stop; two kidnappers broke the rear door window of Schneider's car, Schneider pulled his pistol, several kidnappers started shooting, and Schneider was severely wounded. He died three days later.

The kidnapping attempt was counterproductive. Broad sectors of the population and many officers of the armed forces were upset by the shooting of Schneider. The episode helped strengthen the widespread sentiment that Allende ought to be allowed to take office.

The coup plot was not carried through. Viaux thought that, despite the shooting of Schneider (which he says was unintended), Valenzuela and his co-plotters, Admiral Tirado and Generals García and Huerta, should have acted. Think of it, says Viaux: After the shooting, martial law was declared and General Valenzuela, as the commander of the Santiago garrison, was "the maximum authority, with all forces under his command, and with the plan [for a coup] ready to be acted upon."[39] Viaux doesn't know, he says, why Valenzuela and the others didn't act, but thinks it was because of fear. *The New York Times* says that "the CIA had ascertained that the Valenzuela coup [could] not get sufficient political support to succeed. . . ."[40]

On October 24 Congress confirmed the election of Allende; he received 153 votes to Alessandri's 35. The Christian Democratic Party had formally instructed its congressmen to vote for Allende.

As it became clear that Allende could not be prevented from taking office, *El Mercurio* switched its line. The morning of the vote it granted in an editorial that "an unvarying tradition has caused the Congress always to respect the results of the ballot boxes and proclaim as president the citizen who obtains a plurality." Allende now became "the best guarantee that the process of social change will be realized with full respect for the dignity and security of persons and for human rights."

El Mercurio struck an especially lofty note on inauguration day: "Fortunately, the spirit of patriotic collaboration which animates the citizenry in these moments important for the country should permit the regime of President Allende to take over the administrative and political responsibility for the country without hindrance."

But while sending up smoke to cover a retreat, *El Mercurio* also began to ready its forces for future attack. Noting that the coming struggle between Congress and the president might not be manageable by ordinary means, and that plebiscites might have to be held, *El Mercurio* urged the opposition political parties to prepare themselves for "this direct democracy in good time." It stressed the importance of using the press, radio, and television with maximum effectiveness, since they would be the "orienters of opinion for the popular referendum."[41]

On November 3 Allende was inaugurated.

AMONG the first tasks of the new regime was to name commanders of the armed forces and Carabineros in whom it could have confidence. The old commanders had been acting normally. As though none of them had ever dreamed an unconstitutional thought, the three commanders of the military services had visited President-elect Allende a few days before the inauguration to pay their respects. Immaculate in their full-dress uniforms, they headed delegations of officers to the inauguration ceremonies. Yet, although it was still not fully and generally known, two commanders—Tirado of the navy and Huerta of the Carabineros—had participated in plotting a coup, and a third—Guerraty of the air force—had also been involved, though less actively.

Among the first official acts of the UP government—carried out by the new subsecretary of interior sworn in sometime before the inauguration—was to replace Huerta as director general of Carabineros with an officer from well down the ranks, José Maria Sepúlveda. On inauguration day, Allende named the Commanders-in-chief of the army, navy, and air force. As head of the army, he renamed General Carlos Prats, who had held the post since the death of Schneider. He replaced Tirado with the second-ranking Admiral Raúl Montero and Guerraty with the third-ranking General César Ruiz. By selecting lower-ranking officers to head the air force and Carabineros, Allende procured the retirement of the second-ranking Joaquín García, who had conspired with Viaux, as well as several high-ranking Carabinero officers.

With these changes, the armed forces were headed by—as near as one could tell—constitutionalists. This meant a great deal, but far from everything. Desire for a coup ran deep in the armed forces. Officers of the highest rank had plotted coup. Consider the statement of Karamessines of the CIA that a "dozen or more senior officers" were exchanging views about how to mount a coup. These officers must have thought they would be backed by others. How many such others—unknown to the outside—were there? How many officers were there who, although they might not have backed a coup then, a coup without proper moral and constitutional cover, would nevertheless be prone to back a "properly" prepared coup at the right time?

The solution to the problem of the armed forces was basic to the long-run success of the Chilean revolutionary struggle.

6

Tactics and Strategy

Were the UP tactics in the pre-inauguration period correct? What did this period foreshadow? What does it mean for a socialist movement to have won the executive arm of the government through election? What were the strategies of the UP and its opponents?

Sergio Ramos, in *Chile:¿una economía de transición?* says that the UP leadership "played a decisive role" in the pre-inauguration period, that "judging by the results . . . its direction was, without any doubt, fully successful." Ramos praises the "flexible application of general policies through discussions and compromises with other forces, an example being the discussion of the Statute of Constitutional Guarantees with the CD, which obtained its support for Allende without the UP having to separate itself one tittle from its own program."[1] Others criticize the UP for entering into discussions and compromises with the Christian Democrats, asking why it agreed to the constitutional guarantees which could only hamstring it in any attempt to carry out a true revolution. Alain Labrousse writes in *L'Expérience Chilienne: Réformisme ou Révolution?:* "If there was a moment when the choice between two roads was still possible, it was without doubt that one. But the other road implied the organization of militias across the whole country. . . ."[2]

To understand the tactical problems, not just of this prelimi-
nary period, but of the whole revolutionary struggle in Chile, one
must do something which Lenin once called "the core of Marxism and Marxist tactics"—calculate the balance of forces.[3] With
36 percent of the population on their side and in the face of the
armed forces, a portion of whose members were at best constitutionalist, not revolutionary, what should the UP have done—
taken an intransigent position, which meant feeding the chances
of a coup and a fight? Would a rejection of the Christian
Democrat offer to compromise, which meant pushing wavering
elements in the Christian Democratic Party and the armed forces
to the other side, have created the best conditions for a fight? If
the UP did not want to press for a fight, what could it do except
compromise?

Setting up a militia and arming the people is basic to socialist
revolution. But arming the people is not a simple little technical
formula which one decides to carry out and—*presto*—it is
accomplished. What would the opposition and armed forces have
done while the UP was organizing the militia? One should not be
confused by the relative ease with which militias can be created
in revolutions which have already won state power. For a
revolution which has not yet won power, the problem of arming
the people is a difficult one. The time and manner in which the
people are armed must be part of the strategy for winning power.
If trying to arm the people would provoke a fight when one is not
ready to fight, then it must be postponed.

The significance of the constitutional guarantees must also be
understood. They did not fundamentally change the constitution;
much of what they said was already implicit in it. They had value
in a struggle in which each side was trying to convince public
opinion that the other was violating the constitution. They might
limit some possible tactical actions of the UP. But they were not a
contract that was binding for all contingencies. When, for example, on June 29, 1973, an Army colonel led a group of tanks in an
attack on the presidential palace, Allende—before it was clear
that the attack had failed—spoke of giving the people arms. When
it came to a trial of force, it was the logic of force, not that of
constitutions, that would govern. When the logic of force indicat-

ed that the time had come to arm the people, this would not be prevented by the constitution.

The other elements of Allende's tactics also made sense. His calls to his followers to remain calm and disciplined helped limit the climate of violence the conspirators were trying to create. ITT officials commented ruefully about the UP's unwillingness to be provoked. "You can spit in their face in the street," one quoted Alessandri's brother-in-law, "and they'll say thank you." Some people did not understand the UP's policy, seeming to think that violence is inherently more "revolutionary" than calm, regardless of circumstances. But if the best strategy at a given point in a revolutionary struggle is to avoid violence, then to be violent is to be anarchic, not revolutionary. Even while calling for calm, Allende was using the strength of the UP effectively by calling attention to it and warning that the UP would meet force with force.

Allende's statements on the Chilean armed forces should be judged not as though he were a professor teaching a course on the principles of Marxism, but as those of a political leader trying to deal with the armed forces and influence them. By stressing the constitutionalism of the armed forces, he was trying to strengthen the constitutionalist elements within them.

Yet although the UP's pre-inauguration strategy was correct, Ramos' statements contain flaws. When he stresses that by agreeing to the constitutional guarantees the UP was able to obtain the support of the Christian Democrats without giving up a tittle of its program, he is applying an erroneous criterion. The program was of enormous importance—for advancing the revolutionary process, for helping to win the masses and to win state power. But the primary test to be applied to the compromise with the Christian Democrats was how it affected the problem of power, and the program was only one element in that problem. Throughout the UP years there were to be others who stressed the part, the program, at the expense of the whole, the problem of power.

Ramos's statement that the leadership by the UP "played a decisive role" and was "fully successful" is overdrawn. To hold this view is to fail to appreciate the danger that remained after

Allende was inaugurated. Why did the conspirators not make a coup in 1970? Was it simply that the actions of the UP prevented one? No. The UP acted well, but it was far from being the dominant element in the situation. Its actions—not just its agreement to the constitutional guarantees, but also its threat to meet force with force—helped prevent a coup. But the conspirators also failed to make a coup because the circumstances were not propitious, because Frei wavered, because the death of Schneider upset plans—and because they had the option of making a coup later, if necessary.

WHAT did the winning of the presidency mean? Clearly, it did not mean that the UP had won full state power with control of the armed forces and police, the Congress, and the judiciary. But it was not an insignificant victory either. It meant that the UP had won an important beachhead from which it could wage the struggle for *full* state power.

A struggle for power was inevitable. The UP was committed to the transfer of wealth and power from the rich and the mighty to the people, to starting the construction of socialism. History teaches that the rich and mighty would not simply sit back and watch. They would resist—if need be and if they could, with force.

Winning full state power was the central task of the UP. The planks of the UP program calling for the nationalization of the monopolies, the banking system and foreign trade, and a genuine land reform were of enormous importance. They reflected the desire for change of the great majority of Chileans. These measures were essential for advancing the revolutionary process. But if full state power were not won they could in good part be reversed when the government reverted to the old rulers. What might be allowed to remain would constitute not part of a basic change in system, but reforms. The key distinction between successful revolution and reform is the winning or not winning of full state power.

What was the line-up of forces in the struggle for power? The population of Chile was divided into three parts. Thirty-six percent had voted for Allende and stood decidedly for revolutionary changes. Thirty-five percent had voted for Alessandri and stood decidedly against revolutionary changes. A little less than thirty percent had voted for Tomic; they were for changes, some of them even for socialism, but they had reservations about the kind of changes and how they should be brought about. The members of this group, mostly from the middle class, oscillated in their political sympathies between the Left and the Right.

Within the 36 percent that had voted for Allende lay the bulk of the working class. The UP could count on the support of the Central Workers Confederation (CUT), Chile's most important labor organization, which embraced 70 percent of all union members. But the Christian Democrats, besides controlling two unions which contained the majority of *campesino* union members, had many sympathizers in a number of other unions.

The UP had legal control of the executive arm of the government. The Christian Democrats and Nationals together constituted a majority in the Congress. The judicial system was staffed by appointees of previous administrations, coming from the upper and middle classes and possessing a traditional legal education. The Comptroller General's Office, which not only audited the government's financial operations, but also had the right to decide whether presidential decrees were legal, was headed by a Frei appointee.

THE officers of the armed forces came mostly from the middle classes and fell into three groups: the aggressive anti-Communists who were willing immediately to consider the use of force against the UP; the constitutionalists who backed the government, but only because it had been legally elected, not because they believed in socialism; and waverers standing between these two groups. Not one officer of the High Command, only a scattered handful of officers of any rank, were socialists.

That many officers were willing from the beginning to participate in a coup is shown by the plotting that took place between the time of the election and the inauguration.

Others may not have been ready to participate immediately, but nevertheless held views which foreshadowed implacable hostility to the UP government. Augusto Pinochet wrote a book, used as a text in Chile's military schools, called *Geographic Synthesis of Chile,* in which the following appears: "Day by day the ties of friendship with the great country of the North become stronger; not only in the economic aspect, because the United States offers a broad market for Chilean products and is at the same time a supplier of machinery and raw materials necessary for the industrial development of Chile, but also in the political and cultural aspects, in supporting fully the international points of view of the occidental 'bloc' against the 'red' peril."[4]

The closeness of the Chilean armed forces to the United States tells a great deal about how many of its officers must have felt toward communism. "Close personal and professional cooperation between Chilean and U.S. officers," says *Covert Action*, "was a tradition of long standing. The American military presence in Chile was substantial, consisting both of military attachés, the Embassy, and members of the Military Group who provided training and assistance to the Chilean armed services. In the late 1960s the Military Group numbered over fifty. . . ."[5] During 1950–1969, the United States gave $163 million in military aid to Chile, more than to any other Latin American country except Brazil, training 3,975 Chilean military personnel in the United States, the Panama Canal Zone, and in Chile. It also provided, over this same period, $2.3 million in aid to the Carabineros; 89 Chilean police officers were trained in the United States. Vicente Huerta, the director general of Carabineros named by Viaux as a co-conspirator, had attended the International Police Academy in Washington. The Chilean and U.S. armed forces were tied together in the Inter-American Defense Committee, and the navies of both countries regularly participated in Operation Unitas—joint naval maneuvers. Such manifold cooperation between the U.S. and Chilean armed forces would not have been possible if many of their officers had not been united by common beliefs about communism.

However, along with the coupists and potential coupists, the Chilean armed forces had a sizable constitutionalist sector. Such a sector was bound to exist: It reflected Chile's long tradition of constitutional government, the interest of its bourgeoisie— normally—in ruling by democratic means. Carlos Prats, the successor to Schneider, subscribed to the Schneider doctrine exemplifying constitutionalism. Besides Prats, a number of other constitutionalists, such as Generals Guillermo Pickering and

Mario Sepúlveda and Admiral Raúl Montero also occupied key positions.

Some Chilean officers had become very interested in recent years in the problems of underdevelopment and social unrest. In July 1970 the official organ of the Army General Staff published an article by Major Claudio López, entitled "The Armed Forces and the Third World." López stated that underdevelopment diminished national security and independence: The armed forces were therefore willing to collaborate in promoting development. The function of the armed forces should not be "limited to maintaining order and repressing subversion. More important is . . . avoiding the outbreak of violence" that makes repression necessary. "The Armed Forces should be clear about . . . the changes needed by society . . . and should promote these changes. . . ." But there is also another side to López: The Latin American armed forces guarantee "the solidarity of the occidental bloc"; and "if the military find themselves in organizations incapacitated by a lack of human and material means from fulfilling the mission for which they were created and . . . feel themselves separated from the life of the nation, it is possible that they will react against the constituted power."[6]

The class cleavage in the Chilean armed forces was sharp. Most noncommissioned officers and almost all the rank and file came from the lower classes and had far less formal education than the officers. The possibility of their ever becoming officers was small. Discipline was rigorous; the army followed Prussian standards introduced during the last century, while the navy followed British standards of a long bygone era. The humble social status and lack of education of the rank and file helped keep them in awe of the officers. They were as much as possible kept from having direct contact with politics. Unlike the officers, the noncoms, the rank-and-file soldiers and the sailors did not enjoy the right to vote.

In time of emergency, they were confined to quarters, which meant that they were cut off from outsiders and could get only the news that the officers chose to let them get.

The armed forces possessed a monopoly of arms in Chile. Aside from scattered weapons here and there, the people were unarmed.

THE UP was able to take over the executive arm of the government not because it controlled a preponderance of force which would have backed the carrying out of a revolutionary program by whatever means were necessary, but because the majority of Chileans—including many officers in the armed forces—believed in legality. Having to respect legality would limit the UP government's ability to carry out a revolution; the bourgeoisie had not designed its legal system to further revolution. But except for legality there would have been no UP government in the first place.

Given this situation, the UP could not simply proceed, according to the classic Marxist-Leninist precept, to "smash the bourgeois state machinery." Smashing the bourgeois state machinery would involve replacing the traditional armed forces with revolutionary armed forces and changing the bourgeois parliamentary and judicial systems. The UP government did not have the legal power to do any of these things simply by its own fiat, and it did not have the force to do them any other way.

Yet, although the UP had to follow a legal strategy, it also had to look beyond legality. It had to accumulate force, to be prepared to defend with force its right to govern. It could try to use the law as much as possible, but it could not rely on it indefinitely in the face of implacable enemies who would not give up their power and privileges willingly. Eventually, the issue of power would be decided by force.

The cornerstone of the UP strategy was to proceed by legal means to carry out its program. The UP hoped that by carrying out the demands of a majority of Chileans, the monopolies and large estates would be done away with and that by improving the economic and social conditions of most Chileans, it would gain increased support not only from the working class, but also from the middle class—enough increased support to become the majority. Achieving majority support would permit the UP to carry out by legal means the plank in its program that called for a "new Political Constitution which [would] institutionalize the massive incorporation of the people into state power" and replace the existing Congress with a single-chamber "Assembly of the People." Sticking to legality would help retain the support of constitutionalists in the armed forces, and avoid giving the coupists the legal and moral environment for a coup that they were hoping to create.

The strategy of the UP toward the armed forces was foreshadowed by its actions in the pre-inauguration period. The UP would appeal to the military honor of the constitutionalists and to the interest of the officers, for patriotic and military reasons, in economic development. The government would use officers in public administration, trying to involve them personally in the UP program. It would raise military pay, bringing it into line with pay scales in the rest of the public administration, thus removing a main cause of discontent. The UP strategy toward the armed forces was geared to the officers; it gave little stress to winning over and revolutionizing the rank and file.

Some critics of the UP have accused it of lacking a clear strategy for winning state power. One or two high-ranking members of the UP, engaging in self-criticism after the coup, have asserted the same thing. Formally, the criticism is true. The plank in the program about a new constitution which would bring about the "massive incorporation of the people into state power" does not by itself mean coming to grips with the problem. State power is not so much a matter of a country's constitution as it is of the nature of its armed forces and who in fact—not legally, but actually—controls them. If Chile's old armed forces remained intact, a new constitution, even assuming that the UP government would be allowed to put it into effect, would not mean that the UP had won complete state power.

Yet it is one thing to make the formal statement that the UP should have had a strategy for winning state power and another—infinitely more difficult—to have said concretely at the time what that strategy should have been. The leaders of the UP—President Allende, Luis Corvalán, head of the Communist Party, Carlos Altamirano, head of the Socialist Party, and others—were pondering the problem of state power. But with the correlation of forces as it stood, the UP was so far away from state power that it was impossible for anyone to sketch, with any degree of concreteness, a map outlining the roads for getting to it. To a considerable extent the UP had to follow one of Napoleon's maxims: *"On s'engage, et puis—on voit."* You get into the action, and then—you see.

There were also thoughts which carried the problem further. For example, Allende had said several times that if the bourgeoisie resorted to violence, the UP would answer with violence. Such statements were not made casually, but were tied to a strategic principle—that the UP should not be the first to attack, that it should operate by counteroffensive. Behind this principle lay a central point about the correlation of forces: A UP attack would tend to push the middle classes and the constitutionalists in the armed forces to the other side; an enemy attack would tend to push them toward the UP.

There were many differences about tactics within the UP—differences about how fast the program could be carried out, about the importance and likelihood of the UP's winning over more of the middle classes, and about whether to enter into compromises with the Christian Democrats. But all six parties of the UP agreed on one basic point—the UP would use its electoral victory, the executive arm of the government it had won, to carry out its program, to start the construction of socialism. Even the Movement of the Revolutionary Left (MIR), founded at the University of Concepción several years earlier, which had not believed in the electoral method and was not part of the UP, felt that "the electoral majority of the left and a UP government are an excellent point of departure for the direct struggle and the conquest of power by the workers."[7]

THE U.S. imperialists and the Chilean oligarchy also faced a complicated strategic problem. The opposition to the UP was divided, with important elements vacillating; this limited its effectiveness, and made an immediate coup difficult and dangerous. Yet the longer the UP government remained, the more damage it could do to imperialist and oligarchic interests; it also might grow stronger. All elements of the imperialists and the oligarchy were agreed that the UP government could not be allowed to succeed; but reflecting their different interests and outlook, their tactics varied.

The National Party, representing Chile's arrogant large landholders and the older, more conservative sectors of its industrial and commercial bourgeoisie, contained the traditionally fascist elements, and was the more inflexible opposition party—the one more prone to move quickly toward a coup. Its leaders came under immediate pressure from landholders and other reactionaries to be firm in their resistance to UP measures. These leaders doubted that the problem posed by the existence of the UP government could be solved by electoral means. They would work to create a unified opposition that would not hesitate to do what was necessary.

In the Christian Democratic Party, the situation was more complex. Frei and the right-wing leadership felt just as strongly as the leaders of the Nationals that the UP government must not be allowed to succeed. But Frei had a strong interest in not moving quickly to a coup, in first exhausting all other possibilities of achieving the common aim. If the UP government could be gotten rid of in the next presidential election or by impeachment before then, the chances were that the Christian Democrats, as the largest opposition party, would inherit the government. With a coup, the government would go to someone else, perhaps for a long time. Moreover, Frei's reputation as a democratic leader would be destroyed by participation in a coup. Even if it turned out that there had to be a coup, it was in Frei's interest that the conditions for it be carefully prepared, that it be made to appear justified to a large proportion of the people of Chile and to the rest of the world.

The Frei group faced problems. In the aftermath of the election, the party was under the influence of the Tomic wing. The Frei group had to win back full control. It had to maneuver the party into resistance to the changes that the UP would try to bring about, into collaboration with the Nationals in opposition. This maneuvering had to be done cautiously since many Christian Democrats wanted change and abhorred the National Party. Premature or careless resistance to change could be dangerous, could result in a leftward shift by many party members, some falling more strongly under the influence of its left wing and— what would be more serious—others moving over to the UP.

The strategy Frei and his cohorts chose to follow was later described by Claudio Orrego, a leading CD theorist, as "that of the Russian marshals" in the war against Napoleon. Said Orrego:

This strategy is very simple. It is a matter of not doing battle with the enemy when he first bursts across the frontier with his combat mystique, firepower, and organization all intact. To do battle in these conditions is to jeopardize the survival of your own army. . . . So you retreat to Moscow harassing the enemy . . . burning the earth, and abandoning towns until winter approaches and the first snows begin to fall. That's the hour for the first great battle and the final offensive.

In Chile, this strategy meant not taking a hard line at the beginning. The UP government, said Orrego, needed

Plots, sedition, imperialist aggressions, boycotts, sabotage, crimes, reactionary violence. . . . To play 'the tough guys' at such a time is to do the party in power the favor it hopes for, is to demonstrate to the country that the opposition resists change and will do anything to defend its interests. [The line would become hard later, as the government lost] its mystique, its internal cohesion, its capacity for action, its very prestige among the people.[8]

What could the opposition do when the Christian Democrats were ready to harden their line? With its control of the Congress, many things. It could work to block the carrying out of the UP program—the nationalizations and other reforms. With its power over legislation on budgets, taxes, and wages, it could sabotage the economy. Chile's history—the fight of the Congress against Balmaceda—suggested many ways in which a Congress could be used against a president. It could harass the government by repeatedly impeaching ministers. It could make it impossible to govern.

Although the internal enemies of the UP had differences about strategy, tactics, and timing, they were in agreement on one basic point: They must ensure that the people not be armed, that the rank and file of the armed forces not be infiltrated with followers of the UP or otherwise come under its influence, and that the officers not be purged. They would stay on a constant alert, always prepared to act, to prevent such developments.

The U.S. corporations operating in Chile were fiercely hostile to the UP government—it was a threat to the business interests by which they measured everything. It meant the end of their profitable Chilean operations.

Some corporations were insured against expropriation with the

Overseas Private Investment Corporation (OPIC), a U.S. government agency, but the payments to be expected would not in their eyes make up for the loss of their Chilean businesses. The ITT was particularly concerned about the "domino effect" in other countries if it were forced out of Chile.

The representatives in Chile of these corporations had been in close touch with the U.S. ambassador during the period between the popular and congressional elections; Ambassador Korry has testified that he held regular meetings with them. They knew about the "Alessandri formula"; officials of ITT, and probably other companies, knew a lot more about U.S. involvement in plans to keep Allende from taking office. What should they do now that these plans had failed?

The corporations worked out strategies, dependent on their individual circumstances, to salvage what they could of their Chilean interests. Some companies hoped to negotiate satisfactory arrangements with the UP government and tried to avoid any actions that would jeopardize the negotiations. The Cerro Corporation, for example, which was preparing the Andina copper mine for operations, was a newcomer to Chile, and unlike Anaconda and Kennecott, which had been pumping money out of Chile for more than half a century, it had not yet earned anything. Cerro tried to avoid being identified with the other two copper giants.

Anaconda and Kennecott faced a more complicated problem. Besides large mining interests, they also held, as a result of the complex arrangements made under Frei, many tens of millions of dollars of notes against Chile's Copper Corporation. For them it was a question not only whether compensation would be granted for the expropriated mines, but also whether the notes would be paid. Unlike Cerro, they could have little expectation of a favorable settlement; yet they could not be sure that Chile would not offer them some compensation, and pay the notes. They worked out a strategy that consisted of several parts—drawing as many dollars as possible out of Chile in the months before nationalization, by stopping expenditures for supplies, equipment and the removal of waste materials from the worksites; getting the U.S. government to exert pressure on the UP government to pay "adequate compensation;" luring key supervisory and technical personnel out of the enterprises in Chile, thus making it more difficult for the UP government to run the mines; and exploring the possibilities for a legal counterattack abroad on the UP government if it did not offer satisfactory compensation or failed to pay the notes.

Besides acting separately to defend their own particular interests, the corporations also planned to work together in some of their actions. A few weeks after Allende's inauguration, a number of them—ITT, Anaconda, Kennecott, Bethlehem Steel, Dow Chemical, Firestone Tire and Rubber, W. R. Grace, Charles Pfizer, Ralston Purina, and the Bank of America—formed a "Chile Ad Hoc Committee." According to a memorandum on the committee's first meeting, prepared by a Bank of America official who attended, "the thrust . . . was toward the application of pressure on the [U.S.] government wherever possible to make it clear that a Chilean takeover would not be tolerated without serious repercussions following. ITT believes that the place to apply pressure is through the office of Henry Kissinger. They feel that this office and the CIA are handling the Chile problem." Both ITT and Anaconda representatives told of meetings with Arnold Nachmanoff of Kissinger's staff. The Anaconda representative reported that Nachmanoff had "indicated that the U.S. will apply quiet pressure [on Chile] along economic lines. . . ." The meeting also discussed the need to bring pressure "upon the international lending agencies to cease activity in countries that threaten or actually expropriate private investments."[9] The minutes of the meeting give further information about the discussion of the lending agencies. "Ralph Mecham of Anaconda said that World Bank people had been in Santiago this past week talking to officials of the Chilean government telling them that if they went ahead with their takeovers, it was quite possible that no more loans would be made."[10] A counsel for the Senate subcomittee investigating ITT and Chile summed up: "All of the documents that we have seen in connection with the ad hoc committee . . . refer to a plan to put pressure on the U.S. Government and, in particular, Mr. Kissinger's office, designed to put economic pressure on Chile."[11]

Compared to that of the corporations, the U.S. government strategy had to be comprehensive and subtle. The government did not have simply the specific, narrow interests of a company to defend, but the interests of U.S. imperialism as a whole—economic, political, and strategic interests, not just in Chile, but throughout the world.

The prevention of Allende's taking office in the first place had been tempting for the U.S. government. It would have avoided getting into, even for a time, the messy situation that Allende's presidency would bring—the nationalization of copper and other U.S. properties, the recognition of Cuba, and a bad influence on other Latin American countries. But there were disadvantages to a coup at that time. At a press conference President Nixon noted: "We can only say that for the United States to have intervened, intervened in a free election and to have turned it around, I think would have had repercussions all over Latin America that would have been far worse than what has happened in Chile."[12] Nixon was willing to press for a coup anyway, but still the worldwide repercussions it would have were weighed in the thinking of the U.S. government. A further reason for not making a coup then was that it would be risky: It might lead to a civil war, with all sorts of undesirable consequences possible—difficulties in neighboring countries, problems even in the United States, which was in turmoil over the Vietnam War.

Now, having retreated by accepting the inauguration of Allende, the U.S. government had time to do things right. It could deal with the Chilean problem not through frenzied improvisations, but calmly, systematically. The specific characteristics of the Chilean situation—Chile's worldwide reputation as a democratic country, the belief of its people in the electoral process, the wavering of the leaders of the Christian Democrats, the presence of constitutionalists among officers of the armed forces, the large mass base behind the UP—could all be taken into account. The possibility of getting rid of the UP government without a coup could be fully explored—that would be the best way. If there was no other way than a coup, it could be prepared scientifically.

The U.S. government would follow a policy of "low profile" toward Chile. It would, notwithstanding the pressure from the corporations, avoid any show of open hostility. It had seen in Cuba how open hostility against a revolution can be counterpro-

ductive, how a skillful revolutionary leader can use such hostility
to increase the unity and revolutionary consciousness of his
people and mobilize support abroad. *The New York Times*
editorialized:

> "The point is not that by playing it cool and correct Washington can
> jolly Dr. Allende out of his socialist programs or even insure good
> relations with Chile during his term. It is that for several reasons this
> policy is the only practical one for the United States at a difficult time
> in its dealings with the other Americas. The Allende Government
> must be given no excuse to blame this country either for obstructing
> its programs or for any failures that may ensue. It is essential that the
> United States refrain from threats or provocations. . . ."[13]

So Nixon would state in his foreign policy message to Congress
that the United States would maintain toward Chile the kind of
relations that Chile maintained toward the United States. U.S.
government officials would blandly tell Chilean diplomats that the
problems between the two countries were negotiable. The U.S.
government would avoid even a hint of an economic embargo
such as it had imposed on Cuba in 1960. It would do everything it
could to cause the UP government to fail. But, as far as possible,
it would do so "invisibly."

The U.S. government would hide behind the international
lending agencies, private banks, and exporters, would work
noiselessly through the CIA, the military attachés, and the U.S.
Embassy. The lending agencies, banks, and exporters could say
that they were cutting down credit, not for political reasons, but
because Chile had become a bad risk. While Nixon, with a pious
look, was proclaiming to the world U.S. willingness for good
relations with Chile, the CIA would be quietly sharpening its
troublemaking apparatus there. The work in Chile could be
divided among the CIA, the military attachés, and the embassy
with an eye, among other things, to the necessary cover for what
was being done; sensitive contacts would be carried out through
what are known in intelligence jargon as "cutouts"—
intermediaries.

A central aim of U.S. strategy was to push as many people as
possible into active repudiation of the UP government, to get
even its own followers to become disillusioned with it. The

people could be a great weight for tilting the balance of force one way or the other. To allow the UP to win many more of the people would be dangerous; this would not only increase its political strength, but also its military potential: The people could not only fight, but their sentiments and actions, especially in a crisis, could be crucial to the UP's winning over or neutralizing soldiers and officers of the armed forces. Conversely, if the opposition could win over enough of the people, it might be able to get rid of the Allende government legally. But even if this were not possible, the strong opposition of a large majority of the people would still be valuable for winning over waverers and constitutionalists in the armed forces, and for helping to give a coup moral cover.

The way to galvanize the people into repudiation of the UP government was to reduce Chile to economic and political chaos. The economic warfare which Broe of the CIA had proposed in 1970 was limited to measures which could produce quick results. Now a broader attack that could get to the fundamentals of the economy could be undertaken. The Chilean economy was vulnerable to internal inflation and to foreign exchange deficits. The opposition in Congress would carry out internal economic sabotage. The U.S. government would work on the foreign exchange problem: It would use its influence to dry up Chile's credits from U.S. banks and exporters and the international lending agencies.

The CIA also had its role in the production of economic chaos. It would penetrate labor unions and professional and business associations and promote actions by them—strikes and lockouts—against the UP government. It would concentrate on strategic industries, for example, copper and transportation whose stoppage would be costly in foreign exchange or would cripple the whole economy.

The CIA had other tasks as well. The fight against the government required a climate of violence and anarchy. The leaders of the Chilean opposition, used to working decorously in the Congress, had little experience in such matters. But the CIA's experience was vast. It would use the techniques it had perfected in many countries to produce the necessary street brawls and bombings.

The U.S. government would of course also maintain contacts

with appropriate officers in the Chilean armed forces. Ambassador Korry testified before Congress in mid-1971: "Our relationships . . . with the Chilean military are normal, friendly, and show no change since this government took office. . . ."[14]

7

The Chilean Commercial Agencies In the United States

The evening in April 1971 when Javier Urrutia named me his advisor we were sitting in his Manhattan apartment. The apartment, he told me, had been burglarized the day before. On returning from the office, he had found the lock stuffed with chewing gum. When the house superintendant managed to open the door and Javier went through his belongings, he found only his pistol missing. He had been carrying his papers with him. "It could have been worse," said Javier, "What can the CIA do with my pistol?"

Javier explained his position and responsibilities to me. He was an official of the Chilean Development Corporation (CORFO) and the president of the Chile Trading Corporation, a U.S. company owned by CORFO, used for the purchase of equipment and supplies. He was also coordinator of all the other Chilean commercial agencies in the United States, having been requested by President Allende to make sure they followed policies appropriate to the UP government.

Javier asked me whether I had any suggestions. "Yes," I said. "Let's, as quickly as possible, engage the services of a good law firm, one that a client like us can count on. The struggle in the United States will in part take the form of legal actions and we will need such a firm. It is also important that all the Chilean agencies in New York give all their legal work to this firm no matter who their legal representatives may have been in the past; in this way we can be sure that everything will be handled with an understanding of the problems of a revolutionary government."

Javier agreed and asked whether I knew of a good firm, and I named Rabinowitz, Boudin, and Standard, which has been representing the Cuban government since the early days of the Cuban Revolution. We arranged for Javier to meet the heads of this firm. A few days later he sent a memorandum to Chile outlining the need for engaging a law firm, recommending the Rabinowitz firm. Some Chilean officials wanted to hire the law firm of Sol Linowitz, former U.S. ambassador to the Organization of American States, arguing that for negotiating with American companies and the U.S. government, it would be best to have a firm with connections to the State Department. The problem was thrashed out in Chile and in the end Rabinowitz, Boudin, and Standard was hired.

The first memorandum Javier asked me to write was on U.S. government strategy toward the Chilean Revolution. Here is how it began:

> One thing we must never assume—that because things seem to be quiet here, the U.S. is complacent about what is going on in Chile, and is doing nothing. The very quietness of the U.S. government is part of its present strategy. Talk would for it not only be purposeless, but counterproductive. The U.S. is still very powerful in Latin America, but the days when it could overthrow a government by simply talking against it are gone. Aggressive talk by the U.S. against Chile right now could mobilize further support for the Popular Government in Chile and the rest of Latin America.

Javier talked to me about the problem of security. He and two other Chileans, representing CORFO, ran the Chile Trading Corporation. Three other Chileans, representing the National Electricity Enterprise and the National Petroleum Enterprise helped supervise purchases for their companies. But the sixty persons who made up the staff of Chile Trading—buyers, transport specialists, clerks, secretaries—were hired in the United States. By law, they were required to be U.S. citizens or foreigners with resident visas. How could we be sure that some weren't CIA agents, or that the CIA wouldn't introduce an agent among those constantly being hired?

Javier was especially concerned about the secretaries, about the possibility that copies of our papers would end up in the hands of the U.S. government. I proposed bringing up two or three reliable English-speaking secretaries from Chile, but Javier informed me that for legal and bureaucratic reasons, this could not be done. A secretary could probably not obtain a resident visa from the United States; and Chilean regulations limited the type and number of persons who could be sent here—as he was—on diplomatic status as employees of CORFO.

I promised to try to find a reliable American Spanish-speaking secretary. Meanwhile, we would try to exercise as much care as we could with our papers and conversations. I wrote many memoranda in longhand. Eventually, we obtained a reliable secretary. But we still couldn't tell whether our offices were bugged, so when Javier and I had something especially sensitive to discuss, we would take a walk outside the building.

The problem of what to do about the Chile Trading staff, as a whole, was difficult. We had no means for carrying out personnel investigations that could tell us whether a person was an agent; certainly not the means for investigating more than sixty persons. And Chile Trading needed people—whether we could be sure of them or not—to do the work; it had been importing yearly more than $60 million of equipment, parts, and other supplies for a large number of industries in Chile, and it was important that the flow should not now be slowed down. We decided that the best we could do was to have someone unostentatiously review the personnel records of the existing personnel and the forms submitted by new job applicants to see if any looked obviously suspicious. For the rest we would have to just stay alert.

Javier told me that the two Chileans from the electricity enterprise were strongly opposed to the UP government. It didn't take long for me to learn how deep the opposition was: One, with whom I sometimes walked to the subway after work, became livid whenever the conversation turned to the UP. Repeatedly, Javier recommended to the home office that these two persons be replaced, arguing that an office in the United States was no place for unreliable people. There was no response to this request.

One day, Javier gave me a special assignment. "I want you," he said, "to be the liaison between the CODELCO (Copper Corporation) people here and me. (Representatives sent by CODELCO to New York to make arrangements for providing the mines with supplies after they were nationalized had recently arrived.) "See José, the person in charge of the CODELCO group. Help him in any way you can. Figure out what would be the best organization for them to have in New York and whether they should buy through Chile Trading or set up their own purchasing office."

I saw José and found that he was concerned that Javier and the other CORFO people would insist on having all CODELCO purchasing in New York done through Chile Trading, instead of through its own office. "You know," said José, "how important copper is for Chile. My superiors in Santiago and I feel that we cannot allow ourselves to depend on anyone else for the supplies, we have to make sure of them ourselves. The CORFO people should also understand that assuring the supplies for the copper mines is not the same as doing so for the electric power and petroleum industries. We are much bigger and use a larger variety of supplies."

My own view, after thinking the problem over, was that it would be unwise to rely only on Chile Trading for the purchase of supplies for the copper mines. Chile Trading was a routine-ridden organization; it handled the kinds of purchases it had been making for CORFO and its affiliates for thirty years with painful slowness. Its buyers knew how to fill out a purchase order, and its transport people knew how to arrange ordinary business with freight forwarders. But Chile Trading did not have the kind of imaginative, versatile people who could assume the responsibility for handling a variety of new and difficult problems. It would have trouble with the unfamiliar supplies and suppliers of the copper mines. And when the United States tried to interfere with the flow of supplies to Chile, Chile Trading would be strained enough coping with its ordinary purchases, without adding all the supplies for the copper mines.

I, therefore, told José that, if he agreed, I would recommend to Javier that CODELCO, New York, should be free to set up its own purchasing organization. Chile Trading would help in any way it could, for example, in procuring office space and hiring personnel. CODELCO would immediately give some orders—amounting to say $5 million—to Chile Trading; this would enable pruchasing to get under way even though CODELCO did not yet have its own arrangements. While CODELCO could set up and run its own organization any way it liked, the local personnel it wanted to hire would be reviewed by Javier for security, it would use the same law firm as the other Chilean agencies in New York, and all political and public relations questions—for example, about holding press conferences—would be submitted to Javier for decision. José agreed, and when I submitted the recommendations to Javier, he accepted them.

José turned over several million dollars in orders to Chile Trading and simultaneously began to build CODELCO's own organization. With my help, he borrowed some personnel and telephones from Chile Trading, rented a floor of space in the same building, and began to transmit orders to U.S. companies in the name of CODELCO.

While working with José I met the other members of the CODELCO group in New York. The three highest-ranking officials after José constituted a problem. Two had worked for Anaconda, the third for Cerro, in Chile, and they showed strong loyalties to these companies. "We, the Anaconda people," one would say, "only we, the Anaconda people, can understand the statistics on the import requirements of our mines. The best way of making sure that the mines get the supplies they need is to let the professionals who know about such things procure them."

The three officials carried the bias for professionals to its conclusion. At the time of nationalization in July, Anaconda had offered, for an appropriate fee, to use its purchasing organization to supply its former mines till the end of the year. Cerro had offered to set up an organization for supplying the mines indefinitely. The three officials, who frequently visited the Anaconda and Cerro offices in New York, recommended that we quickly enter into agreements to take advantage of these offers.

José and I discussed the company proposals with Javier. The three of us agreed that to make CODELCO dependent on the U.S. companies for supplies would be—in the words of Javier—"idiotic, like putting our heads into the mouth of the beast." We also agreed that there would be nothing wrong with letting

Anaconda continue buying for its former mines so long as we had no alternative arrangements and were acting as quickly as possible to set up such arrangements. And we decided that José would ask CODELCO, Santiago, to replace the three former employees of the copper companies with reliable people.

Constantly in our minds was the danger of action by the United States to cut off supplies to the mines. A possible way of trying to meet such action was to purchase the supplies indirectly through an independent trading company. José and I began to explore the possibility of entering into contracts with such companies, holding meeting after meeting with representatives of five of them.

The case of one was easy to decide. It was a little company which offered, for a modest fee, to handle a small amount of orders to show that it was efficient and reliable; once we had gained confidence, it would expand its staff and take more business. We felt there was little to lose, and José gave this company $1 million in orders.

But the larger companies posed problems. With them the amount of orders had to be big, and this meant that CODELCO would depend on a single company for a significant portion of the supplies. In judging the companies, we attached greater importance to how well we thought they could do the job than to the commissions they requested. The key point was the organizational capacity of the company. CODELCO would be giving it tens of millions of dollars in orders for which it would have to engage, organize, and train a large additional staff very rapidly. We asked questions designed to help us judge the company's ability to do this: Who would be in charge of the CODELCO work; how the company expected to organize this work; how many additional people it expected to hire; where the additional staff would be located; what sort of statistical and financial data it would maintain, and what sorts of reports it would make?

We also tried to get the companies to agree to arrangements that might afford protection against hostile legal actions by U.S. companies. Our lawyers had told us that if Anaconda, Kennecott, or some other company expropriated in Chile filed suit against it in an American court, the assets of Chile's New York agencies, including the goods they had bought for import into Chile, might be attached. Buying through a trading company was in itself no guarantee against attachment; if the trading company were seen as an agent of Chile, the Chilean imports in its possession could be attached. While there was no sure protection against attachment, certain measures could make it more difficult and less likely. The trading company should act as an independent trader, buying goods on its own account which it later sold to Chile; Chile should not take title to the goods or pay for them until they had arrived at one of its own ports, or at least until they were outside the jurisdiction of the United States.

We found it impossible to work out such arrangements, not because the companies objected to them in principle but because of the financial problems they created. If the companies were to buy the goods on their own account and receive payment for them only later, they would have to lay out large amounts of money. They were unable or unwilling to do this. Chile could provide the money, but we found ourselves unable to do so in such a way that the companies would not be labeled as its agents.

After several weeks of meetings, we rejected all the larger companies but one—a U.S. subsidiary of a German company which did business throughout Europe. We thought that the European connections might be useful. Together with one of our lawyers, we began to negotiate a contract with this company. The contract had to be cleared with Santiago and José spent much time telephoning long distance explaining it. Eventually, he was told that the contract was approved and that he could tell the people from the company that he would be authorized to sign it in a few days.

While we were waiting for final approval to come through, a new CODELCO official arrived from Santiago, one who outranked José. Hugo, the new official, asked to be briefed about the contract and we held several meetings with him. Almost immediately, Hugo questioned the policy of giving the contract to the German company. "Why," he asked, "should we depend on a company with no experience in copper when we can have the best technical experts in the world do the buying for us— Anaconda and Cerro?" He placed himself in charge of contracting a company. José and I didn't learn about it till later but, assisted by the three CODELCO officials who had formerly worked for the U.S. copper companies, he had begun to negotiate a contract with Cerro.

Javier was away on business trips during the time just after Hugo began to run CODELCO, New York, but when he got to town I informed him of what was happening. We met with Hugo. Javier spoke to him about how unwise it would be to give a U.S. copper company—even Cerro with which Chile had better relations than with Anaconda or Kennecott—power over the import of the supplies for Chile's copper mines. But Hugo persisted. He also confided his other plans: He liked living in the United States and was going to ask CODELCO to let him stay here as permanent head of its U.S. office, but he didn't like New York, so he was thinking of transferring the office to a mining area like Arizona.

After the meeting, Javier expressed the opinion that Hugo should be moved out of New York and returned to Santiago. The question was discussed with the leading officials of CODELCO, Santiago, and soon thereafter Hugo was recalled.

CODELCO, however, never signed a contract with the German company. A newly opened office in London took on, among other tasks, that of buying supplies for the mines. And during the long delay in signing caused by Hugo, the officials in Santiago decided that instead of trying to carry out purchases in the United States through an independent trading company, CODELCO would set up its own purchasing office in Canada.

In November 1971 the head of CODELCO's London office arrived in New York with the task of making arrangements to protect CODELCO assets in the United States against legal actions by the copper companies. Such actions might begin with the new year when the first of a series of CODELCO promissory notes held by Kennecott fell due. President Allende, acting under the copper nationalization law, was considering whether to suspend payment. If he decided to suspend, Kennecott might sue.

Carlos, the head of the London office, accompanied by several other CODELCO officials, met with our lawyers. Carlos, himself a lawyer, asked a well-organized series of questions about the dangers to CODELCO assets and how they might be protected. Our lawyers responded that all CODELCO assets within the jurisdiction of the court could be attached—bank accounts; bank transfers, such as checks being used by CODELCO to pay for something; goods in transit to Chile to which title had already passed to CODELCO or in which it had acquired a "beneficiary interest," for example, by making a partial payment on them; and shipping documents on goods in transit. (If someone succeeded in attaching shipping documents, he could take control of the goods to which they referred, even if the goods themselves were outside the jurisdiction of the court.) The best protection against attachment was to keep the assets out of the jurisdiction of the court in which the copper companies were likely to sue.

CODELCO, New York, under the guidance of Carlos, began immediately to take protective measures. It transferred most of the funds in its bank accounts outside the United States. It routed its goods away from New York where the copper companies were most likely to sue. And it began to work out arrangements for safe ways to make payments.

It was recommended to Javier that CORFO-Chile Trading do likewise. But whereas Carlos and CODELCO, New York, had authorization from the home office to transfer funds and take other protective measures, CORFO-Chile Trading did not. Javier requested the authorization from Santiago and recommended that the Central Bank remove its own bank accounts from the United States and try to make sure that no other Chilean agency kept any assets here. We waited, but the authorization did not come. Still, the accounts could not be left where they were—many millions of dollars could be lost. So three days before the end of the year we worked feverishly with a list of the accounts and the funds of CORFO-Chile Trading were transferred out of the country. Instructions were given to the heads of the other Chilean agencies in New York to do the same with their funds.

On December 30, 1971, President Allende issued a decree suspending payment on the Kennecott note for three months, after which time a final decision would be reached. The first law suit and attachment of Chilean property didn't come until February 4, 1972; the note, although it fell due on December 31, allowed a thirty day grace period. Kennecott attached the New York assets not only of CODELCO and the El Teniente Mining Company, but also of CORFO, the Chile Trading Company, the

Pacific Steel Company (CAP), the National Airline (LAN), and the Central Bank. Despite the previous transfers of funds out of the country, Kennecott succeeded in catching over $5 million in Chilean accounts with New York banks. The head of one New York agency had disregarded the transfer instructions and the Central Bank had maintained a large sum in an account for which no one in New York was authorized to sign.

The heads of the Chilean agencies in New York exchanged opinions at staff meetings on whether Chile should pay the note to Kennecott to get the attachment lifted. The head of CAP had no doubts about what to do. "We should pay," he said, "the CAP office is crippled by the attachments; I have written this to my superiors in Santiago." Others held that it was pointless to pay; payment would not appease Kennecott which would simply gobble up the $5.8 million payment and attack again later. A day or so before the court hearings on the attachments were to be held, the announcement came from Santiago that Chile intended to pay the notes.

Anaconda had kept an observer in court during the Kennecott hearings; it held similar notes, the payment of which had also been suspended. On February 29 Anaconda sued, obtaining attachments on the New York assets of CODELCO and CORFO. With the payment of the note to Kennecott, that firm's attachments were lifted, but the Anaconda attachments remained.

A number of Chileans, both in New York and Santiago, now began to raise the question whether it would be possible for the Chilean agencies in New York to continue to function. Javier asked me to prepare a memorandum on the problem, to be sent in his name to Chile. The memorandum was to be based on a broad analysis of U.S.-Chilean relations. Javier was responsible for Chilean negotiations with U.S. bankers and participated in the Paris meetings for the renegotiation of Chile's foreign debt, and provided me with information on both subjects.

What follows is from the text of the memorandum which I prepared:

Background

Since we took over our position in March last year, we have felt that the key to the situation here was that there existed a fundamental conflict of interest between U.S. imperialism and the Chilean Revolution. We felt that the Chilean Revolution would have to cut into large and powerful American interests, that American counteraction was inevitable, and that we should prepare for it.

We have acted on the basis of this analysis, although with care to avoid provocation. One of our first acts was to recommend that we contract the services of a politically reliable, competent firm of American lawyers. Another recommendation was that CODELCO eliminate its dependence on Anaconda for the purchase of supplies required by its former mines as rapidly as possible, and that it not contract the services of Cerro for this task. Still another was that CODELCO, New York, should not staff itself with ex-functionaries of Anaconda, Kennecott, and Cerro, with politically unreliable personnel.

From the beginning, events have been confirming our analysis. We have engaged in constant conversations with bankers here. They have been courteous and personally friendly and have talked about possible future business, lines of credit, etc. But since we have been here, no loans, no lines of credit—none of these—have been forthcoming. From the conversations, it is clear that each banker knows what the others are doing, that they are acting in concert and receiving orientations from Washington. Their policy is to tempt us, to make us believe that we will be able to operate normally in the future, to avoid our breaking off with them and speaking clearly about the U.S. policy of aggression toward Chile. They try to avoid giving us a flat no and hide the reasons for not giving us credits behind a screen of technicalities. But when they have to say no they do so. When we present a request to Ex-Im for a loan to buy three Boeing aircraft it is rejected as a result of instructions from Secretary of the Treasury Connally. And this same Secretary of the Treasury openly instructs the U.S. representatives in international bodies such as the World Bank and the Inter-American Development Bank to vote against any credit applications by Chile and use their influence on other member countries to get them to do the same. . . .

We have also viewed the renegotiation of our foreign debt in the light of the basic conflict of interests. Some people have seen the renegotiation as largely a technical matter. Chile would submit technical data on its balance of payments showing that it couldn't afford to service its debt in the normal manner for the next several years and everyone would sit down and come to an amicable agreement in the interests of all concerned. But it is one thing for a semi-colony of the United States to renegotiate its debt, and another for a country in revolution like Chile to do so. The problem is not primarily technical. It is one of the correlation of forces: from our side what strength can we use to get them to accept our terms; and from their side, how can they use the renegotiation to further their general economic and political aims toward Chile. . . .

So far the initial optimism of many people about the renegotiation has not proved justified. . . . The United States is not pressing matters but rather stalling in the belief that time works in its favor and against Chile. We cannot exclude the possibility that the United States intends to prevent us from attaining a successful debt renegotiation . . . that it intends to push us into default and use the renegotiations to create a breach between us and our European and Japanese creditors.

The Current Situation

Since the attachments were first put into effect Chilean operations here have been crippled. CODELCO, CORFO, CAP, and other Chilean agencies here cannot use money in U.S. accounts and have to pay suppliers through European accounts; there are delays in payment and confusion. We cannot move goods through New York, and we cannot move them anywhere in the United States without risk of attachment.

With this situation, the U.S. Government gains almost all the advantages of a general government embargo on Chile without any of the disadvantages. Everything appears to be happening because of the natural actions taken by private businesses to protect their interests. The U.S. Government does not appear on the scene. . . .

But merely because the U.S. Government does not always appear openly does not mean that it is not acting. An example from the crisis between Cuba and the United States in 1960 will illustrate. That crisis was touched off by the refusal of three giant oil monopolies— Standard, Texaco, and Shell (two American, one Anglo-Dutch)—to accept crude oil from the Soviet Union for their Cuban refineries. At the time they pretended that this was their own decision, taken by each of them separately, and they wrote separate letters of refusal. Now the U.S. Ambassador to Cuba at the time, Philip Bonsal, tells in his book on Cuba what really happened. The three companies had originally intended to accept the Soviet crude oil. Then, Standard and Texaco were called to a meeting with Robert Anderson, Secretary of the Treasury, who told them it was U.S. government policy that they not accept Soviet oil; a U.S. representative in London told the same to

Shell. The companies sent separate letters of refusal, says Bonsal, only to keep up the pretense that this was their own decision. But in reality the action was part of the U.S. government program to choke Cuba economically and then overthrow the Revolutionary Government.

All U.S. actions toward Chile, those of the government, private companies, and the courts, fall into a pattern. They run in one direction—against Chile. Chile has been receiving no benefits—only blows. The U.S. Government has been following the intelligent policy of talking little. It knows that too much talk and showing open aggression could be used to mobilize the people of Chile and also opposition in the United States and Latin America. But despite its silence, it has been coordinating action here and in Chile to choke the Revolution to death.

Future Prospects

In considering future prospects it is important not to limit ourselves to legal considerations or the already existing lawsuits by Braden and Anaconda, but to take the role of the U.S. Government and the basic purposes of its actions into account.

If the U.S. Government is acting as silent coordinator and its basic purpose is to choke the Revolution, then the actions it has taken till now are far from being the end of the story. What is to prevent the U.S. Government from getting Anaconda to sue in other states or other countries according to a plan for doing the most possible damage to Chile? What is to prevent the U.S. Government from getting one of Chile's many other creditors—for example, the South American Power Company—to sue? What is to prevent them from getting at Chilean Nitrate here, which so far has not been touched.

So far, in Chile's relations with the United States, it is not those who have thought of conciliation and compromise who have been right, but those who have faced the fact of an irreconcilable conflict of interest. Our lawyers may be able on appeal, or through some other legal action, to get the attachments lifted, but they say that there is no assurance that they will be able to do so and how soon this might be. Our lawyers may be able to win our basic case. But again there is no assurance. It would be imprudent for our agencies to count on being able to operate here in the future in the same way as in the past. The basic fact is that the United States is waging economic and political warfare against Chile and is on the lookout for all actions that can be taken to hurt it.

Action to be Taken

Notwithstanding this last judgement, we should not immediately and precipitately dismantle all our agencies in the United States. First, this would grant Anaconda, Kennecott, and U.S. imperialism an important victory without a fight and without much cost to them. Second, it will take time to set up alternative arrangements and get them to operate well; if we dismantle the old agencies before we have alternative arrangements working well, we are increasing the chances of a gap in supplies to Chile. And third, for political reasons in Chile, the United States, and elsewhere, it is important that we should not appear to be taking the initiative in breaking off business relations with the United States, but rather as the victims of U.S. action which is forcing us out.

We should therefore follow a double policy:

1) Fight hard legally to be able to operate here and use our agencies to buy here so long as we do not have an alternative or it remains convenient. Only retreat when we are compelled to do so. Try to force the U.S. Government out into the open in its economic warfare against Chile.

2) Build up alternative arrangements as quickly as possible.

The legal fight here must obviously remain in the hands of our American lawyers. But there is one important political matter on which I shall make a recommendation. In his ruling on the attachments by Anaconda, Judge Metzner stated that although our side alleged that these attachments would damage trade relations between the two countries, he doubted this because he had not heard from the State Department that this was so. Further, our lawyers say that we can ask the State Department to speak to the Court on sovereign immunity* in our case.

I recommend that we ask the State Department to pronounce on these matters. They may say yes, the attachments will damage trade

---

* As I, a layman in the law, understand it, the doctrine of sovereign immunity holds that a sovereign of one state (for example, the government of Chile) is immune from the judicial processes of another state. The power the State Department holds, in whether or not to apply this doctrine, can be seen in the following quotation from a Supreme Court decision in an immunity case: "It is a guiding principle in determining whether a court should exercise or surrender its jurisdiction in such cases, that the courts should not so act as to embarrass the executive arm in its conduct of foreign affairs. . . . It is therefore not for the courts to deny an immunity which our government has seen fit to allow, or to allow an immunity on new grounds which the government has not seen fit to recognize." 324 U.S. 30 (1945). (This footnote is not part of the original memorandum.)

relations, and yes, we should enjoy sovereign immunity in these cases. Or they may say no or simply refuse to pronounce, which our lawyers say would have the effect of saying no. I doubt that they will say yes, but if they should, we would, according to our lawyers, win our legal actions. If they say no, we will have pushed the U.S. Government a little into the open where it does not want to be and, also, we will be able to use this action politically in Chile.

While we are engaged in the legal fight, we may still be able to carry out an important amount of business from our U.S. offices. It is possible that we will be sued and subject to attachments in other states of the United States and perhaps in foreign countries. But as of now, we are being sued and subject to attachment only in the Southern District of New York. Our New York office is therefore able to do the following: 1) place orders in Europe with payment from our accounts in Europe; and 2) place orders in the United States outside New York, using freight forwarders outside New York so that the shipping documents cannot be attached, and arranging that the goods be shipped through other ports (Philadelphia, New Orleans, Houston, and St. John, Canada), with payment from accounts outside the United States. Whenever we can, we buy CIF,* with payment to be made outside the United States, so as to keep us from having a beneficiary interest in the goods while they are still in the United States: This reduces the danger of attachment. This arrangement does not permit us to operate with maximum efficiency. There remains a risk that even with our precautions our goods in transit will be attached. But the arrangement permits us to buy an important volume of goods at a time when we do not yet have alternative arrangements for doing so. I strongly suggest that we continue to use this arrangement so long as we are able to do so. . . .

It goes without saying that we should act fast to set up alternative arrangements. But granting the need for speed, we should avoid acting precipitately and in panic. It is natural that our agencies here and in Santiago should be agitated. But if each separate agency here and in Santiago acts individually in a disorderly way, various dangers will arise—the danger that we will fall into the hands of fly-by-night companies who will promise us the moon, charge us heavily for their services, and still not be able to supply us on time with the goods we

---

* CIF refers to one of the standard types of contract clauses under which goods are purchased. The seller, besides providing the goods, pays the insurance and freight which are included in his price. Our lawyers had informed us that there was less danger of attachment with this arrangement than with contracts under which the buyer pays the freight and insurance either from the factory (FOB) or the port (FAS). (This footnote was not in the original memorandum.)

need; the danger that even buying through third parties, the legal arrangements will not be watertight and we will still be subject to attachment. It is important that the alternative arrangements we set up be well thought out from the organizational, financial, and legal points of view. Speed is urgent but it would be wrong to think of this as a matter of hours. . . .

THE New York agencies were not dismantled. Javier and I held discussions with representatives of various companies to explore the possibility of establishing a safe way of purchasing through them. We came up against the same problem José and I had faced in our negotiations to set up purchasing arrangements for CODELCO—how to finance the company without its becoming an agent of Chile whose assets would then be subject to attachment. Using a company domiciled abroad would not solve the problem—if it were an agent of Chile, any of its goods, money, or shipping documents found within the jurisdiction of an American court in which Chile was being sued, could still be attached. It became clear that setting up alternative arrangements for the purchase of American goods would be difficult and take time. Where Chile could manage with goods that were not made in the United States, it shifted its purchases to other countries. But it required a large amount of goods of American design and had to try to buy most of them through its New York agencies.

In June 1972 several officials of The National Automotive Parts Enterprise (ENARA), a company the UP government had formed to import spare parts for motor vehicles, came to New York on a mission to carry out emergency purchases—spare parts were running short in Chile. Javier assigned me to assist and accompany them on trips to Ford and other suppliers. The ENARA officials would decide whether the prices and quality of the parts being offered were satisfactory; I would review the shipping and payment arrangements for safety against attachment. Javier also wanted me to ask the larger suppliers for the 60 to 90-day commercial credit always given Chile previously. "They won't give it," said Javier, "but let's see what they say."

Getting parts to Chile was a slow process. Several small dealers in the New York area were eager to do business, but the ENARA people couldn't be sure of their reliability; two or three asked for exceptionally high prices and then offered kickbacks. Working out payment arrangements—through European banks or American banks outside New York—that were satisfactory to the dealers took time.

After several weeks had passed without any parts having been shipped, instructions came from Santiago to ship certain orders quickly by air. We arranged for several orders to be carried to Miami by truck and then flown to Chile. These shipments were costly.

I made trips with ENARA officials to five parts-suppliers. At each one, I asked for commercial credit. Everyone turned me down, usually with a comment that Chile's balance of payments was too poor to justify such credit. I asked the financial officer of one medium-size corporation where he got his information about Chile's balance of payments. "We can't afford," he said, "to have our own people studying the financial position of all the countries we do business with. We just follow the lead of the State Department."

At Ford, we negotiated mainly with officials of the subsidiary handling exports to Latin America who seemed eager to get the ENARA business. Their job was to sell, and their work was apparently judged by how much they sold. But the key decisions were out of their hands—they continually had to get the approval of the staff people at corporate headquarters. We would agree to some condition with the sales people and they would later tell us that the staff people were insisting on a new one. One condition I found interesting was in a contract that included a clause that said Ford exports would be sold in Chile only through the network of Ford dealers there. I wondered why Ford should be concerned about its dealer network in a country that was moving toward socialism—unless it expected that movement to be reversed. The ENARA officials and I were usually kept away from the staff people, but we did meet some at a business luncheon. I found them different from the sales people and far more informed and subtle in their political judgments concerning Chile; they were responsible for Ford's overall policy toward Chile and the rest of Latin America. They skillfully stalled the negotiations and, although we took two trips to Dearborn and tried to agree to the Ford conditions, we did not obtain an agreement. One Ford official phoned me often afterwards, to tell me of the progress that he was making in ironing out one point or another of the contract. But days, then weeks, passed and somehow the contract wasn't ready. In the summer of 1972 I began to prepare to go to Chile to work, and lost touch with the Ford negotiations.

Shortly before I left, the news came that Kennecott was attacking again. On September 7, 1972, Kennecott announced that it was withdrawing from further legal proceedings in Chile and would "pursue in other nations its remedies for the confiscated assets." Kennecott said that it was "informing all persons who may be concerned with copper" from the El Teniente mine that it had continued "rights" to that copper and intended to protect those rights.[1] Soon thereafter, Charles Michaelson, president of Kennecott's Metals Division, sent a letter to buyers of Chilean copper which stated: "We have been informed that you are or may be buying copper from the El Teniente mine over which we exercise ownership rights. We want to call your attention to the fact that any purchase, acquisition or sale . . . of the above mentioned copper without our express consent violates our rights. We will take any measures we consider necessary to protect our rights."[2]

The Wall Street Journal, The New York Times, and other publications helped build up the Kennecott threat. Said *The Wall Street Journal:* "Kennecott didn't say what [its] action might be. But industry analysts believe it could take this form: A foreign customer buying copper from the El Teniente mine in Chile could get a bill from Kennecott for its claimed 49% share. When the bill goes unpaid, Kennecott could begin a legal action against the buyer. . . . The threat alone could send a chill through Chile's customers, who obviously would prefer to avoid legal battles. More important, though, analysts here say Kennecott may be successful."[3]

A few weeks later, Kennecott obtained an injunction from a Paris court against payment to Chile for a shipment of copper headed for Le Havre. *The Wall Street Journal* quoted a copper trader who explained that the court action has a "nervewracking effect" on anybody who buys Chilean copper. In subsequent weeks, Kennecott started similar actions in other countries—the Netherlands, West Germany, and Sweden.

The Kennecott campaign in Europe, with its letters of warning to copper traders and its newspaper publicity, was not simply a legal action. The only hope Kennecott had of obtaining a "good settlement" with Chile lay in the replacement of the UP government by a new one. The legal actions freezing Chilean assets in Europe and scaring potential buyers of Chilean copper were useful to Kennecott because, regardless of how the lawsuits of which they were a part eventually turned out, they inflicted great damage on Chile. The Kennecott campaign in Europe was part of the economic warfare the United States was waging against Chile.

8

Running the Economy November 1970 to Mid-1972

The initial short-run economic policy of the UP government was largely determined by the state of the economy it had inherited. For four years, the economy had been stagnating. On top of this, the disruption created by the enemies of the UP after the election caused an economic decline. The index of industrial production (1968=100), which had been 116 in July, plunged to 100 in September, and remained at 107–108 during October through December. Unemployment in Greater Santiago, already 6.4 percent in September, jumped to 8.3 percent in December. Given this situation, the initial economic policy had to be one of stimulating the economy, increasing production and reducing unemployment. For a government representing the workers, any other policy would have been inconceivable.

Idle resources created conditions favorable for a policy of stimulation. As a result of the post-election slowdown in sales, inventories were large. Thirty percent of manufacturing capacity was idle. The ordinary statistics on unemployment understated the true reserve of labor power available—one estimate, taking involuntary part-time work and other forms of disguised unemployment into account, put true unemployment as equivalent to

17.4 percent of the labor force.[1] And foreign exchange reserves, accumulated during the Vietnam War, stood at $300 million.

One economic condition argued against stimulation—inflation. Consumer prices increased by 35 percent in 1970, the highest rate since 1964. In most countries such a rate of inflation would pose a dilemma for the policy makers contemplating stimulation. But the problem in Chile must be understood in Chilean terms. In Chile, an inflation of 35 percent was not unheard of; in seven of the twenty years between 1950 and 1970, inflation exceeded this rate. Inflation always hurt the lower classes, but in 1970, the recession hurt even more.

Besides, those in charge of economic policy felt that they could both stimulate the economy and restrain inflation. They could stimulate the economy by pump-priming and redistributing income in favor of the lower classes, and they could restrain inflation by directly controlling prices. Government expenditures on public works and housing would be increased. The 1971 annual readjustment of wages and salaries would be made larger than usual. For almost everyone, it would at least equal the 35 percent increase in the cost of living in 1970; for the lower paid, it would be greater, with minimum wages going up by 66 percent. The large increase in costs entailed by the readjustment need not increase prices. The Minister of Economics, Pedro Vuscovic, explained why: "The income of capital is excessively high in Chile even in comparison with many capitalist countries, and for this reason the major part of the private productive apparatus is in a position to absorb the readjustment through its profits without transferring it to prices. The price policy of the Popular Government means diminishing the rate of profit per unit produced, with an effect on the income of capital that can only be compensated by taking advantage of the increased purchasing power of the workers to increase production and productivity."[2] A government agency—The National Office of Industry and Commerce (DIRINCO)—would control prices.

The reactivation of the economy and the redistribution of income held promise of great political benefits. As Vuscovic put it: "A central objective of economic policy is to widen political support for the government. . . ." The short-run policy for running the economy and the UP program of structural changes are "inter-dependent. It is not possible to make deeper changes without broadening the Government's political support, and economic reactivation and income redistribution will provide an impulse to these fundamental changes."[3]

The UP's economic policy soon began to show results. By Chilean standards, the price line was held. In December 1970 the price increase was zero. During the first four months of 1971 prices rose 5.8 percent, a third of the increase that had occurred during this period in recent years. And industrial production rose sharply. By May 1971 it was 17 percent greater than a year earlier. Employment rose and unemployment declined. Unemployment in Greater Santiago fell from 8.3 percent in December 1970 to 5.2 percent in June 1971. The standard of living of the lower classes began to improve dramatically.

The increase in production, decline in unemployment, and relative price stability continued throughout most of 1971, and the UP chalked up a number of achievements for that year. Gross product, in constant escudos, grew 8.5 percent. Industrial production rose 13 percent—the largest increase in ten years. There were 200,000 more people employed in December 1971 than in December 1970; unemployment was cut from 8.3 to 3.8 percent. Despite the surge in economic activity, the increase in the Consumer Price Index slowed from 35 percent in 1970 to 22 percent in 1971.

The large wage readjustments and the increase in employment shifted the distribution of income. The share of wage and salary earners in the national income grew from 54 percent in 1970 to 59 percent in 1971. The consumption expenditures of the lower classes soared—many of the poor could now afford to eat meat and began to buy decent clothing.

THERE was, however, another side to the economic picture, less visible to most Chileans than the growth in production, employment, and consumption expenditures, but which was still important. First, the UP government ran into bad luck with Chile's balance of payments. The all-important price of copper, which had been running at seventy cents per pound or more during the first half of 1970, began to drop in July; by January 1971 it had plunged to forty-six cents.

At the then physical level of Chile's copper exports, each drop of one cent in price meant, annually, a decrease of $15 million in their value. Not only was this drop in the price of the export on which Chile depended for 75 percent of its foreign exchange earnings not compensated by any similar decline in the prices of its imports, but mostly these moved the other way; in particular, the prices of Chile's food imports—wheat, meat, and milk— began to rise sharply. At the same time, the net flow of capital turned negative—more capital was leaving Chile than entering it. The net flow had been positive throughout the preceding decade; the inflow of new capital had enabled Chile to pay the interest and amortization on its debt and finance deficits in other parts of the balance of payments. Now, just as the burden of servicing Chile's foreign debt was approaching a peak, came the invisible blockade—the U.S. commercial banks slashed their lines of credit, the U.S. government Export-Import Bank and the U.S.-dominated World Bank and Inter-American Development Bank discontinued granting loans. And of course, the foreign corporations stopped bringing in new capital for investment. Added to these factors outside of Chile's control, the physical volume of imports began to grow with the increasing demand for raw materials resulting from expanding industrial production and the increasing demand for foodstuffs resulting from the rise in the income of the lower classes. The balance of payments moved into deep deficit, and the foreign exchange reserves dwindled.

The Central Bank took several measures to meet the problem. First, it restricted the import of nonessential goods. The bank was not empowered to control imports directly by a licensing system. It achieved the same result by setting up a system under which, for certain items, it could, if it chose, require an importer to make a "Prior Deposit" of 10,000 percent of the value of the goods he wished to import. This requirement was prohibitive; for example, an importer wishing to bring in a $3,000 automobile could be required to make a deposit of $300,000. Throughout 1971 the bank kept adding further items to this system, until by the end of the year all nonessential consumer goods, all capital goods, and several other categories were under its control—which was tightly exercised.

The bank also acted to reduce the outflow of foreign exchange for tourist trips abroad. It progressively lowered the amount of foreign exchange granted each traveler, and required that travelers who spent less time abroad than expected, return a corresponding amount. In July 1971 the bank made it much more expensive for Chileans to travel abroad. A separate rate of exchange, different from that for the export and import of goods, applied to tourist transactions; the bank devalued the escudo in tourist transactions by almost 50 percent in relation to the dollar, practically doubling the escudo cost of foreign travel.

The factors worsening Chile's balance of payments were too strong to be more than partially counterbalanced by these measures. Left unaffected was the large outflow of funds to service Chile's debt. On November 10, 1971, President Allende announced that Chile had decided to renegotiate its foreign debt. Chile, he said, had continued rigorously to fulfill its financial commitments during 1971. But now it was facing balance of payments "difficulties not susceptible to correction through . . . change in its foreign trade and exchange policy. . . . The Chilean Government is certain that national and international public opinion will understand that any underdeveloped nation that has accumulated a debt of the relative magnitude of ours, and that at the same time is experiencing a drop in its traditional income, must initiate severe restrictions. . . ."[4] By suspending the debt payments when it did, Chile avoided paying $80 million due in November and December of 1971.[5]

Having devalued the escudo for tourist transactions in July, the bank devalued it for exports and imports in December. A number of considerations lay behind the delay in making this second devaluation.

The economists of the imperialist-dominated International Monetary Fund and World Bank present currency devaluation as the basic weapon for attacking balance of payments deficits— you lower the value of your currency in relation to others, which discourages your imports by raising their price in your currency and encourages your exports by lowering their price in other currencies; the reduction in imports and increase in exports eliminates the deficit. But there is a hitch to this method. It means indiscriminately raising the cost of imported goods, raising the cost of living, placing the main burden of trying to solve the problem on the lower classes. In a country like Chile, most of whose imports and exports are relatively insensitive to price change, there is a further hitch—devaluation cannot solve the problem. A large part of Chile's imports are essential goods— basic foodstuffs, raw materials, and spare parts and replacement equipment for mines and factories. Raising the internal price of wheat will burden the poor with a higher price of bread but, unless carried to the point where people starve, will not bring about a significant decrease in imports; and those who need raw materials, spare parts, and replacement equipment will buy them even at a higher price. As for exports, devaluation by Chile will not lower the price of its copper, enabling it to sell more—the price of copper is set in dollars in the international markets.

For these reasons, the Left in Chile traditionally opposed devaluation, and the Popular Unity program stated that "We shall put an end to the shameful devaluation of the escudo." The UP government was willing to control tourism—a luxury—by devaluation, but it was unwilling to rely on this method to control the import of goods. The sensible way to reduce the import of goods is through direct controls which enable you to discriminate among different items according to how essential they are, and which does not bring about an increase in the cost of living. This was why the bank attacked the problem of controlling imports by the system of "Prior Deposits" rather than by devaluation.

Still, the problem of exchange rates could not be disregarded indefinitely. That most Chilean imports and exports are relatively insensitive to price change does not mean that they are altogether impervious to it. From July 1970, the last time the escudo-dollar rate for exports and imports had been fixed, till December 1971, the domestic price level had risen by 29 percent: Thus the dollar value of the escudo remained the same while its value in domestic goods shrank by three tenths. Such a strong divergence was bound to distort the price structure and create difficulties.

In relation to the prices of other goods, the escudo cost of imports became cheaper and cheaper. The very cheapness of imports stimulated the demand for them, stimulated importers to apply to the bank to bring in more and more. While the bank could in the main control the imports through the system of

"Prior Deposits," the control mechanism was far from perfect, and some increase in imports undoubtedly occurred.

The volume of exports did not suffer noticeably because of the divergence between the dollar and domestic value of the escudo—the value of non-copper exports rose in 1971, the value of copper exports fell but only because of the drop in price in the international markets. However, the finances of the exporters were squeezed; their costs were rising while the escudos they received per dollar of exports remained the same. With a readjustment of wages and salaries coming at the beginning of the new year, many would be facing financial difficulty unless something were done.

Therefore, though the exchange rate was not a main cause of the balance of payments deficit, it finally became necessary to devalue the escudo. The bank devalued differently for different categories—in technical jargon, it instituted multiple exchange rates. For the import of foodstuffs and petroleum, it allowed the old rate to remain; it didn't want to burden wage earners with higher food costs or to force a rise in the cost of mass transit by causing an increase in the price of oil and gasoline. For the import of raw materials, intermediate goods, and machinery, it raised the amount of escudos the importer had to pay per dollar by 56 percent, and for the import of non-essentials, by 100 percent. For exports, the bank raised the amount of escudos per dollar received by exporters by 29 percent, equal to the increase in the domestic price level since the last devaluation; it didn't want the exporters either to suffer acute financial problems or to be placed in a better position than they had earlier enjoyed.

The measures undertaken by the bank could not prevent 1971 from registering a sharp deterioration in the balance of payments. Even with $80 million saved by suspending debt payments, the deficit was over $300 million, and foreign exchange reserves shrank from $333 million on December 31, 1970, to $30 million a year later.[6] One of the most important reserves the UP government had found when it took over was now used up.

ACCOMPANYING the deterioration in the balance of payments was a larger than planned deficit in the public sector (the government and the so-called decentralized agencies such as the Development Corporation, CORFO). The planned deficit was 9.8 billion escudos, equal to 17 percent of planned expenditures; the actual deficit was 14.1 billion escudos, equal to 22 percent of actual expenditures.[7] There was no way of financing this deficit except through borrowing from the Central Bank—in effect printing money.

Several factors account for the actual deficit being much larger than the planned deficit. On the one hand, there was a shortfall in the revenues of the central government. The large copper companies paid less than expected—partly because with the low price of copper and a fixed exchange rate their profits were down, but mostly because seeing nationalization coming they managed their finances in such a way as to pay as little as possible to Chile. Revenues from import duties rose less than expected because of the changing composition of imports—an increasing proportion consisted of items exempt from duty such as foodstuffs. On the other hand, the expenditures of the public sector, other than the central government, increased more than planned. Some newly nationalized enterprises, squeezed between rising costs and controlled selling prices, were running deficits which were now being counted in the public sector, and the costs of land reform arising from programs administered by a multiplicity of decentralized agencies were difficult to control.

One reason the deficit in the public sector exceeded what was planned is basic to the future economic history of the Chilean Revolution: With Congress controlled by the opposition, the government was unable to reform the tax structure and raise progressive taxes as it wished. It presented proposals for modest changes in taxes in 1971. Here is what happened:

> The Government's path was blocked. . . . Congress had opposed the Popular Unity's proposal to tax transfers of possessions valued at more than twenty-five annual *sueldos vitales**. . . . Proposals for a tax on excess profits had been rejected, and a proposed 30% tax on enterprises with a capital of five hundred thousand *escudos* or more

---

* A *sueldo vital* was the legal minimum monthly remuneration of an employee. It was also used as a standard measure of value for other things besides salaries, such a measure being necessary because the rapidly changing value of the currency often made ordinary statements of value meaningless.

had been reduced to 15% and only applied to firms with a capital of six hundred thousand *escudos* and above. A scaled charge on *bienes raices* (land and property) was rejected in favor of a general tax at the lowest rate of the proposed scale; the proposal for a graduated tax on wine and cigarettes, according to their value, was dealt with in the same way. The Government . . . failed to secure approval for a law to punish tax offenders, modifying the existing over-lenient legislation.[8]

The rejection by Congress of the UP's tax bills was not just a defense of the economic interests of big business and the well-to-do; it was also part of a deliberate opposition strategy of stoking the inflation to weaken the UP government.

The fiscal deficit was the most important factor in the pumping of money into the economy, but not the only one. The credit extended by the banking system to the private sector increased by over 3.5 billion escudos, or 45 percent, in 1971. Although this increase was large, it was not as out of line with previous years as the budget deficit—the increase in credit in 1970 had been 35 percent.

Chile's money supply (currency in circulation plus demand deposits) ballooned from 10.1 billion escudos at the end of 1970 to 20.5 billion a year later, a record expansion of 103 percent; the expansion had been 65 percent in 1970 and 35 percent in 1969.[9] Despite the increase in the money supply, the government was able, by direct control, to hold the price line throughout 1971. But the pressure from the swelling money supply was growing.

Chile's economic situation at the end of 1971 thus contrasted sharply with that at the beginning. Inventories, idle industrial capacity, unemployment, foreign exchange reserves were all down; the economy was pressing against its resources. Industrial production was higher than ever before. The supply of foodstuffs had increased both because of good harvests and higher imports, and Chile's lower classes were eating as never before. But the increase in the output and supply of goods that had been going strong a year earlier was now exhausting itself, while the increase in money supply and demand was gathering impetus. In the latter half of the year, sporadic shortages of beef, fish, oil, and several other foodstuffs appeared. There was danger of a powerful resurgence of inflation.

One economist has a simple comment on the problem of

inflation faced by the UP government. Paul N. Rosenstein-Rodan, referring to the government's allowing the money supply to increase so rapidly, says that "Any undergraduate economic student would have known better."[10] However, this same one-dimensional academic standard might be applied not only to Chile, but also to the United States, Great Britain, Italy, France, Japan, and many other countries in which inflation has run rampant in recent years. Any student would have known better . . . yet somehow inflations of tremendous force got started in these countries. Professor Rosenstein-Rodan is reciting a text-book formalism, not grappling with the real problem.

The UP inherited a recession and unemployment combined with an inflation. The pump-priming required to fight the recession and unemployment would expand the money supply and the expansion was bound sooner or later to cause inflation difficulties. The problem was aggravated by the congressional sabotage of the government's attempts to raise progressive taxes; with such taxes the government would have been able both to combat the recession and unemployment and exercise restraint over the money supply. Still, it had managed the initial period successfully. Now, with the recession and unemployment controlled, it had to switch policy and place ever more emphasis on preventing the inflation from breaking loose again. But it could not, like a bourgeois government, fight inflation at the expense of the working class. It could not take measures that would cause recession and unemployment to reappear or that would reverse the redistribution of income it had started. It had to restrain the growth in the money supply by cutting into the income and wealth of the upper classes. But how, with the opposition in control of Congress, and sabotaging?

The problem was not mainly technical, but political. The enemy was counting on economic difficulties, working to ensure that they would occur. Inflation was one of the difficulties counted on most to create the economic and political chaos necessary to get rid of the UP government. The fight over inflation was part of the struggle for power taking place in Chile.

To appreciate how difficult the problem was, one has but to think of how hard it has been for other countries, even without the executive and legislature split apart by a life and death struggle as in Chile, to bring inflation under control. Yet the UP government had somehow to find ways of coping with the problem. An inspired effort was required. The government needed to run scared—to attack the problem as soon as possible, with revolutionary imagination and sweep, overlooking nothing that might help.

But there were obstacles to the prompt action necessary to prevent the expansion of the money supply from gaining the ever more dangerous momentum that would make it increasingly difficult to control later. The UP was a coalition, and it is hard to get coalitions to agree to a single analysis and strategy, and to act quickly. In addition, the government apparatus that the UP was working with—one it had inherited—was a huge, unwieldy mass, many of whose parts were only imperfectly under its control.

Some UP economists didn't see the danger, and held that concern with such things as money supply reflected a narrow technical and bourgeois point of view. The basic causes of Chile's inflation are structural, they claimed; without changing the economic structure, inflation could not be stopped; with the structural changes the UP was carrying out—the placing of the strategic parts of the economy under state control—it would not be much of a problem to control inflation. The success of the government in restraining the price increase during 1971 reinforced this point of view. An article in the November 1971 issue of *Vía Chilena,* a monthly publication of the National Planning Office (ODEPLAN), stated that the UP had succeeded in "attaining control of inflation" while reactivating the economy and absorbing unemployment. "This situation, truly unique, is not easily understood by many economists from the industrialized countries who tie their analysis to orthodox schemes."

No matter what the strengths of an analysis of the structural aspects of inflation may be, when it leads to underestimation of the importance of the financial and money mechanism, it reflects mushy thinking. The UP government was able to reduce the price rise in 1971 through direct controls over prices. But there are limits to how far such controls can hold in the face of an inordinately increasing money supply. Obtaining state control of the monopolies of production and distribution can be of great help with the problems of supply and prices, but it does not guarantee a solution. No economy can be flooded with money without difficulties arising.

In February 1972 the leaders of the UP met in a Santiago suburb, El Arrāyán, to review the political and economic situation. In the document, "New Tasks, for the Popular Government and the Chilean People," presenting their conclusions, they stressed that the economic situation differed from that of a year earlier—the large margins of excess capacity which had permitted an increase in employment, production, and consumption and a reduction in inflation to take place simultaneously were gone. Nevertheless, the leaders—who did not yet have the statistics that were to show a large jump in the Consumer Price Index in January—were only beginning to grapple with the problem posed by the runaway money supply, and provided only loose general guidance on what would have to be done. "Budget policy will have to reconcile a limitation on deficit financing with an increase in public services such as housing, education, public health. . . . The decrease in the excessive quantity of money in the hands of the private sector . . . is another important task which will be confronted by means of certain specific measures and general resolutions on credit norms soon to be issued by the Central Bank."

The expanding money supply was a force that could be contained for a while by price controls, but was bound to explode. The explosions began with the new year. In January the Consumer Price Index jumped by 3.7 percent. The statistics came out in March. *El Mercurio* gloated in an article entitled, "The Floodgates of Inflation are Being Opened."

The Communist Party reacted quickly. In a report to its Central Committee on March 15 one of its leaders, Orlando Millas, stated: "It is imperative for 1972 to maintain the money supply within much stricter limits; the penalty for failure to do this would be that the inflation would tear away the economic and social benefits attained by the workers and the middle class sectors. . . . Any tolerance toward outlays that the country cannot finance would lead to an increase in money supply equivalent to sitting down on the crater of a volcano. . . . It is a matter of life or death not to permit a repetition of the inflationary cycles to which bourgeois governments have accustomed us."

Millas rejected the fatalistic theory that, given the inherited structure of the Chilean economy, nothing could be done about inflation, and also the view—held by some in the UP—that the workings of the monetary and financial mechanism and phenomena like inflation are somehow not "real," that they are less important than the "real" working of the economy. Millas proposed a number of financial measures, including strict control of government expenditures and a determined attack on tax evasion. [Tax evasion in Chile was enormous. The first message of President Allende to the full Congress estimated it at 40 percent. The loss in 1971 just from evasion of the sales tax was estimated at 20 billion escudos, 6 billion more than the budget deficit.[11]] Millas also proposed "a supreme patriotic effort" to increase the production of copper and other exports and "an extremely rigorous plan, a war plan," for economizing foreign exchange.[12]

In the months following January the Consumer Price Index continued to jump—6.5 percent in February, 2.7 percent in March, 5.7 percent in April. The total increase during the first four months of 1972 was 19.8 percent, three times as high as the increase during the same months of 1971, virtually as high as the 20.2 percent increase for the whole of that year.

Inflation, reaccelerated, now began to feed on itself. Government expenditures rose even faster than the price level, while receipts lagged behind it, thus further widening the budget deficit. Ninety percent of expenditures were for wages and salaries, social security payments, and family allowances which received a generous cost of living adjustment at the beginning of the year. Many taxes were being paid in depreciated current escudos on income earned the previous year or on property evaluated for tax purposes several years earlier.

On top of the deficit of the central government, a new problem arose—a large growing deficit in the state's economic enterprises. This deficit had several causes. The previous owners of the enterprises which were recently taken over had milked them and left them in poor financial condition. Difficulties are inevitable in a transfer of management. In some factories discipline relaxed, additional workers were taken on without a corresponding increase in output, and costs rose. But rapidly becoming the most important factor in the deficits was the squeeze of inflation: The government was holding down the prices charged by these enterprises, while their costs were going up with the readjustment of wages and salaries, the devaluation of the escudo, and the general rise in prices.

The UP had hoped with the nationalization of the monopolies to capture their profits and use the funds to develop the economy. Now, instead of profits, there was a growing deficit which could only be financed by inflationary Central Bank lending. *El Mercurio,* always alert, eagerly called the public's attention to this additional problem. On April 27 it ran an article listing state enterprises with their profits or losses: Of the 112 enterprises listed, only 13 showed surpluses; the other 99 showed sizeable deficits.[13]

Many private enterprises also began to incur losses and turn to the banking system for financial assistance. The Central Bank had set up a careful, cumbersome procedure through which it hoped to control the granting of credit to private companies: The companies had to submit evidence that their need for funds was not due to the owners milking them or running them inefficiently. But as costs soared with inflation, it became impossible to tell whether a company was in trouble for such reasons or through no fault of its own. The Central Bank had to permit the commercial banks to grant the loans required by the companies to cover their deficits. The alternative was to allow companies to go bankrupt and throw their workers into the streets. Such loans were not repaid, or were only repaid from the proceeds of later, larger loans. How could companies repay unless the underlying problem causing the deficits was solved?

As inflation accelerated, the shortages grew more severe. At first they were few and mild. Beef—the main missing item—could still be bought several days a week. And there was a rapid increase in the supply of whiting from the factory-fishing ships provided by the Soviet Union; although people preferred beef, the whiting was also a protein-rich food. But rumors began to circulate that later everything would be short. Those with higher incomes rushed to put their money into goods—refrigerators, television sets, cars—and by April a number of other items besides beef had become scarce. They were mostly not the goods consumed by the mass of the people, but still the problem was serious. The middle classes were being hurt, and even the lower classes were beginning to be affected.

A black market arose in which many goods not available in ordinary markets could be found, but at three, four, or five times the regular price. This, too, was serious. The black market would aggravate the shortages: A small part of the population would get all the goods it wanted, leaving that much less for everyone else. The redistribution of income would, in effect, be reversed. The black market would also aggravate the budget deficit—black marketeers do not pay taxes on their illicit operations. And the black market could create all manner of political difficulties for the government—with people upset by the shortages, with small merchants and farmers it was trying to win over or neutralize and who would be lured by high prices or forced by high costs to sell their goods black.

The excess liquidity, shortages, and black market created an excellent environment for speculation and hoarding by private businessmen. With money abundant, they were under no financial pressure to sell their goods quickly. By holding on to them, they could not only realize speculative gains but also—an important reason for many—worsen the shortages and hurt the government.

The interrelationships between prices became distorted. When the government held down the price of sugar beets, farmers switched to growing other things whose prices were far higher; it raised the price of beets and then found that sugar refineries were being asked to sell sugar at a price below that of the beets needed to produce it. Some farmers, instead of selling their wheat and milk at controlled prices through normal channels for human consumption, fed them to livestock so they could have more meat for sale at black market prices. The price of imported goods again became low; and some, such as automobile parts and medicines, were smuggled into neighboring countries, to be sold for foreign exchange which could then be converted back into escudos at astronomical black market rates.

The situation was ominous. With a 20 percent increase in the Consumer Price Index in the first four months of the year, economic writers were predicting by June that the rate of inflation for the year would reach 50 and perhaps 60 percent. What could the government do to prevent the inflation from gathering such dangerous momentum?

The government could do little with fiscal policy. Congress would not let it increase revenues by taxing the well-to-do; and any significant cut in expenditures would have meant creating heavy unemployment. Nor could the government rely on monetary policy; it could not restrict bank credit to industry and agriculture enough to compensate for even a fraction of the budget deficit; this would have meant a sharp decline in output and—again—unemployment. There was talk of trying to soak up excess purchasing power by importing automobiles and selling them at very high prices. But with projections of the 1972 balance of payments showing a probable deficit of $400 million, and with scarcities of foodstuffs and other essential goods, it was impossible to justify the expenditure of foreign exchange on automobiles.

What could the government do about the deficits in the state enterprises, which by now had become an additional key cause of the expansion in the money supply? It could try to improve the efficiency of these enterprises. But inefficiency was not the main cause of their deficits and, besides, to reduce it would take time.

The government was faced with a dilemma. It could raise prices so that the enterprises could again cover their costs—or it could watch the deficits grow. Raising prices was a hard measure to swallow. It entailed obvious political disadvantages. Besides, the increases would be reflected in the Consumer Price Index and, to protect the lower classes, the government would have to permit a corresponding readjustment of wages and salaries—which would mean an acceleration of the price-wage spiral. But the deficits had to be kept from growing even larger, otherwise the economy would be flooded with money, and goods would increasingly disappear from the regular markets with their low official prices into the black markets with their outlandish prices. Moreover, the longer the government waited to take action, the more acute the dilemma would become—the bigger the deficits and the bigger the price increases required to bring them under control.

The government could hope to partially counter the effects of the increase in the money supply by direct action. It could use DIRINCO, the police, and the people to enforce price controls and fight hoarding, speculation, and the black market. In the statement of El Arrayán, the UP leaders had spoken of Committees of Supply and Prices (JAPs), organized by neighborhood, through which the people could help with these tasks. It was important to make the most of all these methods, especially the mobilization of the people.

But there were limits to what these methods could do. Only a small proportion of the chain of distribution had come under the government's direct control through takeover—there were 125 thousand small, private merchants and storekeepers and many small private farmers. Even a number of large wholesale distributing houses were still privately owned. How could the government control all these merchants and farmers as the financial pressures and allurements to trade in black markets became stronger? To control a black market by police action is difficult under any circumstances; here the government was without state power, did not have a police force on which it could fully count. Only half the population supported the UP and would be willing to back the JAPs.

The UP coalition reacted slowly to the worsening economic situation. Statistics began to show what was happening only weeks later. Meetings and discussions of government and party officials took time; it was difficult to find and agree on solutions. By the end of May the Communist Party was insisting that something had to be done. Millas had been arguing that Chile had to solve the problem of the finances of the nationalized enterprises and the problem of inflation. He called for a new economic policy.

The UP was facing a crisis—one not limited to the problem of inflation and shortages, but also involving nationalization policy and the loss of ground politically. The UP leaders held another conference, this time at Lo Curro. With the situation much clearer than it had been at El Arrayán, they agreed that action—though painful—had to be taken to reduce the flow of money into the economy and to correct distortions in the price structure. The

Cabinet was reorganized, the ministers of finance and economics replaced, with Orlando Millas becoming the minister of finance and Carlos Matus of the Socialist Party becoming minister of economics. Action would follow within a few weeks.

9

Structural Economic Transformation

The clearest, most concrete portions of the UP's program covered the structural economic transformation it proposed to carry out. Whereas the sections dealing with the problem of power spoke in generalities, those dealing with the economic structure laid out in detail the measures to be taken.

The process of transformation of our economy will begin with the application of a policy intended to create a dominant state sector, comprising those firms already owned by the state, and the businesses which are to be expropriated. As a first step, we shall nationalize those basic resources like the large-scale copper, iron, and nitrate mines, and others which are controlled by foreign capital and national monopolies. These nationalized sectors will thus be comprised of the following:

1) Large-scale copper, nitrate, iodine, iron, and coal mines.
2) The country's financial system, especially private banks and insurance companies.
3) Foreign trade.
4) Large distribution firms and monopolies.
5) Strategic industrial monopolies.
6) As a rule, all those activities which have a strong influence on the country's economic and social development, such as the production and distribution of electric power; rail, air, and sea transport;

communications; the production, refining, and distribution of petroleum and its derivatives, including liquid gas; the iron and steel industry, cement, petrochemicals and heavy chemicals, cellulose, and paper.[1]

Besides the state sector, there would also be a mixed and a private sector. The mixed sector "will be composed of enterprises combining both state and private capital"—for example, enterprises in which the state would join with foreign companies which could provide technology useful to Chile. The private sector would be made up of non-monopolistic, non-strategic enterprises, which constituted 99 percent of all enterprises in the country.

Even before the UP, the state had played an important role in the economy. The Development Corporation (CORFO) owned many companies—electric power, petroleum, sugar—and held shares in others such as steel. More than 70 percent of all investment funds had been provided by the state. But this state intervention had supported the private monopolies, foreign and national, which dominated the economy. The state had developed the less profitable basic industries which served the monopolies and had supported the private companies financially, providing them capital and credit. During its early years, CORFO's financial help went only to Chilean enterprises, but then it also began to help finance mixed enterprises in which U.S. companies participated.

The creation of the state sector envisaged by the UP would serve several purposes. It would remove the economic power of the foreign monopolies, regain Chile's basic resources, the control of its own market, and its economic independence. It would similarly eliminate the power of the national monopolies. Besides capturing the profits and using them for economic development, the state would be able to plan the economy, to gear it to producing the goods and services needed by the people, rather than those that the monopolies chose to provide.

The UP foresaw important political benefits from the economic reforms. Nationalization of the monopolies (along with land reform) would destroy the material base for the political power of Chile's ruling classes. As they do everywhere, the monopolies in Chile used their money to support political parties and candidates, newspapers and public figures. Here are some comments on how the U.S. copper companies did this:

> It strikes one's notice that companies which did not sell copper inside the country, nevertheless spent hundreds of millions of *escudos* in advertising in the press, and on the radio and television. . . . The North American companies looked after their image within the country very carefully. . . . For many years, the Braden prize . . . was granted to persons and entities it was judged convenient to maintain grateful. . . . Frequent banquets, receptions, parties, and gifts helped keep useful individuals satisfied. . . . For many years, the copper companies had the pleasure of seeing seated on the bench of the Supreme Court more than one member of their legal staff. . . . Not long ago, it became public through the press that sons and very close relatives of the highest-ranking members of the Judicial Branch had held office in these copper companies. But one of the principal and constant concerns of the companies was to maintain the closest contacts possible, preferably of a contractual nature, and better yet if they resulted profitable to the other party, with influential parliamentarians and politicians. . . . Anaconda preferred members of the ex-Radical Party before it split. . . . Kennecott also sought contacts with parties of the right.[2]

Some UP people seemed to think that the destruction of the material base of the ruling classes would by itself solve the problem of power in Chile. By creating a state sector and destroying the material base, one was setting up a new "alternative power" which would somehow take over from the old power. I have never read nor heard a clear explanation of how the transfer of power would come about, or of how destroying the material base would solve the problem of the armed forces of the bourgeois state.

The nationalization program got under way quickly. On November 22, less than three weeks after the inauguration, the government took control of Purina de Chile, an affiliate of Ralston Purina, and of Nibsa, a subsidiary of Northern Indiana Brass, when these companies tried to close down. On December 22 Allende announced at a mass meeting that the government would present a constitutional amendment for the nationalization of copper. In January the Lota-Schwager Company, which produced 80 percent of Chile's coal, and the Banco de Crédito e

Inversiones, the third largest bank, were taken over. In February the RCA Victor plant, a subsidiary of RCA International, passed to state control by purchase. By May 21, 1971, when Allende delivered his *First Message to the Full Congress,* he was able to point to a variety of important takeovers—iron mines, nitrate mines, textile factories, banks, a cement plant, a publishing company—and to say, "We have acted with decision."

By far the most important industry marked for nationalization was copper. The dream of nationalizing this industry had existed for a long time. Left members of Congress, including Allende, began introducing nationalization bills in the early 1950s. The Confederation of Copper Workers and the Central Workers Confederation (CUT) pressed for nationalization. In 1961 Rado-miro Tomic said: "Two thirds of the external economy of Chile consists of copper. Who controls two thirds of the external economy of a country controls that country. Because of this, it is obvious that so long as we want to be a sovereign country, not just formally but in reality, copper should be in the hands of the public powers of the state of Chile, not in those of foreign enterprises."[3]

The Left parties made the nationalization of copper a key issue in the 1964 presidential campaign, and several Christian Democrats spoke in favor of it. The Frei government tried to get rid of the pressure with "Chileanization" and "contracted nationalization," but Chile soon became aware that the copper monopolies still bestrode their country. A reactionary senator—Francisco Bulnes of the National Party—complained in 1965, just after Chileanization, that Kennecott's subsidiary, Braden Copper, with only half its former assets, would double its profits; he was not altogether correct—in the next four years, the profits quadrupled.[4]

Sentiment for full, real nationalization grew even among Christian Democrats and others not of the Left. Tomic, soon to become the Christian Democratic candidate for president, declared shortly after the Frei agreement with Anaconda that the "best hope for the country" lay in nationalization. When Tomic announced in his campaign that he would "immediately and integrally nationalize the principal copper companies," this meant that two of the three candidates, representing two thirds of the voters, were running on platforms calling for nationalization.

The government decided to carry out the nationalization of copper not by an ordinary law, but by a constitutional amendment. Embodying the nationalization in Chile's most fundamental law would present it in the most impressive way, would emphasize that it flowed from Chile's very sovereignty as a nation, and would make it legally as unassailable as possible. A constitutional reform also had, under the Chilean system, another advantage—if the opposition-controlled Congress opposed the measure, the government could call a plebiscite in which the people would decide.

The government originally proposed a different method of nationalization than the one actually used. It wanted to nationalize the property of the copper companies, not the companies themselves, leaving itself free to create a new organization to which it could turn over the nationalized property. But the Christian Democratic bloc in Congress objected. The Christian Democrats didn't want a nationalization in which the mixed companies created under them ceased to exist, in which the "Chileanization" and "contracted nationalization" were undone. To them belonged the "historic honor" of having initiated the recovery of Chile's copper, and the new nationalization must simply complete what they had started. Not just the property of the mixed companies, but the companies themselves must be nationalized. The Christian Democratic method had grave disadvantages: It saddled the nationalized industry with the old organizational forms—one company for El Teniente, another for Chuquicamata, etc.; and it meant assuming the debts of the old mixed companies, which amounted to $700 million.

Allende accepted the Christian Democratic method. As Eduardo Novoa, who was in charge of legal work on the draft law, related: Allende felt that for Chile to be in the strongest position to deal with the international problems the nationalization would give rise to, the backing of a broad majority of Congress was required. "Without the modifications requested by the Christian Democrats, there would be no parliamentary approval and it would be necessary to submit the law to a plebiscite."

This might be difficult—the Christian Democrats were preparing to argue that the copper law was not a proper subject for a constitutional amendment and plebiscite.[5]

When the bill came up for a vote in July it was passed unanimously. Even the Nationals, who had placed obstacles in its way throughout its journey in Congress, voted in favor.

Was Allende right in accepting the demands of the Christian Democrats to obtain their support for the bill? This touches fundamental questions of revolutionary strategy. What was the true goal—simply to get the nationalization of copper accomplished or to promote the revolution in general using nationalization to help increase the strength of the UP? How important was the parliamentary support which the UP obtained for the nationalization? Could it really help in the face of the international difficulties Chile was facing?

The government need not have been quick to accept compromise with the Christian Democratic Party on this issue; it could have insisted on the bill that was best, to the point of deliberately provoking a nationwide debate on the copper law and the need for a plebiscite. The nationalization of copper could have been used to help stir revolutionary fervor, to help unmask the leadership of the Christian Democrats and Nationals as defenders of foreign imperialist interests, to help win over followers of the Christian Democrats and even Nationals to the UP. The nationalization of copper was one of the best issues for attempting these things, and the circumstances were favorable. The issue was tied to national sovereignty and patriotism, lending itself to basic appeals to broad sectors of the population. A great majority of the people wanted nationalization. Because of the improvement in the economy, the government's popularity was high. The Christian Democrats and Nationals in Congress recognized the dangers they faced and treated the nationalization bill gingerly, disguising their opposition, abstaining on many votes, trying to avoid anything that would give rise to a plebiscite. The UP could have tried to force them into open battle. Instead it agreed to a bill they could support unanimously, even while the Christian Democrats and Nationals were preparing to attack the UP mercilessly on issues and under circumstances more favorable to themselves.

The idea that broad parliamentary support was essential to

meet the international problems that Chile would be facing was poorly founded. The imperialists—the copper companies, the U.S. government—would not be impressed by formalities and legalisms. What did they care if the nationalization was voted unanimously by the Chilean Congress, unless this in some way represented strength behind the UP government? Knowing the basic positions of the National and Christian Democratic parties, as well as their strategy in voting for nationalization, how much strength could they attribute to the UP government on the evidence of this vote?

One important problem remained even with the passage of the copper law—the compensation to be paid to the companies. The law contained only procedures and rules for determining indemnization, not the amount. The amount was to be determined by the comptroller general. Compensation was to be paid according to the book value of the enterprises. But the comptroller was authorized to deduct an allowance for the value of properties received in a deficient state. And the president was authorized to instruct the comptroller to deduct the amount of excess profits made by the companies since 1955. If the companies disagreed, they could appeal to a special tribunal, composed of a member of the Supreme Court, the president of the Central Bank, and several other dignitaries.

The president, comparing the profits Anaconda and Kennecott had pulled out of Chile with those they had made in the rest of the world, found that the Chilean profits were indeed excessive. He instructed the comptroller to deduct $774 million for excess profits, equal to the sum of profits above 12 percent annually, from the compensation for these companies. This deduction exceeded the book value of the companies' properties. For the Cerro Company, which began operating the Andina mine in 1971, no excess profits were, of course, found.[6]

The United States government and press had been closely following the moves to nationalize copper. On February 3, 1971, *The New York Times* carried a dispatch from Santiago saying:

> United States diplomats have officially cautioned Chilean officials here that the Government's plan to nationalize American copper interests could seriously damage relations between the two countries. . . . The official United States concern over the form of the

nationalization of the United States interests is . . . a major factor influencing the continuation of 'correct relations' between the Nixon Administration and the leftist Government of Dr. Allende.

Upon the passage of the nationalization in July *The New York Times* editorialized:

> President Allende has now signed the amendment to Chile's Constitution that nationalizes the copper mines. . . . Every one of the 158 senators and deputies present—from revolutionary Socialists and Communists on the left to the Nationalists on the right—had voted for the amendment. In such a climate, Washington wisely kept its official mouth shut on the issue. . . . Any Washington protest would have been not only futile but grist for the propaganda of those forces in Dr. Allende's coalition that seek an open break with this country. . . . Even a Chile bent on building socialism seeks qualified foreign investment and bank credits to carry out ambitious industrial expansion. In determining their response to Chilean requests, investors and bankers around the world are certain to take into account the treatment given the copper companies.[7]

On September 30 just after President Allende issued the decree giving the comptroller the amount of excess profits to be deducted from the compensation, *The New York Times* carried a story from Washington which said:

> United States officials said today that yesterday's decision by Chile's President in effect to pay nothing to United States copper interests for nationalized properties would undoubtedly spur 'get tough' moves in the Nixon Administration. . . . Senior United States policy makers are reliably reported to fear that if the United States continues to appear 'soft' toward underdeveloped countries that expropriate private United States assets, this will precipitate a rush of similar actions.

On October 13 Secretary of State William Rogers stated that "the U.S. Government is deeply disappointed and disturbed at this serious departure from accepted standards of international law" and added that the United States government "hopes that the Government of Chile in accordance with its obligations under international law will give further careful consideration to this matter."[8] Two days later, *The New York Times* said in a story headed "Rogers Stand Spurs Chile Unity Drive":

The statement by Secretary of State William P. Rogers yesterday warning Chile against nationalization of United States companies' interests in large copper mines without compensation touched off a 'national unity' campaign here today. The Foreign Ministry issued a statement rejecting 'pressure against our country.' There was a headline in the pro-Government newspaper *Puro Chile* saying 'Uncle Sam Picks a Fight With Chile.' And there were radio broadcasts calling on Chileans to 'defend our national honor.'

As Anaconda and Kennecott saw nationalization approaching, they took what they considered appropriate measures. With the election of Allende—to some extent even before—they began to run their Chilean properties in such a way as to draw out the most money in the least time, if need be by letting the property run down. The Chilean government arranged in 1971 for two groups of technical experts—one Soviet, the other French—to prepare reports on the state of the mines. Both reports found serious deficiencies.

The Soviet report says concerning Chuquicamata:

> In recent years, the company carried out a policy of extensive extraction without the necessary removal of the overburden. This led to a decrease in the reserves of material prepared for extraction. . . . This problem should be resolved without delay, otherwise the prepared reserves of mineral will continue to decline, which can lead to a decrease in copper production.[9]

For Anaconda there was a double advantage in neglecting the overburden—having more cash to pull out and leaving its successor with a difficult problem. Kennecott also held back on necessary expenditures and investments. The Soviet report also found a shortage of water for treating the mineral at El Teniente. "The concentration plant at Colón, put on stream at the beginning of the year, is only producing 11–12 thousand tons daily, instead of the 28,000 tons for which it was designed, because of a lack of water."

Months before the nationalization, Anaconda passed the word to the foreign technicians employed in its mines to leave Chile, and all but a handful did. Most technicians at Kennecott's El Teniente were Chileans, but the majority also left with the nationalization.

Most supervisors remained. Supervisors had enjoyed great privileges: For example, the companies had paid them in dollars, which enabled them to realize fat gains in the black market. Shortly after the UP government came in, the Central Bank ruled that they were to be paid in escudos and although their salaries were adjusted, they were discontented. They didn't wait long to make trouble. In August 1971 the supervisors at Chuquicamata struck, in protest, they said, against the appointment of three mine executives from outside the old staff. A number of supervisors at El Teniente struck in sympathy. At Chuquicamata, several supervisors committed sabotage, taking over a substation of the electric power plant by force and disconnecting several turbines, which caused a decrease in current not only to the mine but to the whole surrounding area.

The UP government inherited many problems with the copper industry. Besides the obvious one that 95 percent of the spare parts and equipment came from the United States, there was the problem of organization. There were five nationalized mines, including the largest open-pit (Chuquicamata) and the largest underground (El Teniente) copper mines in the world. The companies running each mine were organized and administered differently; often the equipment and supplies used for the same operation varied; and people doing the same work received different wages and salaries. It was necessary to organize the separate units into one whole.

The mine workers constituted a ticklish potential problem. Having seen the barracklike housing of the miners and their families on the steep, bleak Andean slopes at El Teniente, I cannot write glibly of "privileges," but the truth is that the copper miners' wages, fringe benefits, and living conditions were better than those of most other workers in Chile—much better, for example, than those of the coal miners at Lota-Schwager whose work was at least as rough as theirs. There existed among the copper miners, more than among most other Chilean workers, a tradition of "economism," of using their trade union power to wrest specific, immediate economic gains from the foreign employers. Now there was a need to replace the economism with a revolutionary consciousness, a willingness in the interests of the revolution and the longer-run benefits it could bring to forego using the miners' power over Chile's main export to promote as much as they could for themselves.

The copper industry was one of the few the UP was able to transfer to the state sector through a new nationalization law. Almost all other transfers had to be accomplished by other means—purchase or takeover in one legal form or another under laws inherited from the past. Among Chile's 20,000 laws were several which lent themselves to takeovers—to full expropriations, or to "interventions" or "requisitions" under which the administration of an enterprise passed to the government even though legal ownership remained unchanged. For example, the almost forgotten Decree Law No. 520, from the revolutionary period of 1932 gave the government the power to expropriate an enterprise dedicated to the production or distribution of "articles of primary necessity" if it failed to maintain a normal rhythm of activity and this resulted in shortages. The government could also intervene enterprises involved in labor conflicts if one of the parties to the conflict requested it.

ANOTHER strategic sector of the economy was the banking system. Allende, in a speech given on December 30, stressed the need to have a banking system that would serve national development, not a small number of favored Santiago customers, and announced that the government would submit a bill to Congress to nationalize the banks. The government also, he said, offered an alternative—to buy the shares of the banks. Allende explained that small stockholders would receive the best terms, and all who elected to sell their stocks would receive better terms than those who waited for the nationalization law.

The government's position vis-à-vis the banks was strong. It controlled the Central Bank, which was the main source of funds for the commercial banks and governed many of their operations. It also controlled the Superintendency of Banks, through which it could carry out a strict enforcement of banking regulations. Against foreign banks, it could apply such measures as prohibiting them from accepting local deposits.

The government never had to submit its nationalization bill to the Congress. One after another, the banks fell under state control. Several were intervened for irregularities. Others were purchased. The foreign banks—Bank of America, First National City, etc.,—entered into agreements with the government for the sale of their Chilean businesses. By the end of 1971 the takeover of the banking system was almost complete—the government controlled sixteen banks with 90 percent of the credit.[10]

The iron and steel industry was also strategic. One of the first acts of the UP government was to buy up the privately held shares of the Pacific Steel Co., and by mid-December it announced that it had gained control. This company accounted for Chile's entire steel production of six hundred thousand tons, and one third of its iron-ore output. The government then entered into negotiations with Bethlehem Steel to purchase its Chilean iron mines, and in March a contract was signed. With these added mines, the government controlled 70 percent of Chile's iron-ore production. The government proposed to use the Pacific Steel Co. as the core of a metallurgical complex, encompassing iron mines, steel works, machine shops, shipyards, and metal fabricating plants. The Pacific Steel Co. began to acquire majority interests in a number of companies—for example, ARMCO, which produced grinding balls, and SOCOMETAL, which produced cranes, boilers, and railroad cars—with the aim of incorporating them into the complex.

"The nitrates are also ours," said Allende in his message to Congress on May 21, 1971. Chile had purchased SOQUIM, the main nitrates producer, and placed another nitrates firm—the Alemania—under state management.

The textile industry was dominated by a few large firms. In November 1970 The Office of Industry and Commerce (DIRINCO) took control of the textile factory Bellavista-Tomé—owned by the Yarur family and W.R. Grace—because it had shut down. In May the government requisitioned five other large textile companies. By the end of the year, nine textile companies had been requisitioned and four expropriated, giving the state sector 50 percent of the industry.

Soon the auto industry began to fall under Chilean control. In May 1971 Ford closed its assembly plant, claiming it had suffered $16 million in losses during the preceding two years; 600 workers were dismissed. Chile requisitioned the plant. In September General Motors, under investigation for failure to fulfill contractual obligations to use local parts in the vehicles assembled in Chile, announced that it was closing its truck plant, and Chile took over this plant also.

Companies in a variety of other industries were taken over. DIRINCO requisitioned the two main cement companies, a glass company, and several companies producing other construction materials. CORFO requisitioned a producer of dried and smoked meat. The workers seized the beer monopoly. And dozens of bankrupt small enterprises were taken over to maintain jobs for the workers and supplies to the population.

In foreign trade and distribution, the government acquired the old import houses dating from the early days of British imperialism in Chile. It took over the bankrupt Weir Scott and purchased Duncan Fox, Williamson Balfour, and Gibbs. The government created several state distribution agencies—such as the National Distribution Enterprise (DINAC)—which handled 30 percent of the wholesale distribution of groceries.

Like the copper companies, the other monopolies took measures to meet expropriation well before it occurred. Pedro Vuscovic, the first minister of economics, commented that "the bourgeoisie . . . prepared for the expropriation of their enterprises, pulling out working capital beforehand, exhausting the stock of raw materials, neglecting the maintenance of equipment, etc."[11]

How foreign companies lured technicians out of the country can be illustrated by what happened at the Chilean subsidiary of Dow Chemical. According to an article in *Fortune,* Dow passed word to the technicians "that if they showed up at Dow offices elsewhere in Latin America, jobs would be available. . . . Eventually, more than sixty of them accepted Dow's offer of resettlement abroad, and in many cases Dow reimbursed them for expenses, such as airfare, that they had incurred in leaving their native land. Some were given interest-free loans by the company to help buy housing and cars."[12]

Despite the poor condition in which the old owners deliberately left their enterprises and the innumerable difficulties that inevitably accompany basic transformation, the UP government and the

Chilean working class not only were able to keep the expropriated mines and factories running, but generally were able to increase output. In the crucial copper industry, production was 2.5 percent higher in the second half of 1971 than in the first half. The new management was able, despite the departure of technicians, supervisor's strikes and sabotage, and inherited technical problems, to keep the second half-year production at Chuquicamata, El Teniente, and El Salvador within 2.5 percent of the first half, and to raise production at the new mine—Andina—more than enough to make up for the difference.[13]

FOR nine months, the government takeovers proceeded rapidly. Then, just after the nationalization of copper was voted, the opposition mounted a counterattack. On July 19 Héctor Humeres, the comptroller, a Frei appointee, rejected the requisition of Textil Yarur, giving the government thirty days to return it to its old owners. In August Humeres decreed that several other giant textile properties had to be returned. The workers at the different plants assembled and declared that they would not permit the enterprises, under any pretext, to be returned to their old bosses, and the government used "decrees of insistence"—decrees signed by all members of the Cabinet—to force the comptroller to accept the requisitions.

An involved legal controversy ensued. The government maintained that it was for DIRINCO to decide the technical question of whether there existed a "shortage of supply" justifying requisition. The comptroller maintained that his office could judge whether the technical decision of DIRINCO was correct. The opposition accused the government of abusing decrees of insistence, and in Congress the enemies of the UP began to accumulate materials for possible use to impeach the president and his ministers.

Using the legal controversy, the opposition parties and press launched a political campaign against expropriation. The vote of the opposition on copper had strengthened its hand for such action—it could not now so easily be accused of not having the national interest at heart. And the Christian Democrats, who had earlier been reluctant to join in open action against expropriation, because "our party is also in favor of structural change," had now found the way to play their role. They were still not against structural change, but the process must be carried out within the law, and the decisions of the comptroller must be respected.

The opposition worked to win mass allies against expropriation. It stoked fears of expropriation among Chile's thousands of small proprietors. "The way the UP Government is acting, no one can rest easy. Who knows who will be next?" they cried out.

In August *El Mercurio* attacked a proposal to nationalize La Papelera—the giant paper monopoly—which with its plants in Puente Alto, Talca, and other cities not only dominated the Chilean market, but was a big earner of foreign exchange. Nationalization and state control of paper, *El Mercurio* kept repeating, would mean the end of a free press in Chile. This was "a good issue" for the opposition, and its spokesmen missed few opportunities to bring it up. When the government proposed to buy the stocks of the paper company, *El Mercurio* refused to accept government advertising addressed to the stockholders, and opposition spokesmen urged them "not to sell their liberty."

Faced with increasing difficulty in carrying out expropriations by the methods it had previously used and concerned about the fear of expropriation being falsely spread among small proprietors, the government decided to submit a bill to Congress giving itself the power to nationalize certain types of enterprises, but also clearly defining the limits of the social and other areas of property. The bill, announced in October, gave the government the power to nationalize only enterprises whose capital and reserves were above 14 million escudos on December 31, 1969. The government stated immediately that it did not intend to take over all these enterprises, that altogether it proposed to nationalize 150 of them, leaving in the private sector those that were not monopolistic or strategic.

The Christian Democrats also submitted a bill—for a constitutional amendment. Their bill required separate legislation for each act of nationalization, which meant that the government could no longer take over enterprises through pre-existing laws, and that power over nationalization would pass to Congress. The bill also provided that all transfers to the social area [state sector] after October 14, 1971, not authorized by legislation passed according to the new amendment, would be "null and void." This provision made the amendment retroactive—it would have forced the government to return banks and other enterprises acquired after October 14, including those acquired by purchase, to their former owners.

An impasse—never to be resolved—developed between the government and the opposition on the question of passing legislation authorizing nationalization and defining the three areas of property. In December Allende made a list of only 91 enterprises that would pass to public control, but this attempted compromise failed to bring about agreement. Congress refused to pass the UP bill and the president vetoed the constitutional amendment passed by Congress.

In June 1972 representatives of the UP and the Christian Democrats held talks to see if they could work out mutually acceptable legislation. But the Christian Democrats insisted that at least four banks and the paper company remain in the private area. At the end of June the talks broke down.

Even before the breakdown of the talks, Eduardo Novoa, the leading legal theoretician of the UP, commented on the situation that had developed: "To be able to operate, this Government has had to resort to a series of legal dispositions which lay almost forgotten. But once having used these to their maximum, the moment has arrived when there is no legal mechanism by which to proceed any further. . . . [The] few legal mechanisms which would permit no more than moderate implementation of the Popular Unity's Program are being whittled away."[14]

The difficulties over nationalization came to a head at the same time as those over the problem of controlling inflation, and both were part of a more general crisis involving political troubles. The different parties of the UP coalition, and the MIR, outside it, reacted differently to the crisis.

The Communist Party held that there should be a "turn of the helm." "Characteristic of the present juncture," wrote Orlando Millas, "is that the correlation of forces has been shifted against the working class and the Popular Government by political and economic errors. . . . It would be fatal to continue increasing the number of our enemies; on the contrary we must make concessions, and at least neutralize certain social strata and groups. . . ." We should not talk so much, said Millas, of the industries we propose to take over in the future, but rather improve the management and efficiency of those the State already has.[15]

The Socialist Party, consisting of a number of factions, did not speak with a single voice. But the dominant line was against a pause for consolidation, contending that the material base of the oligarchy must be destroyed. Only by advancing could the power of the people be extended. If an industry was "strategic," it was essential that it be placed in the social area.

Among the smaller UP parties, the Radicals favored "consolidation," while MAPU was divided, one group supporting consolidation, another supporting continued advance.

The MIR took the most extreme position, criticizing the negotiations with the Christian Democrats and any policy of concessions or pause. Miguel Enriquez, its general secretary, talked of "mobilizing the masses . . . and advancing with more force than ever on the factories and large estates." There were, he said, two currents on the Left, one reformist, the other revolutionary. The reformists denounced the seizure of factories and estates, and were the source of weakness in the revolutionary process. "Only by advancing will a revolutionary solution to the process be found."[16]

Allende, like the Communist Party, believed a shift in direction was necessary. He said that the middle classes had to be given "absolute confidence" that the UP program would be carried out strictly according to law.

There were among the workers those who wanted to "advance." In June, while the talks with the Christian Democrats were still going on, workers at the Cerillos-Maipú industrial belt in Santiago occupied several factories. And at marches and demonstrations there appeared the sign, "*Avanzar sin transar*— Advance without compromise."

What did the nationalizations mean in the Chilean revolutionary process? What did they mean at different stages of that process? What did they mean for gaining control of the economy and for the problem of winning state power?

The nationalizations carried out by the UP must be seen as part of the overall revolutionary process, and as such they were of enormous revolutionary significance. Had the UP government been able to continue and win state power, they would have given Chile its independence from imperialism, and laid the ground-work for economic planning, industrialization, and socialism. Politically, their import was incalculable. The recovery for Chile from foreigners of its copper, nitrates, and iron ore, the takeover of the monopoly strongholds of homegrown oligarchs like the Edwards and Yarurs, the attempt to create a banking system that would work for the people, fulfilled deep aspirations of the majority of Chileans—and the people were bound to respond.

The nationalizations gave important chunks of economic power to the government. When the UP took office, the state held enterprises accounting for 10 percent of industrial production; by mid-1972, the state-held enterprises accounted for 40 percent. The nationalization of copper, nitrates, and iron ore gave the government control of over 90 percent of exports. The takeover of the banks gave it control of the distribution of credit, and increased the control it already had of the management of foreign exchange. Each enterprise taken over meant one less that private owners could use for sabotage.

Yet even with all this, the government was far from controlling the economy the way a socialist economy has to be controlled. In some respects it did not even have the degree of control which most capitalist governments enjoy. The reason was simple—the UP did not have complete state power. It did not even control the Congress.

Nationalization could not by itself solve the problem of gaining control of the Chilean economy. First, the government could not nationalize anything like the whole economy, with its thousands of small shops and retail stores. Even if its maximum program had been carried out, 40 percent of industry and a higher percentage of retail trade would still have remained in private hands. Besides, an economy is more than an agglomeration of enterprises, and to control it requires more than just nationalizing these enterprises.

To truly control nationalized enterprises requires the power to set up an appropriate state body to run them—a Ministry of Industry. To convert a capitalist into a socialist banking system requires the power to reorganize it, to merge the many individual banks into a single, unified system. The UP government, lacking control of Congress, was never able to do such things.

To run a whole economy requires power over its finances— over taxes, public expenditures, wage-readjustments, and foreign exchange. The UP government's power over all these things was partial. Especially weak was its power over taxes and therefore its power to fight inflation.

To run an economy in a class society with conflicting interests requires the backing of the court system and force. Modern economies, including underdeveloped ones, are complex and delicate. Many different groups have the power to damage them, to disrupt and shut down large parts of them. Even under ordinary circumstances, governments often find it hard to control such groups without resorting to legal sanctions and the threat, or use, of force. For the UP government, the problem was infinitely more difficult. Deadly enemies were carrying out a comprehensive strategy to overthrow it. The CIA was working to provoke various groups to use their power not just to wrest economic concessions, but to dislocate the economy, to create chaos. The government could not count on the courts, the police, or the armed forces to back it in controlling these groups.

The struggle with the opposition over nationalizations was important; but it was not the ultimately decisive one. To insist that the process of nationalization must "advance" without interruption and without compromise so that the "power of the people could be extended" and the "material base of the oligarchy" destroyed, was to create confusion and strengthen the misconception that the basic problem of power could be resolved in this way. Meanwhile the imperialists, with their immense resources, would be supplying money to the opposition political parties and newspapers, and weaving plots among the officers of the armed forces.

The decisive fields of battle were those that could bear most directly and heavily on the struggle for state power. Put another way, on the struggle of the UP government to survive: the ideological struggle to develop the revolutionary consciousness of the people; the struggle to win allies or at least neutralize potential opponents; and the struggle over armed forces. These were the fields that could most strongly influence the correlation of forces relevant to the struggle for survival or state power.

Nationalizations were a part of a larger whole; their effects had to be considered against that whole. If, at a certain stage of the revolutionary process, further nationalizations promised to do more harm than good, if they tended to cause the UP to lose potential allies, if they created problems with constitutionalists in the armed forces, if they could only be carried out by illegal methods which would help produce the political climate that the coupists wanted, then there was little choice but to suspend them for the time being.

By mid-1972 the problem of nationalization was far different than it had been when the UP government first took over. Then it had been a question of nationalizing basic, heavily foreign-held industries, which the great majority of Chileans wanted nationalized. Now it was a question of nationalizations about which opinion was divided. If the nationalizations could only be carried out illegally, the balance of sentiment would tilt unfavorably against the government. The nationalizations the government had been able to carry out before mid-1972 were of incomparably greater significance than any it could hope to carry out thereafter—going from control of 40 percent of industrial production to 50 percent is not the same as going from 10 to 40 percent, or gaining control of Chile's copper and its banking system.

Holding back on nationalizations in mid-1972 permitted the government to concentrate on an economic problem more important at the time than nationalization—controlling inflation. Going on the defensive on nationalization need not mean the government would have to be on the defensive in everything. It could, for example, be on the offensive in the ideological struggle.

The conference of UP leaders at Lo Curro attempted to arrive at an agreed nationalization policy. The Cabinet shifts that followed the conference made it evident that the UP's nationalization program would not be pressed as insistently as before. But with the MIR, outside the UP, disagreeing, and with certain forces within the Socialist and MAPU parties sympathetic to the MIR position, there would still be difficulties.

Thus the problem of nationalization in Chile went through two stages. In the first stage, the UP government realized a basic accomplishment—politically, an enduring accomplishment. The Chilean people will never forget the government that showed it meant what it promised; the government which set out to recover Chile's resources from the foreign monopolies and began the construction of socialism. But the second stage would be characterized by differences among the parties of the UP and with the MIR. The second stage would illustrate the problems of ruling with a coalition, and without a single, unified strategy.

10

Land Reform

The UP government's lack of state power, lack of even a majority in the Congress, determined the kind of land reform it could carry out. It could not simply decree the land reform law it thought necessary, but was limited either to working with the law passed under the Christian Democrats or to submitting new legislation to the opposition Congress. It decided to use the old law. Jacques Chonchol, the first UP minister of agriculture, explained why: "Any changes in such a complex and controversial law as the Agrarian Reform Law would certainly have required many months of discussion, which would paralyze the agrarian reform process resulting in great frustration among the peasantry who are pressing for the acceleration of the process. Also it was felt that, given the political willingness to use the existing law much more thoroughly, it would be possible to accelerate the agrarian reform process."[1]

Besides the 1967 land reform law, the UP also inherited the government apparatus for dealing with agriculture that had grown up under previous administrations. This apparatus was exceptionally unmanageable. Twenty-one different agencies, dependent on five ministries, dealt with agriculture. Credit to *asentamientos* was granted by the Agrarian Reform Corporation (CORA), the Institute for Agricultural Development (INDAP), the Development Corporation (CORFO), the State Bank, and many other bodies. (I used to have difficulty at the Central Bank getting the most simple statistics on agricultural credit.) With the old organizational forms, came the old staff, persons placed in office by the Frei and other previous administrations. Many represented landholder interests, and others a Christian Democratic point of view about agricultural problems. The UP could not, except through new legislation, change the government organization; by law, it could not, except for top officials, get rid of old personnel.

While the Christian Democrats had designed their land reform to help prevent a socialist revolution, the UP government needed a land reform that would help further one. It was vital to try to use the land reform to help with the problem of power. The UP needed to reverse the movement toward division of the *campesinos* promoted by the Christian Democrats, to unify all the lower class *campesinos* into one revolutionary force which together with the urban working-class and middle-class allies would provide the strength for socialist revolution.

To create a unified *campesino* revolutionary force, the UP needed to carry out a land reform that would benefit not just a small minority of the *campesinos*, but the great bulk of them. How? It was not difficult to conceive of ways in which the land reform could be changed to improve it and spread its benefits; the problem was to find ways that the government, given the limitation on its power, could carry out.

The UP explained its proposed land reform in its program and an attached statement called *The Twenty Basic Points of the Agrarian Reform.*

The Agrarian Reform is conceived as a process simultaneous with, and complementary to, the general transformations we wish to promote in the social, political, and economic structure of the country. . . . [It] will involve not only the expropriation of all *latifundia,* the delivery of land to *campesinos* and the provision of technical assistance and credit . . . but also the transformation of the industrial and commercial relationships for the sale and purchase of products needed by the *campesinos* to live and produce. The marketing and processing of agricultural output must be in the hands of the State or *campesino* or consumer cooperatives.

The UP stated that it would accelerate the expropriation of the holdings exceeding the established maximum size. And it told how it proposed to change the reform from what it had been under the Christian Democrats:

> The benefits of Agrarian Reform will be extended to the medium and small farmers, the *minifundistas,* employees, sharecroppers, and *afuerinos* who have so far been excluded from its benefits. . . .
>
> The Agrarian Reform will no longer be carried out farm by farm, but by zones, and in each of these zones productive work will be guaranteed to all *campesinos.* . . .
>
> In certain . . . cases land will be assigned to small farmers, tenants, sharecroppers and trained agricultural workers.
>
> Only small and medium farmers will have the right not to be expropriated; and only those large farmers whose social and economic contributions to agricultural production and rural community development are recognized by the *campesinos* will have the right to a reserve. This right will not mean that the landholder can select which land is to go into the reserve. . . .
>
> Working capital [seeds, supplies, cattle, machinery and equipment] will be included in the expropriations so that the expropriated farms will from the beginning have the capital necessary for their work. . . .
>
> The defence of the indigenous Indian communities which are threatened with usurpation of their land will be assured, as will . . . the provision of sufficient land and appropriate technical assistance and credit to the *Mapuche* people and other indigenous groups.

The UP understood the faults of the Christian Democratic land reform. Its intentions were good. But how, until it won more power, could it carry out the kind of land reform it was proposing? The old land-reform law would prevent it from doing so. Land was the key to a reform that would benefit the mass of the *campesinos.* The UP needed to get at all the land that a true, socialist land reform law would mark for expropriation, and it needed to be able to distribute this land to all *campesinos* in need of it. The Christian Democratic law, with its high 80 basic hectare limit on expropriations, its provision for landlord reserves, and its favoring of the permanent workers on the estates in the distribution of the expropriated land, prevented the UP from being able to get the necessary land and distribute it in such a way as to solve the problem of the temporary workers, the *minifundistas,* and the *Mapuches.* The law limited the UP government in other things besides land. It was legitimate as a statement of aim to say that working capital would be included in the expropriations, but to be able to carry this out required a change in the law.

The main point in the program that the UP government did have within its power to carry out, because it could be done within the existing law, was to accelerate the expropriations—so the government put a great deal of its effort into doing this.

THE government was under pressure to get the expropriations under way quickly. The impatience of the *campesinos,* stirred up under the Christian Democrats, was boiling over. With the approach of the 1970 elections, the number of illegal land seizures had multiplied, especially in Cautín where many were led by members of MIR.

The UP government had no sooner taken office when it was faced with the ticklish problem of what to do about the seizures. It did not want to use force against *campesino* revolutionaries, yet disorders in the countryside ran counter to its overall strategy and could help the opposition with the image of anarchy it wanted to create.

Jacques Chonchol, within weeks after he became minister of agriculture, moved his office to Temuco, the capital of Cautín, to personally supervise "an accelerated agrarian reform." The government announced that it would expropriate 1,000 *latifundios* in 1971 and that it planned to "end all *latifundios* in Chile in two or three years." The actual speed of the expropriations was even greater than these goals. By the end of 1971 the UP government had expropriated 1,379 estates—almost as many as the 1,408 that the Christian Democrats had expropriated during their whole six years in office.[2] By the end of June 1972 the government had expropriated another 1,904, and this practically ended private ownership of estates of more than 80 basic hectares.[3]

Despite the speeding up of the expropriations, the number of seizures remained high, reaching 1,278 in 1971 compared to 148 in 1969.[4] Seizures were especially numerous in some southern provinces where the *Mapuches* had not forgotten that the land had been stolen from their ancestors, and where the percentage of land in estates of over 80 basic hectares was less than elsewhere, while the land hunger of the rural poor was greatest. Often the *Mapuches* seized land in estates too small to come under the land reform.

The wave of seizures was not confined to the south, but swept to the edges of Santiago. A group of *campesinos,* affiliated with a rural federation called Power to the Campesinos, which supported the UP government, seized the Santa Elena estate near Melipilla, 25 miles from the capital. "We don't want any more stalling," their leader told Juan de Onis of *The New York Times.*[5]

Not all the seizures aimed at acquiring land. Sometimes *campesinos* occupied an estate to force the landholder to meet specific economic demands—for example, that he pay the family benefits to which they were entitled; and sometimes *campesinos* engaged in seizures to show solidarity with actions of other *campesinos.*

Even if not all the seizures were for land, they constituted, *taken by themselves,* a true revolutionary movement, similar to the peasant movements of the French and Russian revolutions. Had the situation in Chile been different, the task of all revolutionaries would have been to encourage the *campesinos* to go ahead—to support a land reform propelled from below, as Lenin did during the Russian Revolution. But the seizures in Chile had to be understood not by themselves, or as part of some other revolution, but as part of the revolutionary struggle in Chile. The test of how to deal with a phenomenon like seizures is whether, given the circumstances of a particular revolution, they weaken or strengthen it, help it gain power or do the opposite. The land seizures in Chile did not, as did the seizures in Russia in the spring of 1917, reflect the strength of an overwhelmingly united peasantry which constituted the great majority of the population, backed by an already revolutionized, mainly peasant army. In Chile, the fighting in the countryside that seizures could cause would serve the strategy of the enemy, not that of the UP.

The landholders and their allies fought even more rabidly against the UP land reform than they had against that of the Frei government. In the first months after Allende's election some landholders sold fancy breeding bulls or pregnant cows for slaughter, or drove herds of cattle across the Andes into Argentina. *El Mercurio* worked to show how the UP had let loose a wave of injustice and chaos on the once tranquil Chilean countryside. Stories of how a woman committed suicide the day after her estate was seized, and how a man suffered a heart attack while his estate was being expropriated, were spread over page after page. From time to time an opposition congressman proclaimed that some southern province was "in a state of anarchy." In Cautín, a group of landholders formed a vigilante group calling itself the White Guard. According to a correspondent for the *London Economist,* the group had "a pool of about 60 cars" and "about 600 small farmers [were] ready to join in operations, as well as a small group of professionals, many of them unemployed laborers who knew how to use a gun."[6]

BESIDES accelerating the expropriations, the UP also tried to substitute a new form of organization—the Agrarian Reform Center (CERA)—for the *asentamiento.* The government hoped through the CERA to remedy the deficiencies in the land reform that flowed from the *asentamiento.* CERAs were not to be set up on each estate, but on combined estates, as many as suitable for the organization of production. Membership was to be broadened to include not just those *campesinos* who had lived on the estates, but all who had worked there, no matter where they had lived, and not just heads of families, but all workers, men and women, above the age of sixteen. The CERAs could engage temporary workers, but these workers would participate in making decisions.

As new investments and the increase in the productive capacity of a CERA permitted, new workers would be incorporated into it. A pamphlet put out to explain the CERAs to the *campesinos* stated that they would, "by incorporating all workers and giving them the same rights, eliminate the exploitation of some *campesinos* by others, thus opening the way for a socialist system in agriculture." The government began to organize CERAs on newly expropriated estates in the third quarter of 1971; it hoped also to change the existing *asentamientos* to CERAs.

The opposition reacted immediately. *El Mercurio* and Rafael Moreno, a former high land-reform official in the Frei regime, carried on a campaign against the CERAs. These innocent-sounding bodies were aimed at establishing a "system of state property in the countryside;" state property meant that the *campesinos* would not get the land they had been waiting for; and the *campesinos* would regret it if they allowed themselves to fall under a new boss, "The State Boss." The Chamber of Deputies held hearings on the CERAs, and opposition deputies questioned their legality.

As with nationalization, some in the UP wanted to push ahead fast with the organization of CERAs, regardless of circumstances or political consequences. No matter whether the *campesinos* were ready to accept the CERAs; it was enough that they were "more socialist" than *asentamientos*. Sometimes zealous officials tried to impose on the *campesinos* arrangements cutting into rights long held by them—for example, to limit to one, the number of their own animals that they could have free pasture for on the farms. The opposition propaganda against the CERAs took hold among some *campesinos*. During the hearings, groups of those opposed as well as those in favor came into Santiago to demonstrate before Congress, and clashes occurred.

When the government saw the suspicious or unfavorable reaction of many *campesinos* to the CERAs, it developed a third form of organization—the *Campesino* Land Reform Committee. These committees were to be established where the *campesinos* were not yet ready to form CERAs, their purpose being to win the *campesinos* over to the CERAs by gradually introducing some of their principles.

The government also introduced a fourth form of organization—the Production Center—a kind of state farm. These centers were to be established on farms which, because of their great concentration of capital and developed technology, were exceptionally important, such as the gigantic cattle ranches of the far south.

The government's efforts to change the organization of the agricultural units of the reformed sector were unsuccessful. Those *campesinos* who gained privileges from the *asentamiento* system were uneager to join CERAs. Only 25 were established in 1971, compared to 246 *asentamientos* and 628 *Campesino* Committees.[7] In 1972 238 CERAs were established, compared to six times that many *asentamientos* and *Campesino* Committees.[8] Only a handful of the admittedly exceptional Production Centers were ever set up. And the CERAs, *Campesino* Committees, and even some Production Centers worked out in practice to be little different from the *asentamientos.*

Despite the statement in the UP program that the government would carry out the land reform by zones, it was usually unable to combine two or more estates in the formation of the reformed units. The law favored organization by estate, and the *campesinos* of one estate usually resisted joining with those of others. Because the CERAs, at the time they were set up, admitted women, as well as men who had not lived on the estates, their membership was broader than that of the *asentamientos.* But once they were established, their members, like those of the *asentamientos* and the *Campesino* Committees, were reluctant to admit new members.

The government faced an especially vexing problem in the application of the land reform to the *Mapuches.* Many *Mapuches* distrusted all "white" Chileans regardless of political affiliation, and expected little from a land reform carried out by a government in Santiago. "We know our land," they said; "we want to decide for ourselves which estates will be expropriated and not be dependent on far-away bureaucrats." Government officials might talk to them of the law; the *Mapuche* experience with the law was that it served to rob them.

The *Mapuches* were right in criticizing the land reform law: A reform made according to that law would not provide enough land to benefit more than a fraction of the *Mapuche* poor—the landless unemployed and the *minifundistas* working plots too tiny to support a family. Yet for all the justice of *Mapuche* demands and the importance of trying to make the *Mapuches* into a bulwark of the revolution, the government could not allow them to make land reforms according to their own criteria. It could only begin by doing its best with the existing law and hoping that later its power would permit it to do more.

In sum, although the UP government succeeded in eliminating estates of more than 80 basic hectares, it was unable to solve the problem of spreading the benefits of the land reform more broadly. The bulk of the poor *campesinos*—temporary workers, *minifundistas,* and *Mapuches*—did not receive land. Solon Barraclough and Almino Affonso wrote in an analysis of the land reform from November 1970 to June 1972: "Only about 12 percent of the agricultural labor force is receiving direct benefits in rights over land expropriated. The problem of rural unemployment and underemployment continues to be serious."[9]

Moreover, although the expropriations carried out by the UP government reduced the economic power of the landholder class, they far from eliminated it. As of July 1972 estates of 40 to 80 basic hectares covered more than 27 percent of the total land and those of 20 to 40 basic hectares another 12 percent.[10] Over 50 percent of the total agricultural production brought to market came from the estates in these two categories. A large proportion of the owners of these estates were bound to be hostile to the UP government. Many had received their land when families subdivided their estates under Frei to escape expropriation. Others were the old owners of expropriated estates who were now working their reserves.

EXPROPRIATING large estates and providing land was, of course, not the only benefit the UP government brought to the *campesinos;* it also followed wage and price policies which benefitted them. As part of its policy of stimulating the economy and redistributing income in 1971, the government raised the minimum wages of agricultural workers. It also gave agriculture preferential treatment in price readjustments. While forcing industrial enterprises to hold their prices and absorb wage increases, it allowed farm prices to increase. "In 1971 agricultural prices increased by about 25 percent, and industrial prices by about 15 percent, and the price adjustments of January and February 1972 maintained this tendency."[11]

The UP government increased the amount of credit going to agriculture, a large part of which was in effect a subsidy, since it was either not repaid at all or repaid in depreciated currency. Some new credit went to small farmers. But much of it suffered from the same defect as the land reform as a whole—it went to the *asentamientos* and other reformed units and so benefitted only a small proportion of the *campesinos.*

The government brought about changes in the marketing structure for agricultural products which could have brought great benefits to the *campesinos* in the long run. Marketing had been controlled by middlemen who squeezed the small farmers. The government arranged for state agencies to buy wheat, corn, and other products from the *campesinos*, thus assuring them of an outlet at reasonable prices.

Even without being able to carry out the kind of land reform it would have undertaken had it had the power, the UP government gained ground politically among the *campesinos*. Simply accelerating the expropriations was a big step forward and gave the *campesinos* a feeling of progress. This feeling was strengthened by the increase in *campesino* income brought about by the wage and price policies of the government. Most poor *campesinos* saw that for all the imperfections in the land reform the government was carrying out, it was their government, trying to do its best for them. The political gains showed in the *campesino* unions. The UP confederations doubled their share of union membership from 31 percent in 1970 to 62 percent in April 1972; the share of the Christian Democratic confederations fell from 66 to 37 percent.[12]

But opposition strength in the countryside remained great. The membership of the *campesino* unions came mainly from the rural working class—wage workers, *asentamiento* members, and *minifundistas*. With 37 percent, the Christian Democrats held a strong minority position even among this class. In some provinces their confederations held more than half the union membership. And opposition strength among the rural middle and upper classes was, of course, incomparably greater than among the working class.

Despite the disruptions caused by the seizures and expropriations, and the problems of organizing the new farm units and getting them started, agricultural production rose in 1971. The Instituto de Capacitación e Investigación en Reforma Agraria, (ICIRA) formed jointly by the UP government and the Food and Agriculture Organization of the United Nations, estimated that total agricultural production in 1971 was 5 percent higher than in 1970. The production of livestock products—beef, lamb, pork, poultry, milk, and eggs—was about the same in 1971 as in 1970, with declines in beef and lamb offset by increases in other items. But crop production, including wheat, corn, barley, potatoes, beans, etc., rose by over 10 percent in 1971.[13]

By the end of the year, however, the inflation began to exert an increasing influence on the workings of agriculture. The problems were potentially serious. The inflation and black markets could not only cause economic irrationalities, like the feeding of wheat and milk to livestock, but could also cause difficulties for the worker-*campesino* alliance required for the revolutionary struggle. Ordinarily, the *campesinos* would view with favor the state purchasing agencies which provided them with guaranteed markets at good prices. But how would they view these agencies when black markets offered prices several times higher? How could the government prevent the *campesinos*, especially those sympathetic to opposition parties, from selling in the black market? What coercive measures could it enforce?

By mid-1972 the government faced the following situation: It was near the end of the expropriations it could carry out under the existing law, and there was no possibility of obtaining a new law. It had been trying to make the land reform cover more beneficiaries by changing the organization of the reformed units, but because of the resistance of those *campesinos* who would benefit from the *asentamiento* type of organization, it was having little success. It had reduced the economic power of the landholder class, but large and medium private landholders, most of whom opposed it, still controlled half the agricultural production brought to market. It had gained ground politically among the *campesino* lower classes, but the opposition still had important strength among them.

Now it would have to grapple with the increasingly difficult task of managing agriculture—of maintaining a high level of production and orderly distribution—in the face of an exploding inflation and the sabotage of its enemies.

11

Political Developments
November 1970 to Mid-1972

The collapse of the Viaux-Valenzuela plot, upon the death of Schneider, left the CIA with inadequate "assets" among the Chilean armed forces. These "assets" had not been able, even at full strength, to mount a successful coup. Now the plot and some of the participants were under investigation. Several of the CIA's leading military collaborators had been forced into retirement; and those who remained were in disarray because of the failure of the plot, the investigation, and the elimination of their leaders. The CIA needed new, additional "assets." It set about—in the words of the Senate report, *Covert Action in Chile,*—"to rebuild a network of agents among the cautious Chilean military."[1]

But the retirements forced by Allende's change of Commanders-in-chief did not clean out all who had been involved in plotting a coup, much less those who were potential coupists but had not had a chance to become involved. Allende did not act—did not use his powers as president—to remove more of the potential coupists. Was this a mistake? We must try to keep hindsight from so coloring our judgment that we lose sight of how the problem may have appeared at the time, of the practical difficulties and risks. It was not always easy to know who was a coupist and who was not. An excessive or poorly managed cleanup might have caused difficulties with the officer corps in general, including constitutionalist officers. Yet if a further clean-up could not be made at that time, with the justification that the attempted coup provided, with the coupists themselves in disarray, when could it ever be made? The failure to act not only reflected difficulties and risks, but foreshadowed a general tendency of the UP government to avoid bold, in favor of seemingly safe, action, to fail to seize fleeting opportunities to weaken the enemy and increase its own strength.

Not just the CIA but all the main enemies of the UP were on the defensive at the beginning of the Allende government—waiting, and, where they could, preparing to take the offensive later. They were willing to cede ground, to permit certain things—the nationalization of copper, for example. But there was one thing they would never permit—the arming of the people. On this point, all the enemies of the UP were unceasingly vigilant.

An example showed itself early. Soon after the inauguration, the non-UP leader of a Santiago shantytown declared that "popular militias" would be created in the shantytowns. Allende had his press officer state that "by express instructions of the President of the Republic, I emphatically deny this statement."[2] *El Mercurio* praised Allende for the "new assurance" which "calms public opinion," and then moved to the offensive: Despite Allende's statement, the possibility of illegal armed organizations could not be discounted since there were elements who did not believe that profound transformations could be carried out legally, who were hoping for a revolution that would "spring from violence;" the country wanted an end to violence; the "entire responsibility" for public order rested with the government.[3]

Besides the problems of arms and armed forces, the UP's enemies also faced those of civilian politics. Here again the U.S. government took preparatory action. It needed a vast network of agents among the strategic organizations of civil life—political parties, labor unions, trade and professional associations, student organizations—and it began to expand its already large existing network to the extraordinary size required. "Intelligence sources," talking later to Seymour M. Hersh of *The New York Times,* "depicted the general involvement of the intelligence agency with the labor unions and trade groups as part of a broad effort to infiltrate all areas of Chile's governmental and political life. The sources said that by the end of the Allende period, the agency had agents and informers in every major party making up Allende's Popular Unity coalition."[4]

Prompt action was required to help opposition political parties: Municipal elections were to take place the following April and it was vital to keep the UP from making large gains and building political momentum. On November 19, 1970 the 40 Committee, according to *Covert Action,* approved $725,000—increased on January 28, 1971, to $1,240,000—"for the purchase of radio stations and newspapers and to support municipal candidates and other political activities of anti-Allende parties."[5] It should be understood that because the dollars would be exchanged into escudos in the black market, this sum would go many times as far in Chile as in the United States.

The opposition political parties in Chile also began to prepare themselves immediately. On December 12 and 13, 1970, the National Committee of the Christian Democratic Party met to elect a new executive board, and to fix the party's political line. Containing one wing rigidly opposed to the UP and some groups sympathetic, the Christian Democrats faced a problem of maintaining unity. Both to maintain unity and to be better able to carry out a subtle strategy, the committee elected a middle-of-the-roader as president of the party. The new president, Narciso Irureta, gave out the political line: We will support the initiatives of the government in everything which is positive but if fundamental values are endangered, "we will be inflexible in opposition."[6]

The Christian Democrats also exhibited a key tactic. Benjamin Prado, the outgoing president, attacked the UP for carrying on a "deplorable and provocative" press campaign against leading figures in the Frei government. The leaders of the Christian Democrats recognized the vulnerability of Frei and his associates; they were to work throughout the Allende years to maintain a climate of public opinion in which any criticism of the ex-president and others who had "so honorably acquitted themselves in high positions," regardless of whether it was based on facts, was somehow morally reprehensible.

El Mercurio analyzed the Christian Democrats' actions. The election campaign had imposed on the party, competing with the UP, a "socialist tone." Once the campaign was over, "the forces which under a strong discipline had been forced into support of the election platform returned to their normal channels." Faced with dangers from the "smashing attack" of the UP and municipal elections in April, the Christian Democrats had laid aside their differences with one another. *El Mercurio* showed interest in the formation of a common front between the Christian Democrats and the other opposition parties, but it knew that this could only be done slowly, cautiously. "It would be too much to hope that a front for the municipal elections could be constituted between heterogeneous forces whose doctrinal differences are clear. The most that can be hoped for is that the fragmented opposition does not waste its strength in mutual attacks."[7]

Nevertheless, on January 7, 1972, Sergio Onofre Jarpa, president of the National Party, proposed that "all non-Marxist forces" form a united front. To begin with, he said, his party would support a common candidate, who need not be from its ranks, in the by-election for senator in the southern-most provinces in April. The proposal called forth objections from many Christian Democrats. Luis Badilla, leader of the CD youth, said that its members would not accept the support of the National Party. "When you win with the Right, it is the Right that wins," said others. Luis Maira, who was later to bolt the party, wrote that by joining a "civic front, the Christian Democratic Party would lose all legitimacy with the popular sectors which constitute the bulk of its support. . . ."[8] Jarpa retorted that he could say many things about the Christian Democrats, but this was not the time to look back and open debates that could only deepen differences. "What most truly interests the country is the unity of all Chileans disposed to defend liberty. . . ."[9]

It was not just Chileans who worked to bring the Nationals and Christian Democrats together. "Throughout the Allende years," says *Covert Action,* "the CIA worked to forge a united opposition. The significance of this effort can be gauged by noting that the two main elements opposing the Popular Unity government were the National Party which was conservative, and the reformist Christian Democratic Party, many of whose members had supported the major policies of the new government."[10]

Senator Raúl Morales Adriasola, of the small opposition Democratic Radical Party, who had been accused of participation in the plot against Schneider, but could not be questioned because the Supreme Court had reversed lower-court decisions lifting his parliamentary immunity, made clear what might be attempted with a united opposition: "Adding the votes of the Christian Democrat Party, the National Party, and the [Democratic] Radical Party, we have enough votes in the Chamber [of Deputies] to suspend from their offices the Ministers and even the President of the Republic. And in the Senate we have the democratic majority necessary . . . so that with the suspension agreed upon in the Chamber, we could proceed" with the dismissal of the ministers and the president. [11]

El Mercurio again entered the discussion.

> Some Christian Democratic parliamentarians have reacted . . . as though the situation of the country permitted the democratic sectors to return to the political picture that existed before September 4. This political picture was definitively erased with the taking of power by the Popular Unity, and every day it becomes clearer that the coming struggles are going to be between the democratic elements and those who are moving toward the establishment of a virtual dictatorship. . . . It is evident that the joining of efforts of parties like the Christian Democracy, the National Party, and the Radical Democracy, to channelize without petty rivalries the feelings of the democratic majority of the country, is the best guarantee of the maintenance of liberty.[12]

Most CD leaders thought, however, that it was too early for an open alliance with the Nationals. On January 20 Irureta stated that his party would not form a common front, because it wanted to confront the UP with a "democratic and constructive opposition." But *La Prensa*—the CD newspaper—added that although the opposition parties "don't fit into civic fronts . . . they should act in a climate of conscious responsibility in order to confront, in common, the defense of the democratic regime. . . . And that responsibility presupposes a climate of respect and the absence of petty sectarianism that makes impossible the necessary coming together in the right hour."[13]

While trying to unite itself, the opposition also strove to divide the Left. It worked to separate Allende from the UP parties, praising him as a democrat who was struggling vainly against the totalitarian plans of the Marxist-Leninist parties, against the sinister Communist Party which really "gave the orders" in the UP coalition. It struggled to create troubles between the UP and the MIR and quarrels within the UP over what to do about MIR.

El Mercurio wrote learned editorials on the history of the Radical Party which stressed its democratic tradition and middle-class backing, and then wondered how it would get along with the Marxist-Leninist parties. "Many people think that the Radicals would not stay in power [as part of the UP] one instant if they arrived at the conclusion that the Popular Unity had infringed the constitution and the law."[14] Again the CIA was involved: It made an effort, says *Covert Action,* "to induce a breakup of the UP coalition."[15] One can picture the omnipresent agents spreading "black propaganda," inciting people to statements and actions that would produce discord.

How did the UP propose to meet the maneuvers and attacks of the opposition? By maintaining its unity and mobilizing the people. On January 10, 1971, an Assembly of Popular Unity was held in Santiago at which representatives of the six elements making up the UP spoke. Anselmo Sule of the Radical Party said that the assembly itself was a demonstration of the unity of the UP, and all speakers agreed on the main task—to mobilize the people. Aniceto Rodríguez of the Socialist Party and Volodia Teitelboim of the Communist Party both said that the 15,000 committees the UP had created for the election campaign should be reactivated. Rodrigo Ambrosio of MAPU said that the UP should unmask the Christian Democrats before the people, that it should be able to attract followers of the Christian Democrats, especially if that party followed the line of the Frei wing. He offered the prophetic self-criticism that the UP was "falling behind" in the struggle to mobilize the people.[16]

The UP also placed hopes in its cautious, conciliatory policy toward the armed forces. Besides raising their pay, initiating programs to improve their housing, and incorporating officers into plans for the development of the southern provinces, it was careful not to interfere with their "professional interests"—for example, the military agreements with the United States.

President Allende took personal pains to cultivate good relations with the armed forces, participating in frequent meetings and ceremonies with them. In March he spoke at a ceremony commemorating the founding of the Chilean Air Force, saying that he would do everything necessary to enable the armed forces to develop "a program in accordance with the Government's policy for the people, since the Armed Forces are themselves the people."[17] In April, at a ceremony at which new generals and admirals were being decorated, Allende spoke of the armed forces' "willing submission to the will of the people" and urged them to participate in the economic development of the country.[18]

The opposition showed its usual vigilance in matters concerning the armed forces. When Allende met with 1,500 officers and men of the Santiago garrison in May, two CD congressmen demanded that the president of the Chamber of Deputies request him to explain "What the meeting was about . . ." Allende answered that "What I discussed . . . was discussed in my position as commander-in-chief . . . and I will not give any explanation to anyone."[19]

How did the officers of the armed forces react to the UP's military policy? It is hard to say. Some undoubtedly were favorably influenced. Even potential coupists maintained an outwardly "correct" posture. General Alfredo Canales, who had studied at Fort Knox, Kentucky and in Panama, was interviewed with Allende and others for a television program to be shown in France. According to Agence France Press, Canales "reaffirmed the traditional political attitude of the army, navy, and air force. 'We are constitutionalists and legalists,' a smiling Canales told the newsman, 'and even though we study in many foreign countries, among them the United States, that country's intelligence services have no access to our Armed Forces'."[20] Canales was to be called into retirement in September 1972 after repeatedly trying to incite a coup.

During the early months of the Allende government its popular support swelled. The assassination of Schneider had turned people toward the UP. The opposition was still divided and on the defensive before a government carrying out the structural reforms that most Chileans desired. Above all, the economic situation was improving sharply. Before the municipal elections of April Allende predicted, "We will win by 42 to 45 percent and that would reflect a good victory."

Actually, the UP won just over 50 percent of the vote. Allende commented: "Never in the history of Chile has a popular movement had the increase we have had. We have ceased being the Government that represented only a third of the people and become a majority. . . ."[21]

In judging the UP victory one must keep in mind CIA help to the opposition parties. According to *Covert Action,* "Early in 1971 CIA funds enabled the PDC and PN to purchase their own radio stations and newspapers. All opposition parties were passed money prior to the April 1971 municipal elections. . . ." There wasn't enough in the $1.24 million, authorized in January, to meet the full needs of the Christian Democratic Party so in March the "40 Committee approve[d] $185,000 additional support. . . ."[22] What might the election results have been without the massive intervention of the CIA?

After the elections some Socialists and members of MAPU suggested to Allende that he call a plebiscite in which the people could vote on changing the constitution and on replacing the Congress with a single-chamber Assembly of the People as called for in the program. Allende rejected the suggestion. He was later to call this the most serious single mistake he had made as president.

The elections showed that the process of polarization, typical of revolutionary struggles, was under way. The center parties, both outside and inside the UP, lost votes. Compared to the parliamentary elections of 1969, the proportion of the votes won by the Christian Democrats dropped by 3.5 percent, that of the Nationals by only 1.5 percent. Within the UP, the proportion won by the Radicals dropped by 5 percent while that of the Socialists increased by 10 percent.

IN JUNE an event occurred which helped Frei move the Christian Democratic Party more quickly into alliance with the National Party, and accelerated the process of polarization. Pérez Zujovic, Frei's hard-bitten, right-wing minister of interior, under whom the Carabineros had massacred the squatters at Puerto Montt, was assassinated by members of the Organized Vanguard of the

People (VOP), a small, far-left underground group which the left parties accused of being filled with lumpen and common criminals.

The assassination created an uproar. The UP said it had been instigated by the Right, that only the Right could benefit from it. The opposition said it had been carried out by revolutionaries, trying to link the VOP to the MIR, and to the UP. Although the Nationals participated in the clamor, it was the Christian Democrats, especially Frei, who made the most of the assassination. From Europe, where he was travelling at the time, Frei sent a message of condolence in which he said, "the atrocious crime has one author: those who systematically lie, slander, incite to hatred, and are destroying Chile with impunity."[23]

Frei dramatically cut short his travels, and on his return spoke at a large demonstration. After eulogizing Pérez, he presented two demands: that "illegal armed groups" be dissolved and that the "campaign of hate," the attempt to divide the Christian Democrats, to destroy the image of their leaders, cease. Frei sharpened the CD propaganda attack on the UP: National solidarity cannot be created through "collective statism or bureaucratic centralism;" the UP wants us to take a route which in other countries has led to "hunger, rationing, and political police." Frei dealt delicately with the question of alliance with the Nationals, calling for a Christian Democracy without "sectarianism . . . open to the entire country, without inhibitions. . . ."[24] With this speech, Frei accomplished several things—he reassumed open leadership of the Christian Democratic Party, pushed it closer to a common front with the National Party, and began to move it from the defensive to the offensive.

Within the next several weeks, signs of further polarization followed one another. On July 18 there was a by-election for deputy from Valparaiso. (As usual, the 40 Committee approved funds—$150,000—to help the opposition.) With Frei and Irureta declaring that the Christian Democrats would accept the support of the Right, the opposition united behind a single Christian Democratic candidate who won with 50.9 percent of the vote. At a meeting of the Christian Democratic National Committee on July 27 the representatives of the left wing requested guarantees against any future alliances with the Nationals. The request was rejected. Eight of the party's seventy-five deputies, half the leaders of its youth organization, and a number of rank-and-file members bolted, forming a new party, the Christian Left (IC).

In August a reshuffling within the UP took place. Two groups had been struggling for leadership of the Radical Party, one consisting of traditional Radicals, the other of people who had been moving leftward with the revolutionary struggle. At the convention of the party on August 1 the leftists put through a party declaration containing statements like "we are socialists because we use historical materialism and the class struggle for interpreting reality" and "we are a political party in the service of class interests and our class is that of the workers." The traditionals accused the majority of the party of having abandoned the middle class. Twelve of the party's twenty-eight senators and deputies left it to form the Left Radical Party (PIR). The dissidents told Allende that they would continue to support the UP, but within nine months, they had left it.

A shift also took place to the left of the UP: The MIR began to emphasize its differences with the government's policies, and to promote alternative courses of action. MIR's discontent with the government culminated in a speech by its Secretary General, Miguel Enríquez, in which he declared:

> Although the Government has struck at interests of the dominant class and begun to take positive economic measures . . . , by not incorporating the masses into the process and by not striking at the state apparatus . . . , it has failed to gain force, but instead made itself increasingly weak. It is precisely these two measures—the incorporations of the masses and blows at the state apparatus—that define a process as revolutionary and make it irreversible.

Then came crucial words about MIR promoting an alternative to the UP government.

> In spite of the positive measures of this Government . . . , its weaknesses and concessions and the tendency of some of its sectors to convert themselves into referees of the class struggle do not leave the workers any alternative but to take back a part of the confidence they have granted, and while supporting the positive measures of the Government and combatting its concessions, to define their own

road. . . . We the militants of the MIR . . . will press these forms of mobilization of the masses and seek to assume their leadership.

Enríquez explained where the new road was supposed to lead.

The workers will obtain the necessary force and sufficient consciousness and organization to pass to tasks which define the problem of power. . . . The first task will be the dissolution of parliament. . . . Its replacement by an Assembly of the People in which are represented the workers, the *campesinos,* the squatters in the shantytowns, the students, and the soldiers; the creation of forms of local power of the workers in the country and the city, through which they assume tasks which lay the basis for revolutionary and popular power. . . . [25]

But Enriquez never explained how the workers were to achieve a sufficiently favorable correlation of forces to be able to dissolve Congress and perform the other tasks he was pointing to.

With the passage in July of the constitutional amendment on copper nationalization, the retreat of the opposition ended. Besides using the Congress, the comptroller, and the courts to block, or try to reverse the UP's actions to nationalize the monopolies, it mounted a political offensive against the government.

Even while switching to the offensive, however, the Christian Democrats remained cautious, letting the Nationals take the lead in the more obviously disruptive actions. In September the National Party introduced a bill to impeach the Minister of Economics, Pedro Vuscovic, but the Christian Democrats did not go along; it was still too early for this type of measure.

Besides supporting political parties, the U.S. government carried out a gigantic progaganda and research effort. On September 9 the 40 Committee approved $700,000 "for support" of *El Mercurio*—in the words of *Covert Action*—"the most important channel for anti-Allende propaganda;" seven months later it was to approve $965,000 more. The CIA

produced several magazines with national circulations and a large number of books and special studies. It developed material for placement in the *El Mercurio* chain . . . ; opposition party newspapers; two weekly newspapers; all radio stations controlled by opposition parties; and on several television shows on three channels. . . . The CIA also funded progressively a greater portion . . . of an opposition research organization. A steady flow of economic and technical material went to opposition parties and private sector groups. Many of the bills prepared by opposition parliamentarians were actually drafted by personnel of the research organization.[26]

As the struggle sharpened, the opposition took to the streets. On September 16 CD youths demonstrated in downtown Santiago against the president's veto of a bill that would have permitted the opposition-controlled Channel 13 to broadcast in the provinces as well as in the capital; Carabineros blocked them from reaching the Congress, and several were hurt. On September 21 demonstrators against the government's "repression" marched from the Catholic University to the presidential palace. On October 2 a street fight took place between followers of the fascist Patria y Libertad and of the UP.

In Washington the 40 Committee was gauging the situation, now different from that at the time of Allende's inauguration. Aside from the polarization and the opposition's shift to the offensive and taking to the streets, there were changes behind the scenes. "By September 1971," says *Covert Action,* "a new network of [CIA] agents [in the armed forces] was in place and the Station was receiving almost daily reports of new coup plotting. The Station and Headquarters began to explore ways to use this network." Further, in October a group "which might mount a successful coup . . . [came] to the Station's attention," and it began to spend a "greater amount of time and effort penetrating this group" than others.[27] In mid-October the 40 Committee ordered the CIA—according to an "inside" informant of *The New York Times*—"to get a little rougher." Another *Times* source stated that a message was sent to Ambassador Nathaniel Davis saying, "in effect, 'from now on you may aid the opposition by any means possible.' "[28]

On November 10 Fidel arrived in Chile. A great outpouring of people, carrying signs saying "Welcome Fidel" and crying "Viva" lined the twelve-mile route from the airport to the Cuban Embassy. But in Santiago's swanky residential districts, some persons greeted Fidel with obscene gestures. Fidel's stay lasted twenty-three days, and he went from one end of Chile to the other, visiting copper, nitrate, and coal mines, farms, factories, and universities; conversing with workers, students, *campesinos,* soldiers, police; observing, giving talks, and expressing solidarity with Chile's revolutionary struggle.

Among the questions Fidel was asked at meetings was whether the UP government was reformist or revolutionary. "I would say," he answered, "that in Chile a revolutionary process is taking place. . . . A process is a road, a phase that is getting started. . . . We must take into account the conditions in which this process is developing, with what means, what resources, what strength, and what the correlation of forces is."[29]

Fidel repeated again and again a theme he had dealt with years earlier in the *Second Declaration of Havana*—the desirability of unity among the revolutionary forces. Sectarianism, he said, is a "great evil" and "our duty is to combat" it. "Revolution is the art of uniting forces . . . of gathering forces together to wage the decisive battles against imperialism. No revolution can afford the luxury of excluding or underrating any force. . . . One of the factors which determined the success of the Cuban Revolution—in which we were initially a small group fighting under difficult conditions—was the policy of uniting, uniting, uniting."

"To unite and wage the struggle," said Fidel, "it is not necessary to get everyone to agree on everything," to wait till people have an "advanced, superadvanced, or Marxist consciousness." What is needed is to agree on four or five essential questions, to unite as many forces as possible into a broad front, and to concentrate this front against the principal enemy.

Fidel returned to the strategy of a broad front in his answers to many different types of questions. A worker asked, "Having in mind that there exists a large sector of private property in Chile which obtains surplus value from an increase in production, what does Comrade Fidel Castro think that Chilean workers should do in the face of this reality?" Fidel answered that the problem must be seen in relation to the situation as a whole, to be handled in subordination to the main strategy. This meant that the workers must make sacrifices in the interests of the revolution: "good parents are those who sacrifice for their children." And what should be the strategy to which this particular problem must be subordinated? "The working class must unite the maximum of forces from the other oppressed social classes" behind a broad program, into a broad front, and concentrate on fighting the principal enemy—imperialism—as was done in Cuba, as the National Liberation Front has been doing in Vietnam.[30]

EVEN within the few weeks of Fidel's visit, the struggle sharpened further as the opposition took to direct physical action. At the University of Chile, opposition students and faculty members had, a few weeks earlier, seized the law school and other buildings. Now there was turmoil—daily assemblies and demonstrations, attempts by UP students to free the seized buildings, and pitched battles. As opposition students at the Catholic University also moved into action—marching through the streets, clashing with the police, and occupying buildings—the turmoil spread.

On December 1 the first important result of the 40 Committee's instructions to the CIA "to get a little rougher" showed itself.[31] The opposition mounted "the March of the Empty Pots"—its first mass street demonstration, its first large effort to draw political benefits from the economic difficulties it was helping to foment. This was its counteroffensive against the visit of Fidel.

Several thousand elegantly-dressed women from the well-to-do suburbs marched on the presidential palace, the Moneda, beating pots and pans in protest against shortages, and shouting "Chile is, and will be, a country of liberty." On all sides of the women marched formations of youths wearing helmets and masks, carrying wooden clubs. Fights broke out between the youths and UP supporters. Some of the youths tried to set fire to the large UNCTAD building which was being constructed for a UN conference in 1972, but the construction workers fought them off.

Traffic through the central streets was blocked, and stores closed their steel shutters. To enable Allende to get to the Moneda, the police had to open a corridor through the crowds; as his car drove through, the women screamed abuse, while UP supporters cheered. When the youth brigades found themselves blocked by the police from the Moneda, they retreated into the wealthy districts, taking over the streets, blocking traffic with barricades and bonfires. President Allende decreed a state of emergency in Santiago and the army in the person of General Augusto Pinochet, assumed control of public order.

The day of the march, *The New York Times* carried a story headed "2 Nixon Aides See Allende In Peril, Finch and Klein Feel Chile's Leader 'Won't Last Long.' " The story explained: "Two top White House aides conveyed to President Nixon today a 'feeling' they had gained during a Latin American trip this month that the Socialist Government of President Salvador Allende Gossens in Chile 'won't last long.' "[32] Robert H. Finch was counselor to Nixon and Herbert H. Klein was White House director of communications.

On a trip to Chile a few days later, I was asked by Jaime to comment on the story in a memorandum I was writing for him. I said that such a remark by such high officials would never be made public casually, that this had been done deliberately to serve some well-thought-out purpose, perhaps that of signalling various groups in Chile that a new stage in the action against the UP government had arrived.

At a farewell mass meeting for Fidel on December 2 Allende spoke of fascism. "A fascist germ is mobilizing certain sectors of our youth, especially in the universities." Referring to the use of disorders to create the setting for a coup, he said, "the events are similar to those experienced in Brazil during the Goulart government." Then he declared, "I am not a martyr. . . . [But] I will leave the Moneda only when I have fulfilled the task entrusted to me by the people. . . . Only by riddling me with bullets can they stop me from fulfilling the people's program."[33]

In his last few talks and a final press conference, Fidel also spoke of fascism. "When fascism shows itself," he said, "let us arm our revolutionary spirit. It is the spirit of the masses that can contain the fascist offensive."

"No social system," said Fidel, "resigns itself of its own free will to disappear. . . . When a revolutionary process is begun, when a revolutionary crisis is produced, the struggles and battles become tremendously acute. . . . The measures carried out . . . let loose the ire and resistance of the exploiters, of the reactionaries. . . . Fascism appears with all its tricks and schemes and techniques of struggle. . . . We have seen fascism in action.

We have been able to verify a contemporary principle—the desperation of the reactionaries . . . today tends toward the most brutal, most savage forms of violence and reaction. . . . You are at a point in the process in which the fascists are trying to win the streets and gain ground among the middle strata. . . . They are trying to spread fear and uneasiness among broad parts of the middle strata. . . . They are trying to demoralize the revolutionaries." Fidel asked, "What is the objective of the fascists?" And answered, "Sedition. To overthrow the revolutionary government."

Fidel spoke frankly of weaknesses in the revolutionary process. "Who," he asked, "will learn most rapidly in this process? The people or the enemies of the people?" From the audience came shouts of "The people." But Fidel said, "Permit me to differ . . . we sincerely believe that the apprenticeship of the enemy, of the reactionaries, has been going more rapidly than that of the masses." Referring to Finch and Klein's statement, he asked, "Why are they so optimistic, so assured?" and answered: "Because of weaknesses in the revolutionary process, weaknesses in the ideological battle, weaknesses in the mass struggle, weaknesses in the face of the adversary."

Fidel offered the opinion that the "success or failure of this unusual process will depend on the ideological battle and on the mass struggle—on the art and science of the revolutionaries, their ability to add, to grow, to win the middle strata of the population."

The revolutionaries, said Fidel, "should not allow the adversary to gain the initiative. These are conflicts between classes and have their rules. Passivity and the defensive spirit are very bad. The revolutionary forces must be on the offensive."

"Your most important task," said Fidel to revolutionary journalists, "is to unmask the counterrevolutionaries, to help the masses visualize the enemy. . . . The masses need to know and visualize the enemy. If they don't know him, if he is disguised, they can't visualize him. When fascism launches a challenge," said Fidel, "when it takes to the streets, we can only expect that the masses will mobilize, even if just for a peaceful act like this one at the stadium, and that there will exist adequate mechanisms for such mobilization."

But even while Fidel was telling the UP to take the offensive, he kept the correlation of forces in mind. About suppressing parliament, he said, "I am not an unconditional devotee of bourgeois legality. And I have said that Parliament is an anachronistic institution. But nobody suppresses it until he is able to suppress it."

The UP, Fidel emphasized, must grasp the initiative and advance in the mass struggle, in the ideological struggle. The revolutionaries must unite and grow and arm the spirit. "When the spirit is armed, the people are strong."[34]

Two days after the March of the Empty Pots, the National Committee of the Christian Democratic Party voted to introduce a bill to impeach José Tohá, the minister of interior. The polarization, street disorders, and shortages had created a climate in which it was safe for them to start using this procedure through which they hoped later to remove the president. Among the charges against Tohá was that he had failed to prevent street violence and disband armed groups. The opposition was using one of its standard techniques—to do all it could to create troubles and then blame them on the government. In January the Senate voted to dismiss Tohá from office, but Allende immediately named him minister of defense. Thus was started a procedure through which the opposition, in twenty months, impeached and dismissed seven UP ministers.

Meanwhile, the U.S. government had been discussing how to use the network of military agents that had been reestablished through the CIA and the U.S. military attachés. "In November the Station suggested that the ultimate objective of the military penetration program was a military coup."[35] But Washington was cautious about committing itself exclusively to this one course; other possibilities were still considered open, such as the removal of Allende by impeachment. "U.S. officials . . . were instructed to seek influence within the Chilean military and to be generally supportive of its activities without appearing to promise U.S. support for military efforts which might be premature. . . . The Station was instructed to put the U.S. government in a position to take future advantage of either a political or a military solution to the Chilean dilemma, depending on developments within the country and the latter's impact on the military themselves."

Among the methods used by the CIA to influence the armed forces were some imaginative ones. "The Station proposed . . . to provide information—some of it fabricated by the CIA—which would convince senior Chilean army officers that the Carabineros' *Investigaciones* unit, with the approval of Allende was acting in concert with Cuban intelligence (DGI) to gather intelligence prejudicial to the army high command. It was hoped that the effort would arouse the military against Allende's involvement with the Cubans, inducing the armed services to press the government to alter its orientation and to move against it if necessary. . . . In December 1971 a packet of material, including a fabricated letter, was passed to a Chilean officer outside Chile."[36]

At the beginning of 1972 an important but little noticed event occurred: Pinochet became Chief of the General Staff of the Army. The CIA evidently made contact with him at this time. Since October it had been monitoring the group which "might mount a successful coup" and, according to *Covert Action,* "by January 1972 the Station had successfully penetrated it and was in contact through an intermediary with its leader."[37]

Pinochet's promotion, as *El Mercurio*'s quasi-official account of the coup points out, placed him "in a position of great influence, but did not give him an operative command. The General Staff is a body for planning and advice, but command belongs to the Commander-in-chief of the Army, in this case General Prats, with whom Pinochet collaborated loyally in the service of the Army." Still, Pinochet, even while "collaborating loyally," began to promote his own purposes. Within a few months he would be using the general staff to prepare for a coup.[38]

In mid-January the opposition, united behind one Christian Democratic and one National candidate, won by-elections for a senator and a deputy. The elections showed that the alliance between the Christian Democrats and Nationals had become firm, that the Christian Democrats could now make a pact with the Right without their followers deserting; and that the UP had lost popular support as compared to the municipal elections of April 1971.

THE election results disturbed the UP. While the opposition was uniting, increasingly in possession of the initiative, resorting to ever stronger measures in Congress and on the streets, the government was being thwarted from carrying out its program or even governing effectively, and its popular support was receding.

What should the government do? "Arm the people," yelled a few in the crowd listening to Allende address them from a balcony of the Moneda one night in January. But an attempt to carry out this measure would have quickly brought about action by the armed forces to remove the government; and just because some leftists seemed to be ready to take to arms didn't mean that the overall correlation of forces favored the UP. What should the government do about the Congress? "Suppress it," said some. But as Fidel said, first you have to be able to suppress it.

The electoral setback widened the differences among the parties of the Left. The MIR said the UP was losing ground "to the degree that it had not decided to gain force by mobilizing the masses, pointing out the enemy, and advancing on the farms and factories." The PIR, the new party formed by the traditional Radicals a few months earlier, issued a document stating that "changes should be carried out within the law," and implying that if they were not, it might leave the UP. Carlos Altamirano, the leader of the Socialist Party, declared that the results of the election showed that "the Government would have to radicalize its program." The Communist Party said that "for the purpose of dealing with the middle strata we must take into account the real character of the revolutionary tasks we must now solve. We work with the perspective of constructing socialism. But today the tasks are fundamentally anti-imperialist and anti-oligarchic."

The meeting of the UP leaders at El Arrayán was a first attempt to thrash out agreed new policies to meet the growing problems facing the government. Enough agreement was achieved to issue a document entitled "New Tasks for the Popular Government and the Chilean People." But the title was a misnomer: The document did not so much present new tasks and policies as insist more firmly on the old ones. It proclaimed that the solution to the UP's problems lay "not in slowing down, but . . . in carrying out even more rapidly the integral fulfillment of the Basic Program . . ."[39]

There was some justification for defiantly holding high the program, even from a weakened position—the program was what the followers of the UP had voted for and believed in. But to say that "each step of advance in the fulfillment of the Program weakens the power of reaction" was to delude oneself, to fail to grapple with the full problem of power facing the UP government. This problem could not be solved by nationalizations alone. Moreover, the UP was promising more than it could deliver: how, given the correlation of forces—for either legal struggle or armed conflict—could it carry out the "integral fulfillment" of the program "even more rapidly"?

With different elements of the UP holding divergent views on inflation, the leaders at El Arrayán not only made little progress in grappling with the economics of the problem, but failed to think through how to present it to the people. Instead of explaining how congressional sabotage was preventing the government from dealing with the problem of the ballooning money supply, the document spoke glibly of new credit norms; instead of itself predicting that the problem of inflation would worsen, it left it to the opposition to gain the political benefits of foretelling what would happen.

Above all, the UP with its hands full—trying to run the government in the face of opposition sabotage, trying to solve a growing, endless series of particular problems, trying to get its different parties to agree—was not facing some of the central problems of how to deal with the plans and machinations of the enemy. Its key potential weapon was a strong ideological struggle that would make the people of Chile and the world aware of what the imperialists and the oligarchy were working toward. This weapon could mobilize the people against a fascist coup. The UP was calling for the offensive in carrying out the program—the nationalizations—where its ability to maintain the offensive was limited by the political and military correlation of forces, while its strategy for the ideological struggle, where it could have attacked, was defensive.

Because the UP leaders thought that the elections showed a loss of support from small businessmen and farmers worried about expropriation, the Arrayán document assured these groups that they had nothing to fear; it spoke out against illegal seizures.

This was important, but not enough. The middle strata were being moved not just by fear of expropriations and illegal seizures, but by the general development of the revolutionary struggle; they were being tugged in contrary directions by the increase in economic activity, inflation and shortages, the violence at the universities and on the streets, and the threat of fascism.

There was the need to mount an ideological offensive that would explain plainly, concretely, vividly, how the revolutionary struggle was developing and why, who the enemies of the revolution were and what they were planning, how they were working to carry out their plans, what fascism would mean to the people of Chile, and what socialism would mean. Such an ideological offensive could not consist of sporadic, isolated speeches and articles; it would have to be a planned, systematic, developing campaign in which the UP analyzed and explained each different juncture of the revolutionary process, trying to present such an accurate picture that the people—including those in the opposition—could see from their own experience that it was true.

The UP would have to discuss difficulties openly; difficulties are inevitable in a revolutionary struggle, and any attempt to pretend that they don't exist plays into the hands of the enemy. The UP would have to unmask Frei and those other leaders of the Christian Democrats who were collaborating with the imperialists and the fascists to overthrow the government. It could not allow itself to be stopped by the CD tactics of shouting "scurrilous" whenever it started to do this; it could not allow its opponents to determine the rules of the ideological struggle and keep it from taking the offensive.

There was the need to do more about the armed forces. It was concentrating on placating the officers while neglecting to make any strong attempt to win over the troops. To placate the officers was necessary, but a policy restricted to this was dangerous. Such a policy could gain time; it was apparently keeping the constitutionalist officers neutral, even winning the sympathy of a few. But it was not reducing the power of the three officer corps—bodies containing almost no revolutionaries, only constitutionalists, imperialist sympathizers, and fascists. This meant that if the coupist officers could win over or eliminate the constitutionalists, if the officers of the different services could unite behind a common policy, the officer corps would dominate the situation. The UP could not depend indefinitely on the unwillingness of the officers to make a coup; it needed to render them unable to do so: To a great extent the unwillingness would depend on the inability.

Reducing the power of the officer corps required winning away their control over the troops by spreading democratic, anti-coupist, anti-fascist sentiment, eventually revolutionary and so-cialist sentiment, among them.

Action to win away the troops would be difficult and risky, both politically and personally. The enemies of the UP watched for signs of such action with the same lynx-eyes that they used to make sure that the people were not being armed. Here is an example.

On March 1, 1972, *El Mercurio* carried a headline: "Secret Mission of the Communist Party, Infiltration in the Armed Forces." The story explained: "The Communist Party has confid-ed to its youth cadres an ambitious plan for infiltration of the Armed Forces. . . ." Documents found in the possession of a militant "reveal that members of the Communist Party Youth have the mission of establishing contacts with conscripts to propagandize them." *El Mercurio* did not state how the docu-ments happened to be found, who found them, or how it acquired them. But for five days it continued the story, explaining that, for the Communist strategy, "the Achilles heel [of the armed forces] is the Obligatory Military Service which covers the whole nation-al territory and all social strata," giving details of alleged methods of infiltration. Many of these methods, said *El Mercurio,* were of course known to the military intelligence services; it was simply alerting public opinion to the danger.

Action to win over the troops ran the risk of provoking the officers. Nevertheless, it had to be undertaken. It would have offered greater promise if it had been started early in the regime when the UP's position was most favorable. But even starting somewhat late, it could still be crucial.

The UP position deteriorated further after the meeting at El Arrayán. With each passing week, the accelerating inflation and spreading shortages made it clearer that the government's strate-gy of increasing its popular support by improving the state of the economy was in serious trouble. The president and the Congress were locked in an across-the-board impasse—over the budget, impeachments, nationalization, and the constitutional question of whether a simple or two-thirds majority was required to override the president's veto of the Christian Democrats' proposed constitutional amendment on nationalization. The impasse favored the opposition since it prevented the government from carrying out its program or running the country effectively.

In April the Left Radical Party (PIR), citing the president's veto of the nationalization amendment and the government's failure to put a stop to "indiscriminate seizures" as reasons, resigned from the UP with its two ministers, seven deputies, and five senators. It was in this same month that the "40 Committee approve [d] $50,000 for an effort to splinter the Popular Unity coalition."

Both the UP and the opposition were now carrying out large demonstrations. The CUT organized a mass meeting on March 24; the opposition carried out a "march for democracy" on April 10; the UP held a "march for the *patria*" on April 18. The newspapers disputed whether the UP or the opposition had brought out more people. But, like the constitutional struggle between the president and the Congress, the demonstrations were a draw; they showed that both sides had mass support.

In March an event occurred which could have helped the government take the offensive in the ideological struggle: Jack Anderson published the ITT papers which showed how the U.S. government had conspired with leading Chileans to keep Allende from taking office; Frei was implicated. The UP could have used the papers for a sustained, systematic attack, on a perfect issue, foreign intervention—an issue which united rather than divided most Chileans. And it could have tied the pre-inauguration plotting, about which it could now present unchallengeable documentary evidence, to the continuing efforts to create conditions for the overthrow of the government.

The government did publish a collection of the papers, and the left newspapers turned out a wave of articles about them. But most leading UP figures were timid about attacking, about using the documents to show what was still happening, and about not just referring in the abstract to sinister plots but naming names and giving details so people could really understand. The opposition saw the damage the ITT papers could cause and acted quickly to contain it.

El Mercurio, knowing that the government was going to publish the papers, raced to get them out first and weaken their impact. It patriotically condemned foreign intervention, then blandly asserted that the papers themselves showed that Frei had not plotted to make a coup but rather resisted one—successfully. The twenty Christian Democratic senators issued a statement condemning both the ITT intervention and the efforts to "besmirch" Frei who had really "done the opposite" of what the foreigners had wanted.

Frei gave a speech in which he treated his own patriotism and integrity as beyond discussion and accused the government of favoring hate and violence and failing ruinously in its land reform and copper nationalization. The "Secret Documents of the ITT," published by the government, became a best-seller. But within weeks, the opposition had moved the public discussion away from foreign intervention into issues in which it felt itself stronger—inflation, shortages, illegal seizures, alleged violations of the law by the government, and the democratic right of the people to hold demonstrations to protest these things.

Pinochet now began to prepare concrete military plans for a coup. "On April 13, 1972," he was to tell reporters for the magazine, *Ercilla,* six months after the coup, "the possibilities were analyzed at the General Staff."[41] And according to the *El Mercurio* account, "he ordered [the preparation of] a plan for anti-subversive counterintelligence in April 1972, and from June on, the Army began to bring its national security plans up to date and carry out studies which contemplated eventual confrontations. All this material would be useful for future actions."[42]

With the government stymied by the Congress, some *campesinos,* urban workers, and others on the Left became frustrated, and the MIR, preaching direct radical action, was able to increase its influence. The MIR's Revolutionary *Campesino* Movement was the most aggressive of the *campesino* organizations. Its Movimiento de Pobladores Revolucionarios also controlled some urban shantytowns. And its Revolutionary Worker's Front began to gain adherents among the workers.

The MIR led seizures of land, public housing, and factories. In Melipilla, the Revolutionary *Campesino* Movement seized the county building and held a judge who intended to order the return of seized lands; the government was forced to intervene to get the judge released. But for all the stir its actions caused, the MIR's following remained only a tiny proportion of the total Left.

How serious the strains within the Left had become was shown by an event that occurred in Concepción on May 12. The Christian Democratic Party had received permission to hold a march there on that day. The MIR, along with the local headquarters of the Socialist, Radical, MAPU, and Christian Left parties, as well as the local trade union, *campesino,* shantytown, and student organizations decided to take over the streets and prevent the Christian Democrats from holding their march. When rioting broke out, the Communist governor of the province ordered the police to break it up. One student was killed, over 50 persons were injured, and much damage was inflicted on the center of the city.

Luis Corvalán, secretary general of the Communist Party, denounced the MIR and the other groups that had allied themselves with it, saying that "very serious differences have been produced among the parties of the UP." The proper answer to the Christian Democratic march, he said, was not to try to prevent it, but to organize an even bigger UP march. The most revolutionary thing to do was not to engage in street fights or illegal seizures, but to close ranks behind the government. The national headquarters of the Socialist, Radical, MAPU, and Christian Left parties issued statements repudiating the action of their local headquarters in Concepción.

The Lo Curro conference, unlike its predecessor at El Arrayán four months earlier, resulted in several important shifts in UP policy—changes in economic and nationalization policy and the naming of new ministers of economics and finance to carry out the changes. The worsening of the government's position helped make possible agreement on the changes. Not only was it now obvious that something had to be done about the economy, but the UP's loss of ground politically lent weight to the argument that it must avoid creating new enemies.

Obtaining agreement on changes in policy was important but it was only a beginning. The new policies would have to be carried out in an enormously difficult situation. They would have to be carried out by a UP which, despite the general agreement achieved at Lo Curro, suffered from differences and strains that were bound to show up in day-to-day action. They would have to be carried out—as always in battle—in the face of the counteractions taken by the enemy to keep them from succeeding.

The UP was entering a period in which its very existence would be at stake.

12

Running the Economy
July 1972 to September 1973

Carlos Matus, who became minister of economics after the Lo Curro meeting, enjoyed the reputation of being decisive. He quickly resolved to take the painful action that, he felt, could no longer be avoided—an increase in the fixed prices and another devaluation of the escudo. Prices would have to be raised to reduce the deficits of the state enterprises which, being financed directly or indirectly by central bank lending, were helping to swell the money supply. The escudo would have to be devalued because exchange rates were again out of line with the rapidly rising internal price level. Both the price increase and the devaluation would have to be large.

It would, of course, have been better if the government had not been forced into the need for such harsh action. Had it possessed a majority in the Congress and the ability to increase taxes on the well-to-do, the government could have controlled the original budget deficit and kept inflation from gathering momentum in the first place. Even given the problem as it stood in mid-1972, with the government facing accelerating inflation and enormous deficits, both in its own budget and in the state enterprises, the ability to increase progressive taxes could still have made a great difference; the government would not have had to rely exclusively on price increases to reduce the deficits and restrain the growth of the money supply. But what might have been was of no help to Matus. He had to select—and quickly—between the grim alternatives available. It was either raise fixed prices and control the deficits or have the money supply continue its astronomic rise, causing more and more goods to disappear from legal markets into black markets; either correct irrationalities in the price structure or watch farmers feed more and more wheat and milk to livestock; either devalue the escudo or watch imported goods become ridiculously cheap in relation to other goods, stimulating excessive imports and the smuggling of imported goods out of the country.

Matus's policy was to carry out the price increases in a frankly discriminatory way. The prices of luxuries—automobiles, for example—were to be boosted drastically. The cost of telephone service was to be made especially high for those living in rich districts. The prices of mass-consumed goods were to be raised only as much as necessary. In this way, the price system could serve as a partial substitute for the tax system which the Congress would not let the government use as it wished.

But there were limits to how far a discriminatory price policy could be carried out. Increases in the prices of luxuries could not by themselves provide enough additional revenues; the price of other goods would also have to be jacked up. Besides, there were specific reasons for large increases in the prices of many goods—including mass-consumed goods; for example, the prices of foodstuffs would have to be raised enough to provide an adequate return to Chile's farmers or to cover the large increases in international prices that had occurred.

Since the new price increases, to begin in August, would bite deeply into the purchasing power of the people, the government entered into discussions with the Central Labor Confederation (CUT) on how the real income of the working class could be protected. It was agreed to advance to October the readjustments of wages and salaries which usually took place in January. As of October 1 wages and salaries would be raised by 100 percent of the cost of living increase, from the beginning of the year through the end of September.

To avoid having the state enterprises kept in deficit by the wage and salary readjustments, the government decided to make the price increases large enough to cover the rise in pay. To finance the readjustments for its own employees, the government intended to submit to Congress proposals for increasing taxes.

Matus knew that the price increases, gigantic and concentrated in a short period, would shock the economy. But he hoped to bring the basic problem—the increase in the money supply—under control by eliminating the deficits in the state enterprises. He hoped, in his own words, that "after the squeeze, an acceptable degree of stability at a higher level would result."

The devaluation came on August 5. The escudo cost per dollar for the import of raw materials was raised by 58 percent; for foodstuffs and fuels by 64 percent; for machinery and equipment and luxury items by even higher percentages. Some economists estimated that the devaluation alone would bring about an increase of 15 percent in consumer prices.[1]

The price adjustments had to reflect not only the devaluation and the wage and salary readjustments to be carried out in October, but also the inflationary increases in other costs since the last time prices had been fixed. These adjustments continued throughout August and into September. Every few days brought an announcement of new, massive price increases: August 1, cigarettes—100 percent; August 12, soft drinks and beer—85 to 100 percent; August 13, automobiles—220 percent; August 16, textiles—60 to 90 percent; August 19, beef—200 percent; August 20, milk—40 percent, and bread—75 percent; September 9, shoes—100 percent.

The increase in the Consumer Price Index during the seven months from January through July had been 33.2 percent. In August alone the index shot up 22.7 percent—and then in September 22.2 percent. The price increases were gigantic, not only for luxuries, but even for essentials. For foodstuffs, the Consumer Price Index rose 38.1 percent in August and 30.4 percent in September.

The opposition missed no opportunity to make the difficulties worse. *El Mercurio* fanned inflationary psychology. As government spokesmen talked about establishing stability once the devaluation and price increases had worked their way through the economy, *El Mercurio* declared that the devaluation would not be the last, that the price increases would not solve the problem of controlling the money supply. With pictures of lines outside stores, it played up shortages which worsened as merchants withheld goods while waiting for the price increases. Christian Democratic union leaders, trying to provoke discontent among the working class, called upon the national leadership of the CUT to prevent the increases. The Christian Democratic and National Parties organized protest marches in Concepción, Valparaiso, and Santiago. Orlando Saenz, president of The Society for the Development of Manufacturing, issued a statement saying, "The economic restoration of Chile has to start with the reintroduction of habits of order, discipline, and hard work, and we may legitimately doubt whether these are attainable by the present Government."[2]

There was also Congress. Try as the government would to reduce its dependence on Congress, to bring the money supply under control by price increases instead of the tax increases over which Congress had power, it still remained vulnerable to congressional sabotage. The financing of the wage and salary readjustments for government workers could not be provided, as could the financing for workers in state enterprises, by price increases; it depended on Congress. If Congress refused to vote the new taxes required, the government's own deficit would go up. The government might succeed in stemming the flow of money into the economy from the enterprises, only to be confronted with an overwhelming increase in the flow from its own expenditures.

The increases in the Consumer Price Index during August and September brought the January-September increase to 99.8 percent. The October readjustment would therefore double wages and salaries—an increase which if not adequately financed would obviously cause the government deficit to skyrocket. The opposition in Congress was, of course, interested not in curbing the deficit or the inflation, but rather in producing economic chaos; as it had done since the government came to power, it went along with the expenditures, but refused to vote adequate financing.

The government economists had not expected the increase in the overall price level that accompanied the adjustments of fixed prices to be as gigantic as it turned out. They had hoped to bring the deficits of the state enterprises under control without causing such a great leap in the cost of living, without making necessary quite such a massive wage and salary readjustment.

The very size of the surge in the price level shocked people, and in midstream the authorities became worried about pursuing the price adjustments to the end. Additional price adjustments would cause the increase in the cost of living to be still greater and the wage and salary readjustment to be still more massive. And with Congress refusing to provide adequate financing for the wage and salary readjustment of public employees, additional price adjustments would cause the future deficit in the government's administrative budget to be still greater. How could one be sure that these adjustments would not increase the government deficit more than they reduced the enterprise deficit?

The Government stopped raising prices even though some enterprises had not yet had their prices adjusted. Since these enterprises would have to confront enormous increases in costs with the old frozen prices, their deficits would now be larger than ever. Alongside these enterprise deficits, there also remained the government deficit. Drastic though the government's new economic measures had been, they had not brought the money supply under control.

Some in the UP and other leftists criticized the devaluation and price adjustment, claiming that it had accelerated the inflation and created an economic crisis. But these critics didn't say what would have happened if the government had not applied the new policy. Actually, the conditions for acceleration of inflation and the crisis were being created by the inordinate growth of the money supply long before the new policy was applied. This growth in the money supply, left unchecked, would have led to a crisis anyway. And the longer one waited to attack the problem, the worse the crisis would have been—the bigger the deficits and price distortions to be eliminated, the more painful the corrective measures to be taken. The government's action was at least an attempt to grapple with the problem.

Would the new measures, even though they did not bring the money supply under control, have at least slowed its growth and improved the situation? It is impossible to say. The government had expected it to take a few months for the effects of the devaluation and price adjustments to work their way through the economy, hoping that then the inflation would ease. But in the third month, the opposition shook the economy with a tremendous blow—the "October stoppage."

THE OCTOBER stoppage was an employers' shutdown directed against the government—an attempt to paralyze the economy. It was started by the Confederation of Truck Owners and then joined by the Confederation of Retail Storekeepers, the associations of doctors, dentists, engineers, and lawyers, many bus companies, taxis, bank employees, secondary schools, parts of universities, and some *campesinos* belonging to unions controlled by the Christian Democratic and National parties.

Behind the shutdown stood the CIA. As *The New York Times* reported on September 20, 1974: "The Central Intelligence Agency secretly financed striking labor unions and trade groups in Chile for more than 18 months before President Salvador Allende Gossens was overthrown, intelligence sources revealed today. ... Among those heavily subsidized, the sources said, were the organizers of a truck strike that lasted 26 days in the fall* of 1972, seriously disrupting Chile's economy. ..."

The striking truck owners used goon squads to prevent truckers who wanted to keep working from doing so; the roads were strewn with *miguelitos*—three-pronged steel tacks—to perforate tires. Many storekeepers who opened for business were attacked, sometimes with guns. Sabotage was attempted against road tunnels, railroads, an oil pipeline. The government had to declare a state of emergency in twenty-one of Chile's twenty-five provinces, which meant placing these provinces under military control.

The UP's enemies were unable to paralyze the economy. The Society for the Development of Manufacturing called for indus-

* In Chile, of course, it was spring.

trialists to shut down their factories, and many tried to do so, offering to continue to pay the workers even though they would not be working; but the workers took over the factories and kept them going. Many doctors worked emergency hours to provide the services their striking colleagues were withholding. Some retail stores, especially in the poorer neighborhoods, remained open. Teams of workers and youth, improvised by CUT and other organizations, transported and distributed foodstuffs and other essential goods.

Still the stoppage inflicted great damage: It imposed heavy financial losses on both government and enterprises, aggravating the problem of deficit and inflation. Government revenues plummeted, and remained low for several months even after the stoppage had ended. The minister of finance estimated in mid-November that receipts for that month from the sales and turnover tax—Chile's most important tax—would be only 50 percent of normal.[3] Countless enterprises suffered losses.

Not only did the stoppage cause an immediate wastage of perishable agricultural products which could not be transported to market, but it interfered with spring planting and the feeding of livestock, ensuring future reductions in output. Ten million liters of milk and an immense quantity of vegetables were lost during the stoppage. Planting for the coming year's crops had already fallen behind during the preceding winter because of excessive rain, but there was a chance to catch up in the spring. The stoppage supervened and disrupted the distribution of seeds, fertilizers, pesticides, and fuel for trucks and tractors. Five million hectares ordinarily planted to sugar beets were left unsown. The distribution of seeds for planting potatoes, beans, and corn, of guano to fertilize potatoes, and of sulphate to spray grapes, was delayed. The distribution of feedstuffs for livestock was disrupted and animals had to be slaughtered prematurely.

Losses of critically short foreign exchange resulted. Some agricultural losses had to be made good by increased imports; the five million hectares of sugar beets lost meant an additional foreign exchange outlay of $6 million. Exports were reduced. And five thousand tons of copper production, then equivalent to $5 million, were lost.[4]

The stoppage caused a dangerous reduction in inventories

throughout the economy, from factories, farms, and import houses to retail stores. Chile was left with inadequate reserves of oil, wheat, flour, and many other goods.

From the CIA point of view, the stoppage was well timed. If there had been any chance that the government would realize some of the purposes for which it had carried out the price adjustments of August and September, the strike guaranteed that it would not. Coming on top of Congress's refusal to vote adequate financing of the wage and salary readjustment, the stoppage guaranteed that the deficits, the inflation, and the shortages would get still worse.

The Consumer Price Index rose by 32 percent during the months October through December, bringing the increase for the year to 163.4 percent. The specter of a need for ever more frequent wage and salary readjustments arose. When the government decided to grant an extraordinary readjustment on October 1, 1972, it had hoped not to have to grant the next one till a year later. Now with 32 percent of the purchasing power of the October 1 wages and salaries cut away in only three months, it was clear that the next readjustment would have to come much sooner.

The shortages after the strike were far more severe than before. My wife and I, finding it impossible to obtain meat, lived on whiting and, occasionally, other fish. Many goods—coffee, tea, sugar, toilet paper, detergents, bedsheets—were available only sporadically, or not at all.

The hoarding of goods by manufacturers, wholesalers, and storekeepers grew. The government and the UP parties called on the people to fight against the hoarding. Government inspectors and community Price and Supply Committees (JAPs), often accompanied by reporters and photographers from Left newspapers, carried out searches of establishments suspected of hoarding. When hoards were found, the newspapers publicized them and their owners were forced to place the goods on sale. The actions of the inspectors and the JAPs were useful, but they were trying to hold back a tide too strong for them to control.

With the inflation skyrocketing and the regular market mechanism breaking down, some in the UP argued that the best policy would be simply to forget the inflation and to stop using the regular market mechanism—to establish rationing and guarantee everyone a "people's market basket" at controlled prices. Some found in this idea the truly "revolutionary" way of solving Chile's economic problems. Providing everyone with an equal share at a time of scarcity would, of course, be the fairest method of distribution. But the idea of simply forgetting about inflation was dangerous; and most of those arguing for rationing were not asking themselves how well, given Chile's circumstances, it would work.

Jaime asked me in April 1973 to prepare a memorandum on the problem, of which the following are some key paragraphs:*

Subject: *Shortages and Inflation*

It is important to understand well on what the functioning of a rationing system depends and not give ourselves illusions about how well one would function in Chile's concrete circumstances. We must also bear in mind that we cannot solve the problem with direct controls alone (rationing, people's market basket, etc.). We must at the same time fight strongly against the monetary inflation.

The economic situation is very delicate. First, the foreign exchange situation is critical. The projection made recently by the Research Department of the Central Bank shows that even without paying one cent for the service of debt to the United States, Chile will have a cash deficit of $300 million or more. . . . So far the internal economy has not felt the full force of the foreign exchange situation because we have used reserves. . . . But the foreign exchange outlook is such that we shall perhaps have to reduce imports of items which are not luxuries, including not only capital goods, but articles of consumption and raw materials for industry.

Second, the outlook for agriculture is also not encouraging. . . . We cannot exclude the possibility of a strong decline in agricultural production.

On top of these two factors comes inflation. We should not delude ourselves with the argument that because production has increased x percent since 1970, there are therefore no shortages. It is a great achievement that production has increased and there is great political

---

* I was unable when I left Chile to take any of the memoranda I had written there. But somehow *El Mercurio* obtained a copy of this one and, with the omission of some paragraphs, published it a few weeks after the coup. It was originally written in Spanish.

value in indicating the increase. But if the effective demand grows even more than production, there can be shortages which people feel in a tangible way when they go to buy. It seems obvious that an inflation of 160 percent has great force for creating shortages, not only directly, but also by distorting production and distribution, helping hoarders and saboteurs, placing pressure on the precarious foreign exchange reserves, etc.

It appears obvious that with the economic situation outlined, a system of rationing, people's market basket, etc., will be under strong pressures. What will be its ability to resist these pressures?

We do not have in back of us a population united in a patriotic fervor [such as] is produced by a war.

Specifically, we do not have all the *campesinos*. Even in the reformed sector, which covers 40 percent of the agricultural land, there are *asentamientos* and federations controlled by Christian Democrats and even by Nationals.

Many private merchants are not with us and the public sector controls only part of distribution. The public sector controls only 65 percent of imports and 25* percent of industrial production.

In sum, a large proportion of the links of the chain that goes from production or importation to the consumer is in private hands. Many of the people who control them are not with us; and a part of the population is disposed to buy outside of legal channels.

With this economic and political situation, it can be seen why the problem of shortages is not just a problem of arithmetic, of computers, etc. It is essentially a problem of political economy.

The solution of partial problems depends to a great degree on the solution of the problem in general. For example, if the supply of materials which the *campesinos* require, or of the industrial goods which interest them, fail to reach them, or if there arises a black market in these products, with what success are we going to be able to insist that they sell their wheat to the state monopoly at the official price? Another example: You ask a storekeeper why he charges illegal prices and he answers, "Because I have to pay such prices." I do not defend dishonest storekeepers, but it is necessary to recognize that even storekeepers who are honest and sympathize with the Government can find themselves in a difficult situation. To be able to request that they charge official prices, we have to make it possible for them to buy at such prices.

The political aspect of the problem is perhaps obvious. We do not

*This differs from the figure of 40 percent cited on page 144 because it excludes mining.

want to lose ground, above all with the *campesinos,* but also not with the storekeepers. Our policy toward them has to be realistic, taking into account their situation and problems.

Besides not having the whole population behind us, we also do not have state power. This limits our capacity to use the coercive force of the State against those who do not comply with their economic obligations, who would commit infractions against rationing regulations, etc. The opposition says that rationing, the JAPs, etc., are illegal and the tribunals are with them. We can and should use the actions of the masses to apply sanctions. But we do not have all the masses and, besides, their utilization is not always easy or advisable. For example, if a significant part of the *asentamientos* did not collaborate with the system it would not be easy to use the masses against them.

Three main arms can be used to make a system of distribution function: 1) The market; 2) Political-moral incentives; and 3), Coercion. To the degree that one of these arms doesn't work, one is forced to depend more on the others.

There are people, apparently, who think that there is something non-revolutionary in taking inflation seriously, that the monetary factor isn't real, etc. But what will happen if the country gets flooded with money is quite real. Something in the economy will have to give way. Even if it were possible to control distribution and avoid a black market, there would still be ugly consequences: Many people with an excess of money in their pockets would work less; absenteeism would increase, etc. In Chile's circumstances, however, the system of distribution will not work well. We could see ourselves forced to recur more and more to coercive measures even against sympathizers, to our political disadvantage. There is nothing revolutionary about ideas that do not work and entail political disadvantages. . . .

While it was not difficult to marshal arguments about the dangers in the foreign exchange situation and inflation, finding solutions to these problems was another story. Jaime asked me to prepare recommendations on foreign exchange to present to the Council of the Central Bank. Talking to those in charge of foreign exchange at the bank showed me that exchange control was severe. I did feel, however, that some additional savings might still be wrung out from two or three secondary categories of outlays, such as debt service and tourism. The memorandum published by *El Mercurio* illustrates my recommendations:

We should not bet on optimistic projections of the foreign exchange situation, but cut to the bone on the payment of debt, tourism, and the expenditures of Chilean missions abroad. (I have traveled with Chilean officials abroad; the travel allowances are generous. It would be worthwhile to review the salaries of Chilean officials abroad: They reflect criteria of the period before the Popular Government.) . . . We should also review the projected expenditures of foreign exchange on capital goods to see which can be postponed. We are entering a decisive period, and the state of the economy now is more important than the fruits of the investments in the future. . . .

Jaime presented the recommendations to the council. A decision to cut down the payment of foreign debt had already been taken, and the council accepted the recommendation to cut down on tourism. But while such measures might help a little, they could not solve the exchange problem, which remained critical.

Jaime and I discussed many times how to try to control inflation. The problem was baffling. The government could not try to control inflation as bourgeois governments did, at the expense of the working class, by lowering its real income and creating unemployment. Yet how, with only a minority in the Congress, could the government control inflation at the expense of those best able to pay?

All elements of the problem—credit policy, fiscal policy, price policy, and wage and salary policy—had to be seen as parts of one whole. They had to be managed jointly in such a way as to maintain production and employment, preserve the redistribution of income which the UP government had carried out, and yet somehow slow down inflation.

Restriction of credit could not be a major weapon against the inflation. To try to control a money supply growing as rapidly as that in Chile, by a general restriction on credit, would have meant depriving industrial and commercial enterprises and farms of the funds they needed to operate, and would cause a sharp decline in output and a tremendous increase in unemployment. Credit had to be kept from growing *even faster than* the economy required, but had to be allowed to grow *as fast as* it required. There were, however, one or two areas in which strong restrictive measures could be taken: For example, some types of credit to farmers had gotten out of hand and could be reduced.

The best potential weapon for fighting inflation—if it could be used—was taxation. With increased taxes, the government deficit—a main source of the increase in money supply—could be reduced. The increased taxes could be made to fall on the well-to-do, not the poor.

Another way of reducing the budget deficit was to trim government expenditures. Some trimming was desirable; the budget still contained items left over from previous administrations which, for a government aspiring to establish socialism, were not necessary—for example, projects for superfluous roads. But the extent to which the budget deficit could be reduced by cutting expenditures was limited. Since 90 percent of government expenditures went to pay wages and salaries, any large reduction would cause unemployment.

The increase in the money supply could also be curbed by a reduction in the deficit of the state enterprises, which could be brought about by raising the prices of the goods they sold. Some use of this method could not be avoided: The deficit of the enterprises was enormous and growing and had to be restrained. Yet, as the experience of August and September 1972 showed, this method had to be used carefully. Raising these prices meant either that the next wage and salary readjustment would be that much larger, giving an additional fillip to the price-wage spiral, or if the wage and salary readjustment were held down, that the real income of the working class would shrink.

Even while defending the real income of the working class, a program to control inflation had to do something about the price-wage spiral. Periodic readjustments to make up for past increases in the cost of living could not be avoided. For the lower levels of wages and salaries, these readjustments could not be less than 100 percent of the cost of living increase. To give less would cause great hardship, and be unjust and politically unwise. But like all incomes in Chile, wage and salary incomes were very unequally distributed. Eighty-five percent of wage and salary earners received less than three *sueldos vitales,* while there were others receiving salaries of twenty or more. Those with the higher wages and salaries—say those receiving five *sueldos vitales* or more—could afford to receive readjustments of less than 100 percent.

Of all the weapons, the principal one was taxation. It did not suffer from the disadvantages the other methods entailed. Taxes could be increased without causing a rise in unemployment, a reduction in the income of the lower classes, or an aggravation of the price-wage spiral.

With a large increase in revenues from taxation, the other measures for controlling the money supply would have to carry only part of the burden. Without additional revenues from taxation, the other measures would have to be pushed to drastic extremes. With additional taxation, inflation could be controlled without reducing the employment and income of the working class. Without additional taxation, inflation could only be controlled by drastically reducing them—an impossible solution for the UP government.

Jaime and I deliberately tried to make our analysis as independent as possible of the policies the government was following. When we finished we could see that our analysis and the government's policies were in line with one another. The government was constantly trying to get progressive taxes passed; it was preparing to adjust prices, but cautiously; and a wage and salary readjustment in May 1973 granted a higher percentage increase to those earning less. But the government was stymied: It could not try to control inflation at the expense of the working class; Congress refused the taxes necessary to control it at the expense of the well-to-do. And so inflation grew.

What could the government do without having control of the Congress? Try to exhaust the possibilities inherent in the executive arm of the government? Jaime and I thought that the government ought to try to obtain more revenues through stricter enforcement of the existing tax laws, that it ought to mount a sweeping revolutionary campaign, one which mobilized the people to help, against tax evasion. We also felt that the organization of the government for handling financial matters was faulty. Lines of authority and responsibility were divided and confused; one organization and one individual ought to be given authority for the fight against inflation and ought to be held accountable. Jaime asked me to prepare a memorandum giving our analysis and suggestions, which he sent to the Office of the President.

IN June 1973 Carlos Matus became president of the Central Bank and Jaime became economic advisor to President Allende. Matus asked me to work with him, as well as with Jaime, to help thrash out measures for fighting inflation. I suggested to Matus that remedying some faults in the organization of the government for handling financial matters, although it could not solve our basic problems, might nevertheless be useful. I pointed to the inherited irrational division of authority and responsibility between the Ministry of Economics and the Central Bank as a key fault, one that was helping to worsen the troublesome deficit in the state enterprises. The Ministry of Economics had the authority to fix low prices without responsibility for grappling with the deficits they would entail; the Central Bank had the responsibility for financing the deficits without any authority over the price fixing which was causing them.

The advantages and disadvantages of fixing prices low were not being properly weighed against one another: The Ministry of Economics saw mainly the advantages, leaving the Central Bank to cope with the disadvantages. Besides, it was wrong to have the banking system administering the distribution of funds to the enterprises to cover the deficits, under the pretext that the funds being advanced were loans. The funds would, in fact, never be repaid and were therefore not loans, but subsidies. Bank employees, whatever their qualifications to judge the merits of loan applications, were not qualified to judge the pros and cons of granting subsidies.

Matus agreed and asked me to prepare a memorandum for the Economic Committee of the Cabinet. The memorandum suggested that a committee composed of representatives of the ministries of economics and finance, the Central Bank, and the CORFO (which administered the state enterprises), be formed and placed in charge of fixing both prices and the total amount of money to be budgeted for subsidies. Having these bodies represented on the new committee would enable their different points of view to be expressed. Having the committee responsible for both price and subsidy policy would keep it from looking at only one aspect of the problem.

If it decided to hold fixed prices low, it would have to take responsibility for the subsidy required; if it decided to hold the subsidy down to prevent the money supply from growing excessively, it would have to take responsibility for the price increases required. The memorandum also suggested that the task of determining the amounts of subsidy to be granted individual enterprises be carried out by the financial department of CORFO, which was better informed than the banks about the financial problems of the enterprises and better suited to make the economic judgments required. The Economic Committee approved the proposal.

Matus also asked me to explore possible measures for a systematic attack on inflation—to meet with the budget director about obtaining increased tax revenues and reducing government expenditures, and to discuss with Ministry of Finance economists the problem of reducing the deficit of the state enterprises by raising the prices of non-essential goods. We also talked with the economists of the Investment Division of the Central Bank about reducing government expenditures by postponing investments. Many hours were spent in consultations and in examining statistics.

The budget director was not encouraging. We knew, he said, that Congress was refusing to vote the necessary taxes. Some reductions could be made in government expenditures, but not enough to matter. The best time for mounting a campaign against tax evasion had passed. Such a campaign could still be undertaken, but it would take time to get under way—a new crew would first have to be installed at the Bureau of Internal Taxes. I pressed him with deliberately strong questions, and then concluded that despite the discouraging prospects every possible method of increasing revenues and cutting expenditures, especially a campaign against tax evasion, should be used—something would be gained and everything helped. There was no single, magic method for fighting inflation; and no front on which possible gains might be made should be overlooked.

The Ministry of Finance economists were enthusiastic about what could be done with discriminatory price increases. They presented me with thick sets of statistical sheets giving proposed price increases for different types of goods, the additional revenues and reductions in deficit of the state enterprises that would result, along with the effects of the price increases on the Consumer Price Index. The proposed increases on essential goods were much lower than on luxuries. I did not share the enthusiasm about what could be done to control the money supply through price increases alone. I felt that if we were forced to rely only on them and were unable to curb the deficit in the government budget, we would end up in the worst possible position—the real income of the working class would be reduced, while inflation would continue.

When I met with the economists of the Investment Division of the Central Bank, I found them reluctant to consider reductions in investments. Investments were sacred: The future depended on them. Investments were important, I argued, but something had to be done about inflation, otherwise it would grow even worse and produce economic chaos. Our means for fighting inflation were limited, and we had to make hard choices.

From time to time, I reported to Matus the results of my explorations. He agreed about the importance of trying to get additional tax revenues. One day in August he told me: "I am having lunch today with Admiral Montero [the Commander-in-chief of the Navy, just appointed minister of finance] and will try to get him to press Congress for tax increases; maybe as an admiral he will have better luck than the ordinary ministers of finance." When I next saw Matus, he told me that Montero had impressed him as very patriotic, concerned about what inflation was doing to the economy, and interested in all possible methods for combatting it, including additional taxes. But those preparing a coup were already working to get high-ranking, constitutionalist military officers, like Montero, out of the way. Within days, he was forced to resign as minister of finance.

WHILE the opposition in Congress was blocking the only way through which the government could cope with inflation, the UP's other enemies, including the CIA, were active elsewhere. In April a strike broke out at the El Teniente mine; a majority of the supervisory employees and a minority of the workers went out, demanding a wage and salary readjustment more favorable than that for everyone else. The strikers were mainly followers of Christian Democratic union leaders. Opposition newspapers and congressmen, who had never during previous governments shown an interest in higher wages and salaries, now came out in support of the strikers' demands. The cost of the strike in reduced copper output and lost foreign exchange was great.

On July 26 the truck owners started a second stoppage, to be joined by the same groups that had been with them the previous October—storekeepers, bus companies and taxis, doctors and other professionals. Again there was violence and sabotage. By August 20 the second stoppage had lasted as long as the first. The "intelligence sources" of *The New York Times* specifically named this strike, along with the first one, as having been subsidized by the CIA.[5]

With the second truck owners' strike, the U.S. government and the internal opponents of the UP brought to a climax their campaign to produce economic chaos. Their long, well-planned effort, skillfully coordinated and executed on many fronts, had met with success. Even before this stoppage, the economy was in a grave state. During the seven months, January through July 1973, the Consumer Price Index rose by 114 percent. In July it was 320 percent higher than in July 1972. The second truck owners' strike gave the finishing blow.

All goods, even bread, became hard to get. My wife and I used to get up early on Saturdays, walk to what we thought was the most likely bakery—a big one, a mile away, on the Avenida Providencia—and get on the line, three to six blocks long. Sometimes, after we had been waiting three or four hours, the flour ran out before our turn came and we had to try a different bakery or go back the next day.

The leaders of the different groups of strikers didn't even pretend that the strike could be ended by the government meeting any specific demands. They made it clear through statements to the press and television interviews that what they wanted was—in the words of *El Mercurio*—a "radical change." The strike was part of a broad series of actions to create the most propitious conditions for the approaching coup.

13

Political Developments July 1972 to the Coup

In July 1972 divisions among the parties of the Left erupted again. The MIR issued a call in Concepción for the formation of a People's Assembly—as a form of dual power apart from the UP government. The call was supported by some local elements of the Socialist, Radical, and MAPU parties; the Communist Party spoke against it. Allende immediately wrote a letter to the heads of the UP, rejecting any attempt to set up parallel tactics, a parallel movement, or parallel power. "The enemies of the UP," said Allende, "are engaged in destroying the Government's image" so that they can attempt to overthrow it. "Nothing better serves this enemy tactic than divisionism. . . . In Concepción, for the second time in three months, an attack on the unity of the UP has occurred. . . . People's power cannot spring from the divisionist maneuver of those who wish to set up a political mirage, which they call, without any justification in reality, a People's Assembly."

An authentically revolutionary People's Assembly, said Allende, would represent the people, would assume all powers, would govern. "In other historical circumstances, such assemblies have arisen as a dual power against a reactionary government which has lost its social base and become impotent." Those who would impose a People's Assembly "by the simple act of will of some impassioned persons have not made a correct examination of the correlation of forces in the country." Such an assembly could only be a "verbalistic tribune," at best "full of empty talk," but also dangerous, because it could become a source of provocation.[1]

While the left parties were wrangling, the opposition parties were progressing toward greater unity. Some dissensions between the National and Christian Democratic parties and among the different wings of the latter still troubled them. Renán Fuentealba, of the left Christian Democrats, argued against the division of Chile into two irreconcilably opposed blocs and proposed the formation of a center "Zone of Democratic Stability." The right Christian Democrats disagreed, and since they controlled the party, nothing came of Fuentealba's proposal. The Nationals protested against the willingness of the Christian Democrats to enter into negotiations with the UP government. But a good part of the difference was tactical. The Christian Democrats mainly entered into negotiations to keep up appearances as defenders of constitutional democracy; they pitched their demands beyond what the UP could accept. In August the opposition parties—National, Christian Democrat, Democratic Radical, and Left Radical—formed the Democratic Confederation (CODE), through which, by running only one opposition candidate in each district, they could present a united front against the UP in the congressional elections of March 1973.

The National Party began at mid-year to press for decisive, final action against the UP government. In a report to the General Council of the National Party at the end of June, Congressman Fernando Maturana laid down the party's position: "If, as is evident, they are the ones looking for a respite . . . we, the democrats, are obliged to look for a rapid denouement."[2] But the Christian Democrats did not want to overthrow the government immediately, since they hoped to be able to get rid of it legally by impeaching Allende after the March 1973 elections; and as a matter of day-to-day tactics, they were cautious about being identified with harsh measures against the government before its image had been sufficiently destroyed.

Taking the UP's enemies as a whole, the U.S. strategy of getting into "position to take future advantage of either a political or a military solution to the Chilean dilemma" was being followed. While the Christian Democrats served as a restraint on the impatient Nationals, the General Staff of the Army under Pinochet was, with Prussian thoroughness, preparing plans for the coup that might prove necessary. *El Mercurio*'s account of the coup states that "in July, General Pinochet ordered the offices dependent on the General Staff to revise the planning of the Interior Order, orienting it toward a 'more offensive or preventive character, so that the system of force already previously deployed and organized could act in anticipation of the facts.' Analogous plans were formulated, brought up to date, and revised by the other armed services."[3]

The August 1972 price increases, coming on top of the government's other troubles, created a situation which made all its enemies ready to increase the intensity of their attack. The CIA had the occasion it had been planning and waiting for; its economists were doubtless saying, "Now is the time to deliver a body blow." The Nationals smelled victory drawing close. The Christian Democrats became less cautious. Just as in December 1971 the government's enemies had timed their first major street demonstration to the outbreak of shortages, now too they launched an offensive to take advantage of the situation. This time the offensive was stronger and more ambitious.

Within days after the price increases started, actions began that were to culminate in the October stoppage. On August 21 the retail storekeepers staged a one-day shutdown—the first opposition attempt at a national strike. The shutdown was accompanied by other actions designed to create disorder and violence. Women in Santiago's wealthier districts leaned out their windows and banged pots; gangs of youths set up bonfire barricades across the Avenida Providencia, or stormed through the downtown streets stoning automobiles; teams of Patria y Libertad goons, armed with iron bars, blocked traffic. The police, using clubs, tear gas, and water-shooting trucks, clashed with the demonstrators. The government had to declare a state of emergency.

For weeks, on and off, the violence raged. It was during this furious offensive that Kennecott started its legal action against

Chile in Western Europe. On September 14 Allende announced the existence of a "September Plan" to overthrow his government. He implicated prominent members of the National Party, some sectors of the Christian Democratic Party, and Patria y Libertad. The plan called for shutting down truck transport, creating violent disturbances, and making a provocative attack on the armed forces during the Independence Day parade on September 18, giving them a pretext to act. Allende said that the conspirators had been unable to involve the armed forces in their plans.

Juan Marinakis, president of the National Confederation of Land Transport declared the next day that the president's assertions were "false, absolutely false"—the association "had absolutely nothing to do with seditious plans." After a secret session of the Senate, called to discuss the September Plan, opposition senators sneered. "Very weak, almost for children," said a Left Radical. A Christian Democrat added, "I am leaving feeling calm . . . to take a Turkish bath and spend the weekend with my wife and children."[4]

Although the September Plan was not carried out in September, parts of it were put into effect in October when the truck owners went on strike. They had already been granted a 120 percent rate increase, so they now used as a pretext the government's intention of creating a state trucking enterprise to serve the far-away, sparsely-inhabited province of Aysén. Once the stoppage was under way, nobody bothered to pretend that this was the real reason.

Much foresight and preparatory work by the UP's enemies went into the stoppage. The CIA not only subsidized the strikers; it first penetrated their organizations. If you were in charge of CIA operations in Chile, in which organizations would you try to place agents? Philip Agee, in his book *Inside The Company: CIA Diary,* recounts his experiences as a CIA official, and writes of the truckers federation of Ecuador that it "can stop the country completely. . . . It's not really a union because many of its members are owners. . . . Its orientation, then, is middle class rather than working class but for our long-range planning it's the most important of the organized trade groups to be brought under greater influence and control."[5] All this also applies to the truckers association of Chile.

Work also was done among U.S. suppliers of automotive parts. A key grievance of the truckers was a shortage of parts which they claimed resulted from government restrictions on their import. The foot-dragging by Ford and other suppliers that I had seen when the ENARA officials were trying to get them to ship quickly was not accidental.

The opposition parties did their part. Claudio Orrego, the Christian Democratic theorist, writes: "The grave tension in which the country had been living for months allowed one to suppose that in both camps important forces were grouping themselves to play a decisive card. . . . On Tuesday, October 10, the Confederation of Parties of Opposition convoked the people of Santiago to a protest demonstration. . . . A gigantic multitude filled the principal avenue of Santiago. . . . The next day the Confederation of Truck Owners agreed to carry out a stoppage beginning at 0 hour, October 12."[6]

The leaders of the Christian Democrats worked to mobilize mass support for the stoppage, and to spread it. Orrego later boasted that the stoppage was "generalized by means of the successive joining of more and more associations, many of which were responding to the mobilization at the base of the militants of the Christian Democratic Party."[7]

Frei gave a television address in which he agitated for the stoppage, not just with specific grievances of different striking groups, but with "national issues." The stoppage, he claimed, was not the result of a "political machination." An "economic disaster" had been produced in Chile, a situation that would not get better, but worse. Frei ridiculed the UP's talking about coupists and fascists. "Words," he said. Only a "profound rectification" could provide a solution to the "anguish" Chileans were suffering. The March elections, said Frei, must "have the value of a plebiscite." We are "fighting for the reconstruction of Chile."[8]

What could the government do about the stoppage? It was seditious, an insurrection against the government. Ordinarily, a government faced with a seditious strike can wield the full force of the state machinery against the challenge. It can treat the strike as illegal. It can, if necessary, use the police and armed forces against the strikers.

But for the UP government the situation was different. When the truck owners' strike broke out, the government declared it illegal, clapped the leaders into jail, and moved to requisition trucks. But the courts didn't back it. On the contrary, at the height of the crisis the Supreme Court sent Allende a letter accusing the government of a tendency toward illegality. The courts were providing the sedition with legal cover and protection.

Nor could the government use the police and armed forces with the necessary decisiveness and vigor. Whatever strength the government had among the officers came from the constitutionalists who would support only those of its actions that were legal—and legal meant as defined by the courts. Many officers shared the views of the strikers about the UP government, economic conditions, and socialism. The fascists among them had a simple reason for not lending themselves to break the strike— they wanted the government weakened and overthrown. So the government could not press the armed forces too hard, and they served not to choke off the strike at the beginning, but to maintain a minimum of public order while it lasted.

Blocked from immediately suffocating the stoppage, the government did what it could. It was strong wherever the workers were present—in the factories, at constructions sites, in the large distributing houses—and it took over many enterprises.

The industrial working class fought as one against the stoppage. In the mobilizations to keep factories working and goods moving, Christian Democratic workers stood side-by-side with workers from the UP parties. The middle class was split. Many professionals, students, and small merchants took the side of the government and the workers.

Two new forms of people's organizations developed out of the mobilization against the stoppage—Industrial Belts (*Cordones Industriales*) and Community Commands (*Comandos Comunales*). The Santiago area has about ten belts (*cordones*) of factories concentrated along main avenues and roads in and around the city; other cities also had them. The workers developed organizations by *cordon* to run and defend the factories taken over from owners trying to shut them down. While the *cordones* mobilized workers by industrial area, the *Comandos Comunales* mobilized people by community. Set up in the poorer neighborhoods, they were made up of the local mass organizations—Price and Supply Committees, Mothers Centers, unions—and undertook the distribution of goods and the education of people about the meaning of the stoppage.

While the leaders of the government were occupied with the stoppage, the opposition in Congress pushed through an important law, one that was to cause great trouble for the UP later—the Law for the Control of Arms. The bill for this law had been introduced months earlier by Juan de Dios Carmona, a minister of defense under Frei, who enjoyed close relations with high military officers.

The law provided that the control of arms would be exercised exclusively by the armed forces. Only they could authorize the production, importation, storage, distribution, or possession of arms. Everyone outside the armed forces and Carabineros was prohibited from possessing "major arms"—submachine guns, machine guns, gases, bombs, etc. The law also tightened the prohibitions on private militias. "Those who organize, belong to, finance, supply aid to, instruct, or incite to the creation of private militias or combat groups" would be subject to imprisonment of one and a half to five years or exile. Violations of the arms law would be subject to trial by military court.

When the law was passed, Carmona called it "the first great triumph of those who desire the reign of democracy in Chile." It has taken away, he said, from the "political power"—meaning the president and his appointees—all ability to meddle in the control of arms; it shows our "faith in the independence of our Armed Forces."[9]

How did the arms bill get through without a veto, without the changes that the president was allowed to make unless overridden by two thirds of the Congress? The episode is, as several commentators have stated, "confusing." According to writers for the leftist weekly *Chile Hoy,* who closely followed the problem of arms and the armed forces, the law was allowed to pass through "carelessness" and "error" by the government. "The Executive ... got mixed up with the vetoes, [and] sent its observations [proposed changes] late. . . ." The opposition called a surprise session of Congress and "proceeded rapidly to pass the law, without giving the UP Congressmen a chance to get together the third of the votes necessary to give validity to the vetoes of the Executive."[10]

THE stoppage might not have ended in a settlement if the working class had not been firm and disciplined behind the government. If the working class had divided, if the economy had been brought to a complete breakdown, and if political chaos had been produced, those who were thinking of a coup might have seized the opportunity to make one at the time.

But with the working class firm, a coup did not occur. For most elements considering it, a coup was a reserve possibility, to be resorted to if the March elections did not give the two-thirds congressional majority necessary to impeach Allende. In the midst of the stoppage, on October 26, the "40 Committee approve[d] $1,427,666 to support opposition political parties and private sector organizations in anticipation of [the] March 1973 Congressional elections."[11] The U.S. government was wary of a "premature coup;" if a coup turned out to be necessary, better later anyway; with time, optimum conditions could be "scientifically" prepared. Frei and his henchmen were hoping that the March elections would create possibilities for the Christian Democrats to take over the government. The highest-ranking coupists in the armed forces were concerned over the possibility that a coup would split them; they needed time to win over or to get rid of constitutionalist officers. All recognized a basic danger: A coup against a government with as strong a mass base as that of the UP would not be an ordinary one—it could provoke a civil war. A coup must therefore not be undertaken until all elements of the opposition were convinced that it was the only way out, until the coupist officers were sure of controlling united armed forces. The military must prepare and organize the coup meticulously to assure lightning success, and thus prevent a civil war from developing.

Eventually, therefore, the stoppage had to be settled. The settlement came in early November when Allende named three officers of the armed forces to his Cabinet. Prats, without resigning his post as Commander-in-chief of the Army, but only leaving it temporarily to Pinochet, became minister of interior. When, speaking in firm, clipped language, he called for the strike to end in 48 hours, it ended.

Some in the UP criticized Allende's move. Who ever heard, they asked, of a Marxist government with bourgeois military officers in its Cabinet? Jaime told me that when Allende proposed his intended action to the leaders of the UP parties, one or two objected. All right, said Allende, give me an alternative. Since no one could think of a satisfactory alternative, the leaders had to go along.

The MIR declared: "The incorporation of some generals in the Cabinet has in important measure changed the character which the Government has till now had—the traditional people's parties cease being the political axis of the Government. Now they have to cede an important part of this role to the Armed Forces."[12] But it was not the inclusion of the military men that created the weakness of the government; it was the weakness of the government that made the inclusion of the military men necessary. And for all the abstract language about changing "the character" of the government, the inclusion of the military men was not intended to be permanent—it was to last only as long as necessary.

Some in the UP took the ending of the stoppage as a victory for the government. But it was a victory only in the sense that the worst had not occurred. The Nationals and a few others who wanted the stoppage to lead to a coup did not see their hopes realized; for the remaining enemies of the UP, the stoppage accomplished what they wanted it to accomplish.

The inclusion of military men in the Cabinet was a retreat—necessary, but still a retreat. It strengthened the government against an immediate coup, but reduced its freedom of action. It was not to promote revolution and socialism that the armed forces allowed their officers to serve in the government. The different groups in the officer corps had other reasons. The constitutionalists wanted to defend the constitution, the coupists were not yet ready for a coup, and an intermediate group hoped that the military ministers could brake the government and make it more tolerable.

The new Cabinet was able to achieve a half-truce between the warring classes. Among the tasks which Allende assigned it was to assure public order and prepare the way for "honest elections" in March 1973. Apart from being unable to prevent sporadic individual acts of violence, it fulfilled these tasks. The armed forces stood behind the government's request for public order, and none of the warring civilian groups wanted to challenge them.

But the new Cabinet could only dampen the struggle, not eliminate it. To the existing points of conflict were now added several that arose as an aftermath of the stoppage. The stoppage brought the takeover by government and workers of 150 enterprises; now the opposition clamored for their return, while many in the UP, including often workers in the plants, said they should be kept. The new Cabinet declared that no reprisals would be taken against the strikers, but various government agencies held that this did not apply to those who had committed crimes or had held high-ranking or sensitive positions in which they were forbidden by law from striking. The Central Bank dismissed 28 leading officials. And the opposition pressed for their reinstatement.

The military members of the Cabinet could not escape being involved in the struggle. According to Chilean constitutional theory, they were to remain apolitical, like the armed forces they represented. But that someone could participate in a Cabinet and remain apolitical was as much a fiction as the notion that the armed forces were apolitical. Every day the military men in the Cabinet had to participate in decisions involving politics. How could Prats—who as minister of interior was head of the Cabinet and who became acting president when Allende left the country on a trip—avoid politics?

The actions of the military ministers could only strengthen the government or weaken it—there was no middle ground. They could recognize the primacy of the president, which meant in fact strengthening the government by backing its decisions with the authority of the armed forces. Or they could try to avoid backing the government on decisions they did not like; they could even try to dominate the government.

Prats, as Commander-in-chief of the Army and the most important military minister, had clear views about the participation of military men in the government. The Cabinet, he declared, is not a "co-government" of soldiers and politicians, because this would mean that it was made up of two powers, each with separate policies. "The Cabinet is a working body that acts according to the direct instructions of the President of the Republic."[13] Prats's statement was in line with Chile's constitution, which provided for a presidential, not a parliamentary, system of government: The president was empowered "to name at his discretion the Ministers of State," who were to "maintain their posts so long as they enjoyed [his confidence]."[14] But Prats's point of view was far from mechanically legal; he had judgements on the issues behind the legalisms. Referring in veiled language to a possible military coup, he asked: "Where would this lead? To a dictatorship. The Armed Forces would have to convert themselves into special police and this could only bring about the Tupamarization of the people."[15]

Prats acted with decisiveness as minister of interior. Soberly yet firmly, he asserted the government's right to take the actions necessary to defend itself and govern effectively. He was, of course, aware that his actions strengthened the government. But as he once commented, the government had been legally elected and was entitled to its full term in office.

As soon as the opposition saw which way Prats's actions as minister were tending, it began to criticize the participation of military men in the government. Senator Patricio Aylwin, Frei's mouthpiece, insinuated that the armed forces were becoming accomplices of the "illegalities" the government was committing. Senator Francisco Bulnes of the Nationals warned of the presence of "a further element of the UP in the Armed Forces."[16] But the opposition was not really objecting to the participation of the armed forces in the government, just to the manner of participation. What it wanted was one that would weaken and tame the government, not strengthen it. Some in the opposition were thinking that one way to get rid of the UP government was to have the armed forces take over, while allowing Allende to remain as a figurehead.

Increasingly, the enemies of the government saw Prats as an obstacle to their plans. If a coup turned out to be necessary, he, like his friend Schneider in 1970, would stand in the way. He was also an obstacle to solving the problem without a coup. The opposition began to attack Prats, and to mount a campaign to destroy his prestige.

The participation of military men in the Cabinet helped increase tensions in the officer corps. Previously, the armed forces had been able to avoid identification with the government, to maintain the image they wanted for themselves—guardians of "the permanent values of the *patria,*" undefiled by partisan strife. They had been able to keep their independence, to avoid strengthening the government. Now, just when the worsening of inflation, the August-September disorders, and the October stoppage had brought the polarization of the civilian population to an extreme and turned many officers more strongly against the government, there were military ministers in the same Cabinet with members of the UP, participating in making and carrying out decisions.

Prats's actions as minister were received with grumbling by the fascists among the officers, some of whom anonymously made their discontent known through newspapers friendly to them, like *La Tribuna.* These officers were unconcerned with constitutional considerations except when they could use them to argue that Prats was compromising the independence of the armed forces; they saw Prats as favorable to the government and therefore an opponent.

Prats's actions also caused concern among constitutionalist officers who disliked the government. It had been easier previously for these officers to reconcile this dislike with their professional respect for Prats and his constitutionalism. But now they were confronted every few days with government statements or decisions they did not like, with which Prats as the leading minister was associated. For these officers, Prats's actions meant facing more frequently and acutely the conflict between their class interest and outlook and their constitutionalism.

A FATEFUL consequence of Allende's maneuver to end the October stoppage was that when Prats became minister of interior, Pinochet became acting Commander-in-chief of the Army. This brought him from a post in which he was in charge of the preparation of plans, to one in which he exercised, for the time being, full command. He has related one action he began to take immediately: "I constantly visited the units, leaving them with the hope and the faith that Marxism was not going to prevail in the country. . . . Always when I opened a meeting, I told them openly, without concealment, he who is talking to you is not a Marxist."[17] Pinochet also—says *El Mercurio*'s account— "ordered General Arellano to inspect some garrisons, a task which served to join together many officers and tie them to the brother services."

The preparations for a coup moved from isolated plotting and planning within the separate services to the organized planning of coordinated action by them. "By late November," wrote Jonanthan Kandell in *The New York Times* on September 27, 1973, "army and air force colonels and navy commanders began to map out the possibilities of a coup. They also contacted leaders of the truck owners, shopkeepers, and professional associations, as well as key businessmen, who had backed the October strike."

Favored by the rising tensions in the officer corps, the coupist officers worked more actively to win over constitutionalists. "I could have pulled my hair out for teaching my students for all those years that the armed forces must never rebel against the constitutional government," an officer who formerly taught history at a military academy told Kandell. "It took a long time to convince officers that there was no other way out."

Ismael Huerta, representative in the Cabinet of the navy, traditionally considered the most reactionary of Chile's armed services, acted differently than Prats. He did not wish to "commit himself" to the actions of the Marxist government. Besides, even if he were not directly privy to the plans for a coup, he could undoubtedly smell a coup in the air.

Soon after he joined the Cabinet, Huerta began to leak stories to *La Tribuna* about the horrible inner workings of the UP government. Then he trumpeted his disagreement with several measures, such as rationing, that he said the government was considering. In January he submitted his resignation as minister and presented a "detailed exposition of his impressions of the Allende government to the Naval Council."[18]

"The plotting [for a coup]," wrote Kandell, "subsided somewhat in the weeks of political campaigning leading to the March legislative elections." What this meant, exactly what subsided, is unclear. But it seems reasonable that the coupists, without neglecting any opportunities to strengthen themselves or weaken the government, held some of their plans in abeyance while awaiting the election results.

In the campaign, the opposition parties worked not only to elect their candidates but also to mobilize their followers to support the removal of the government. The National Party was blunt. It presented itself as "more firm" against Marxism. Its candidates were Jarpa, who had a fascist history, and Colonel Alberto Labbé, the ex-director of the Military School, who had been retired after making seditious remarks in Allende's presence at a graduation ceremony.

The National Party's slogan was, "A New Congress Is Not Enough. A New Government Is Necessary." Frei and the other Christian Democrats were only slightly more roundabout. Although some opposition spokesmen talked about winning the two thirds of the Congress necessary to impeach Allende, Frei declared that if the opposition won more than 50 percent of the vote, the government would have to accept the result as a plebiscite through which the country was rejecting it.

The UP was on the defensive in the campaign. Its spokesmen asserted that the election was not a plebiscite, but a mid-term election. They attacked Jarpa, but they did not try to explain fully the fascist menace, in which others, not as avowed as Jarpa, were involved.

The UP did much better in the elections than almost everyone had thought it would: It won 43.4 percent of the vote to the oppositions' 56.7, gaining six additional deputies and three additional senators. Again, to understand the vote, one must keep the CIA intervention in mind. In February 1973 the 40 Committee approved $200,000 for opposition parties in addition to the $1,427,666 approved the previous October.[19] The election reflected continuing polarization: Within the UP the Radicals lost ground while the Socialists gained; on the opposition side the Nationals increased their share of the vote.

What conclusions did the UP's enemies draw from the vote? A secret memorandum on the significance of various possible election results was prepared for the Society for the Development of Manufactures whose contents became known to left newspapers which published them. If the UP won less than 36 percent of the vote, its overthrow by constitutional means would be feasible. If it got between 36 and 40 percent, the situation would be uncertain; but if it won more than 42 percent, the only way to get rid of it would be through armed confrontation.[20]

Some coupists were not displeased with the vote. Kandell quotes one military officer: "Frankly, many of us gave a sigh of relief when the Marxists received such a high vote because we felt that no politician could run the country and that eventually the Marxists might be even stronger."[21]

IN late March a new, completely civilian Cabinet was formed and the half-truce of the preceding five months ended. The opposition began the last phase of its campaign to destroy the legitimacy of the UP government. The Nationals, as usual, led the way. On April 13 Jarpa gave a speech, saying: "The moment has arrived for the Congress to . . . declare that [the government] has definitively lost its authority and the legitimacy of its mandate. . . . Nobody is obligated, either by law or morality . . . to continue obeying an illegitimate authority."[22]

Soon after the elections, Jaime was given the assignment of preparing a draft of the speech to be delivered by Allende at the opening of the Congress on May 21, and he asked me to help him. We set to work eagerly. We both felt that one of the gravest weaknesses of the UP lay in the manner in which it carried out the ideological struggle. It lashed out sporadically, instead of keeping up a systematic campaign serving a clear goal. It didn't make enough effort to force the enemy to fight over issues that were unfavorable to the enemy, but rather allowed the reverse to happen. It was pressured into timidity by the accusation that it was sowing hatred in Chile.

We began our draft with a discussion of plotting against the UP by the U.S. government and American corporations, citing extensively from the ITT papers, large new batches of which had just been provided us. Anti-imperialism, we thought, was one of the best issues to fight on, as could be seen by how gingerly the opposition had handled the copper nationalization law, or how it had been put on the defensive when the first ITT papers were published. We attacked Frei, using the ITT papers to show how he had been in collusion with the imperialists—and undoubtedly still was.

Finally, we developed the theme that the alternative to the UP government was fascism. Some people seemed to think that it was possible for Chile to have an immaculate, painless coup after which it would quickly become once again the "tranquil little country" they liked to remember. It would be useful, we thought, to tell these people what a coup would really lead to, to try to get them to think about what fascism would bring to themselves and their families and to Chile.

Several days after we finished the draft, Jaime told me what happened to it. The president had listened to it, and said with enthusiasm that it was "*magnifico*," but added that he couldn't use it. The reasons were not clear—he thought that it was too strong, that it would cause turmoil in the Congress. Only four paragraphs on foreign exchange were used.

While Jaime and I were working on the draft, we had a chance to observe the effects of the UP being drawn into a fight on an issue which was as unfavorable as the anti-imperialist issue was favorable. In January the Ministry of Education had announced a project, called the National Unified School (ENU), which was designed to reform Chile's educational system. The project was presented in high-flown language which made it sound more radical than it was.

How children are to be educated is a sensitive issue which—as I had seen in Cuba in 1960—counterrevolutionaries love to exploit. *El Mercurio* immediately mounted a campaign for "mobilization" against the project. It spoke of "the danger of premature indoctrination to which infants and children would be subject," of the "conversion of the Ministry of Education into a Ministry of Propaganda a la Goebbels."[23] Although the Catholic Episcopate found "some merit" in the project, several bishops spoke out against it, and the church asked that it be postponed. Military officers grumbled, and the minister of defense found it necessary to arrange a meeting between the minister of education and high-ranking members of the armed forces so he could explain the project to them. *El Mercurio* reported that most of those present "flatly rejected" it. Anti-ENU street demonstrations began in April. Day after day, Jaime and I, working in his tenth floor apartment, were interrupted by the turmoil in the streets below. We watched as the streets flooded with demonstrating high school students, as Patria y Libertad goons rampaged through, as fights broke out with UP supporters, and as the Carabineros moved in with tear gas.

From this time on, the disorder and violence were continuous. In Santiago there were disturbances over educational reform; in Temuco, demonstrations and violence over food shortages; in Rancagua, dynamiting and shootings over the strike at El Teniente. . . . The government had to declare states of emergency in one province after another. When they were lifted, the violence erupted again.

Meanwhile, the campaign to destroy the legitimacy of the government moved ahead. In the midst of the shootings in Rancagua, a strike of Santiago bus owners, and the bombing of a television tower, Enrique Urrutia, Chief Justice of the Supreme Court, sent a letter to Allende which said: "This Supreme Court must point out to Your Excellency, for the umpteenth time, the illegal attitude of the Executive Branch, manifested by its unlawful interference in judicial matters, as well as its obstruction of the Carabineros in the fulfillment of judicial orders. . . ."[24]

The turbulence affected the armed forces, although this was not easily visible from outside their ranks. *Chile Hoy* wrote of the air force: "In April and May, a strong movement arose among the troops and noncoms for an improvement in their meager incomes." Besides being hurt by inflation and shortages, the airmen also faced difficulties in the neighborhoods where they lived. "For months . . . complaints have been heard that the wives of airmen have been abused, insulted, and even struck when they tried to get on line to take care of their household needs. . . . The others on line prevented them from joining it, accusing them of being 'privileged,' of getting supplies at the cooperatives of the Fach" (air force). Some airmen complained of rocks being thrown at their houses, or of insulting signs being painted on their walls. The officers worked to convince the airmen that these aggressions came from the Left. In June "the moment seemed to have arrived to exploit the series of real or created situations for

promoting the participation of the Air Force in a coup. . . ."
Officers "began to make special trips to the provinces to agitate
the discontent."[25]

On June 29, as I was walking to work, I noticed that cars were
streaming back from the center of town to the outskirts. One
driver asked me, "Where are you going?" When I answered, "To
the Central Bank," he said, "Don't go, its surrounded by tanks
and soldiers, a coup is under way, you'll get killed." I decided to
walk back to the Institute of Economics of the University of
Chile where my wife was working. There, I found everyone
listening grimly to a transistor radio. Carlos, the head of the
Institute, an old Chilean friend with whom I had worked in Cuba,
was preparing to distribute a few small arms for the defense of
the institute building. On the radio, Allende spoke several times.
In one talk, he said, "I call on the people to take over the
factories . . . to be alert. . . . If the time comes, the people will
have arms."

After a few hours, we could tell from the radio reports that the
attempted coup was being put down. Then came a call for UP
supporters to congregate in the center of town for a demonstration of solidarity with the government. My wife and I joined
others to march downtown. There, the Alameda boulevard over-
flowed with a gigantic crowd of demonstrators, and lines of
soldiers were filing into trucks to be taken back to their quarters.
Jaime and I had been studying Lenin and B. Neuberg's *Armed
Insurrection* on the behavior of armies in revolutionary struggles
and had learned how important it was for the people to be brought
into contact with the troops. I looked now for signs of fraterniza-
tion. The demonstrators were shouting, *"Soldado, amigo, el
pueblo está contigo"* (Soldier, friend, the people are with you),
but the soldiers sat stolidly in their trucks.

Later, more information came out about the *tancazo,* as the
attempted coup came to be called. A Colonel Souper, with ties to
Patria y Libertad, had led several tanks and a few hundred men of
the Second Armored Regiment in an attempt to take the Moneda.
But Souper was not supported by any other units of the army.
Prats personally directed the action against the uprising.

For a day after the *tancazo,* Jaime and I thought that the
success in putting it down might strengthen the government. An

investigation of those implicated and their removal from the army could strengthen the constitutionalists. In addition, Allende seemed to be trying to form another "civic-military" Cabinet which might give the government more authority to deal with the disorders. But the case of Souper was subject to military justice. An order of the Santiago military zone prohibiting the news media from saying anything about the uprising soon made it apparent that the army was going to bury the case. And, as Jaime told me, the generals and admirals were making trouble for Allende over the participation of military men in the government.

For the coupists, the *tancazo* served as a military exercise to study. Two days later, *El Mercurio* published its conclusions: "First . . . the unity and internal discipline of the Armed Forces permits them to smother any uprising . . . and second . . . the Armed Forces are today the most effective power in the country. . . . The dispersion and disappearance of civilian groups when the noise of the first explosions was heard, demonstrates that the population was for the first time getting a clear picture of the efficacy of military power in the streets."[26]

The conclusions which the coupists in the armed forces drew were not of course made public then, but they have since come out in *El Mercurio*'s account of the coup. The coupist officers noted "the non-existent response of the *'cordones industriales'* to the energetic offensive of the troops. The Popular Power disappears before the noise, smoke, and bullets of true war. . . . The silence before tanks reveals that the Marxist people still lack preparation. . . ." The officers also noted "the basic fact that the soldier obeys his commander, that the Armored Regiment went out as one man upon a movement by Souper's arm, while the School of Non-commissioned Officers and the Buin Regiment [used to quell the uprising] responded to orders even though perhaps many of their men would have liked to fraternize with the tanks." The coupist officers had drawn a crucial conclusion—they could count on the troops to obey them.

The day after the *tancazo,* according to the same account, a committee composed of five general officers from each service was formed and met. Admiral Carvajal began by saying that in view of what was happening, there was need for increasingly close coordination of the armed forces. Pinochet said that the meeting should not discuss political matters, only economics; in this way—as *El Mercurio* half explains—Pinochet was able to preserve his cover as a constitutionalist who avoided politics, and still steer the discussion to where he wanted it to go. One officer said that economics and politics were inseparable, and the country was suffering from a grave crisis; "we should therefore justify our posts" and discuss the subjects that worry us. Prats spoke of the danger of civil war, the need to avoid a blood bath; the opposition, he said, deserved the blame for what was happening because it passed wage and salary readjustments without providing financing. There was, says *El Mercurio,* "contained impatience" in the room, and one general manifested his "stentorian nonconformity" with the "burlesque management" of the government. An agreement was adopted to present Allende with the "rectifications . . . the committee of fifteen believed necessary to overcome the crisis, if [he] advanced further with his hinted purpose of bringing military men into the Government." The memorandum listing the "rectifications," drafted two days later, contained 29 points.[27]

Three days after the *tancazo* the armed forces began an action which showed that they were maneuvering into position for a coup. Using the Law for the Control of Arms, passed the previous October, they began a series of searches for arms. Troops carried out searches throughout the country—in the *cordones* of Santiago, the National Distribution Agency in Valparaiso, and a lumber mill in Villarrica. Here it was the army that executed the operation, there the navy, elsewhere the air force; the services were acting in coordination. The searches were directed against the workers and poor, not against Patria y Libertad and other rightist groups.

Everywhere they were carried out with brutality—rifle butts and bayonets were used to make workers move; helicopters with machine guns kept watch over men and women forced to lie on the ground with their hands on their necks. A number of people were wounded, one killed. The main purpose of the searches was not to find arms, but to overawe and frighten the workers, to test the soldiers and accustom them to treating the people with brutality, to find out the leaders of the workers organizations, and in some southern cities, where *cordones* had not yet been formed, to keep the workers from forming them.

Both the people and the government resented the searches, but it was hard to know what to do about them. The armed forces had both force and the law on their side. The Chilean ruling class had constructed the state apparatus well—the armed forces enjoyed an almost autonomous status; they were a state within a state. Now, they were not only arrogantly bullying the people with their searches but also, using the martial law the government had found necessary to impose in various provinces, taking over power wherever they could. In several southern provinces, they were, in effect, becoming the government.

Jaime, who had access to information that I did not, expressed his judgment of the correlation of forces between our side and the enemy. He had always been sober, saying much earlier that the odds in a fight would not be on our side. Now he said the odds were getting worse; the enemy seemed to be gaining the whole of the armed forces. We looked again at our revolutionary literature to help assess the significance of not having part of the armed forces on our side. Lenin said in his "Lessons of the Moscow Uprising" of 1905: "Of course, unless the revolution assumes a mass character and *affects the troops,* there can be no question of a serious struggle."[28] The conclusion for Chile's case seemed clear: The UP's hope in a fight lay in a split in the armed forces, but it was becoming clearer every day that the chances of a split were small and getting smaller.

The arms searches were part of the armed forces' visible preparations for a coup; there were also "invisible" ones. "In July," says *El Mercurio*'s account, "General Herman Brady received instructions to prepare secretly at the Academy of War an anti-subversive plan for the control of Santiago against any extremist group. The plan assumed that the rest of the territory would be easy for the Armed Forces to dominate and that the point at which the subversion would be most active and complex was Santiago. In this study were carefully analyzed the different shantytowns, the terrain, the points of greatest urban concentration, the routes of communication, the public services, and even the headquarters, characteristics, and leaders of the movements that might promote subversion. Greater Santiago was divided into four sectors to be dominated by a lightning operation, carried out with surprise and such shocking force that the possible adversary would not dare to face the war material of the Armed Forces. Sectoral plans, photographs of known personages, calculations, and diverse analyses testify to the meticulousness of the study. The same was, of course, done at the national level at the General Staff of Defense."[29]

Besides preparing plans of attack, the coupist officers took measures to meet the problem of anti-coupism in their services. They tried to isolate the men from civilian influences; getting the navy, for example, to issue an order that uniformed personnel and civilian workers at the Talcahuano base, who had formerly eaten together, must now eat separately. The navy also issued orders that only officers could carry personal weapons; that stores of small arms be moved to new locations known only to officers; that marines—known as "cossacks"—be placed on ships where they could help control the sailors. Coupist officers in the three services increased their efforts to ferret out possible anti-coupists among the non-commissioned officers and men.

Several elements of the Left now began a campaign to win the rank-and-file of the armed forces away from the coupist officers. On July 17 *El Mercurio* carried the headline, "MIR calls For Military Subversion." Members of the MIR were stationing themselves near military bases and handing out leaflets which said: "Soldier, don't die for the bosses. . . . Disown the officers who are inciting to a coup." The MIR weekly, *El Rebelde,* called for the *Comandos Comunales* to form Committees of Unity with the soldiers which would demand the immediate democratization of the armed forces.[30] Carlos Altamirano and the Socialist paper, *La Aurora de Chile,* called for soldiers, sailors, and noncoms to disobey coupist officers, to rise against them, if necessary.

On August 6 the navy announced that its intelligence service had detected the "gestation of a subversive movement in two units of the fleet" and was charging those involved with the "grave infraction" of having "deliberated with elements foreign to the institution."[31] The navy was never able to show that those arrested did anything more than discuss not participating in a coup, but by the definition of the coupist officers any threat to *their* discipline and control was "subversion." Since there was nothing the coupists feared more than a threat to their control, they resorted to terror. The navy arrested over 100 persons, not just from the two original ships, but also from several others and from the bases at Valparaiso and Talcahuano. Torture was used to try to extract information about other possible "plotters" and to intimidate other noncoms and sailors. Various prisoners were given electric shock treatment, awakened every 15 minutes while trying to sleep, beaten about the genitals, forced to eat excrement, suspended upside down and dunked into the sea.[32]

Carlos Altamirano and Oscar Garretón of the MAPU had attended a meeting with some of the noncoms and sailors who were later arrested, a meeting to which they had been invited to hear of the preparations by the coupist officers to overthrow the government. The armed forces started legal proceedings against Altamirano and Garretón, as well as Miguel Enríquez, the leader of MIR.

With the preparations for a coup visibly moving forward, Allende called in late July for a dialogue between the government and the Christian Democrats. "It is necessary," he said, "to make a supreme effort to avoid a confrontation and . . . getting dragged into a civil war." The Christian Democrats accepted, and then in the discussions called for the government to form a "Ministry with the institutional participation of the Armed Forces."[33] Institutional participation meant that the military ministers would be responsible, not to the president, but to the armed forces, who would determine policy. This proposal was an invitation to Allende to submit to a legal coup; he could then remain as a figurehead. As if this were not enough, the Christian Democrats also called for the immediate promulgation of their nationalization law and the restitution of "usurped industries" to their "legitimate owners." Allende resolutely rejected the Christian Democrats' terms, and the dialogue broke down within ten days.

To add to the government's problems, differences within the UP and the Left became even more numerous and strident than earlier. There were differences concerning what to do about the arms searches and the torture of imprisoned sailors, whether to try to infiltrate the armed forces, whether to enter into a dialogue with the Christian Democrats, whether to form a Cabinet which included Prats and other military men.

While Allende was searching for a way out of the desperate situation without surrendering, leaders of various *cordones* were announcing that to "deepen Popular Power" the factories seized by workers during the Souper uprising would not be returned regardless of the wishes of the government; and the MIR, to back this position, was organizing workers to set up barricades blocking roads and highways, including the highway from Santiago to the airport.

The true answer to Allende's call for a dialogue was given the day after he made it by the truck owners who began their second stoppage. Again, the goons attacked those trucks that continued to work, railroads were bombed, and people were wounded and killed. The government had even less strength for dealing with the problem than they had the previous October. The leaders of the stoppage spoke on television with arrogant assurance, like small boys acting tough because they know they will be protected by a strong older brother. They were in collusion with the CIA and the armed forces, and knew that their job was to keep the stoppage going until the coup.

A few days after the "dialogue" with the Christian Democrats broke down, Allende again formed a Cabinet containing military men. The Commanders-in-chief of the armed forces and the Director General of Carabineros were all incorporated into the Cabinet.

There was no contradiction between Allende's rejection of the military Cabinet proposed by the Christian Democrats and his formation of this one. This Cabinet was not based on the "institutional participation" of the armed forces, was not a disguised way of forming a new government controlled by them, but was rather a grasp at a possible way of strengthening the UP government. The presence of constitutionalists like Prats and Montero in the Cabinet might make it harder for the coupist officers to unite the officer corps behind a coup; the military presence might make it possible, as it had the previous October, to end the truckers' strike. Allende said that the new Cabinet constituted the last chance to avoid a confrontation.

But the situation differed from that of the previous October. The position of the constitutionalists, like Prats and Montero, had weakened. Montero had received a visit from his second in command, José Toribio Merino, along with the commander of the marines, Sergio Huidobro, during which they had asked him—"in the name of the Naval Council"—to resign as Commander-in-chief. And the army generals on the Committee of Fifteen opposed Prats' entering the Cabinet.

In fact, the Committee of Fifteen opposed any military men entering the Cabinet on the terms set by Allende. The policy of almost all its members resembled that of the Christian Democrats during the dialogue: "All or nothing"—the armed forces should enter the Cabinet only if given "complete responsibility to pacify the country;" otherwise they should "remain entirely outside the Government and await events." Allende was able to get the Commanders-in-chief into the Cabinet only by pressing them hard, and because Prats decided to join despite the wishes of the other generals. Montero followed, and General Ruiz Danyau of the air force, who had originally been opposed, decided that he could not stay out while the other two went in.[34]

In October there were many officers who did not object to the entry of military men into the Cabinet. They knew that since they were not yet ready to act, the stoppage would eventually have to be settled, and didn't mind Prats using his authority to settle it. Now, however, the coupists were finishing their preparations for a coup, which was to take place soon. They wanted the stoppage to continue. They not only wanted the Commanders-in-chief out of the Cabinet, but out of the way altogether. They wanted coupists in place as Commanders-in-chief to minimize the chances that when the coup came, the armed forces would split.

The day after the new Cabinet was announced, the Christian Democratic Party declared that it could not solve Chile's problems; only through the "institutional participation" of the armed forces with full powers could the "spiritual and material disarming" necessary to reestablish "normality" be attained.[35] A few days later, Frei carried the line a step further: "There is much talk," he said, "of coupism and fascism, but those who are endangering the rule of law . . . are those who have conducted the country to this crossroads. . . . Without a profound rectification, there will be no solution. . . . The problem is not that some want respect for the Constitution and others a coup. The problem is that no country in the world has been able to withstand such economic destruction without its stability being menaced." When he was accused of supporting a coup—of saying in effect that the government must give in or be overthrown—Frei indignantly rejected the accusation. Soon the National Party carried the line to its conclusion. It declared that all members of the Cabinet "without exception"—that is, including the military ministers— would be held responsible for the "grave deterioration in national security that persistence in Marxist action would involve," and repeated that it stood ready to vote in Congress the "illegitimacy" of the government.[36]

The first Commander-in-chief the coupists succeeded in getting rid of was Ruiz. Ruiz was a vacillator. He was opposed to the government, but as he had said at the first meeting of the Committee of Fifteen, he did not want to take the responsibility for leading a coup—if it came to that he would retire. He had opposed joining the Cabinet, but had joined when Prats and Montero decided to do so. Now, as minister of Public Works and Transport, he had the impossible task of dealing with the truckers strike. He didn't want to, nor could he settle it against the wishes of the powerful coupist officers. Yet if he didn't settle it, he would appear to be ineffective. Within ten days of becoming a minister, he told Allende he wanted to resign. When Allende responded that if he left the Cabinet, he would also have to give up command of the air force, he resigned both posts.

The coupist generals in the air force had earlier agreed not to accept a successor to Ruiz if Allende retired him as a result of his actions as minister; they were worried that Allende would try to "behead the Air Force," that is, try to place an anti-coupist at its head. But now they felt they were too strong for this to happen and saw a chance to replace Ruiz with someone more suitable to their purpose. So they went along with his retirement. Allende couldn't get any of the leading air force generals to accept the post of Commander-in-chief, except the decisively coupist Gustavo Leigh.

The coupists now went to work on Prats. The day Ruiz turned over his command, a crowd of 300 wives of officers of the

Santiago garrison marched on Prats's house to deliver a letter to his wife calling on her to intercede with him to end the "indecisive and confused attitude of the army toward Allende."[37]

The 300 constituted a high percentage of all the officers' wives in the garrison, and among them were a number of generals' wives. The demonstration was a means by which the officers could tell Prats, without themselves committing an open breach of discipline, that they no longer recognized his authority. The next day Prats called a meeting of the Generals' Council and asked the members to take a position on the demonstration. The majority refused to condemn it; several avoided taking a position; only a few supported Prats. Prats already had an idea of the correlation of forces within the army, having recently taken a trip to the garrisons in the south to sound things out. Now he concluded that his position was untenable, and submitted his resignation.

For the coupists, getting Prats out of the way was an important victory. Two other constitutionalist generals, Mario Sepúlveda, commander of the Santiago garrison, and Guillermo Pickering, director the the military institutes (Military School, Non-commissioned Officers School, etc.), also resigned during the Prats crisis. Pinochet was second in seniority after Prats, and Allende moved him from acting to titular Commander-in-chief. A year later Pinochet spoke about what this had meant: "When I was given the appointment on August 23 the decision [on the coup] crystallized."[38]

Within a day after Prats's resignation, Montero resigned as minister of finance, and reassumed his post as Commander-in-chief of the Navy. The Naval Council requested him to resign from this position also. But Allende refused to accept Montero's resignation, and he stoutly remained as nominal head of the navy. The real head was now the coupist second in command, José Toribio Merino.

IN the midst of the crisis over the Commander-in-chief, the Chamber of Deputies passed the resolution it had long been preparing on the "illegitimacy" of the government. The resolution stated that the "government has not committed isolated violations of the Law, but has made them a permanent system of conduct." It accused the government of "usurping the principal function of Congress . . . ," of "trying to undermine the authority of the judicial system . . . by leading a campaign of insults and calumnies against the Supreme Court," of violating the judgments of the Controller General's Office, of acting against liberty of expression, freedom of education, the autonomy of universities, etc.[39] Together with earlier statements—a joint declaration by the president of the Senate (Frei) and the Chamber of Deputies, and public letters by the head of the Supreme Court and by the controller general—which similarly accused the government of illegalities, this resolution was designed to create the moral basis for a coup.

To help create the proper psychological atmosphere, a terror campaign was carried out. One day an oil pipeline was blown up, another day, a bridge. One night several electric transmission towers were toppled—in the middle of a television address by Allende. Santiago and many other cities and towns, along with the surrounding countryside, were in darkness for an hour. My wife and I were reminded of the explosions and fires which took place in Havana in the weeks preceding the Bay of Pigs invasion.

El Mercurio now carried articles about "Djakarta," and on walls in Santiago appeared the words *Ya viene Djakarta* (Djakarta is coming). "Djakarta" referred to the slaughter, after the coup in Indonesia in 1965, of several hundred thousand persons "suspected of communist ties."

The UP's enemies—the U.S. government, the Chilean conspirators in political parties, business circles, and the armed forces—were now nearing the end of their preparations. They had waited a long time, not allowing the impatient ones among them to drag them into premature, unprepared action. They had waited until they could be sure that a coup was the only way of solving the problem, until the conditions for a coup were as good as they could ever hope them to be.

The sabotage of the economy had "made it scream." Frei had maneuvered the Christian Democratic Party into collaboration with the reactionary Nationals, and had swung around most of its hierarchy to support the overthrow of the government. The economic difficulties and the skillful exploitation of them by Frei and others had moved many Christian Democratic rank and filers to the right, creating among some a receptivity to a coup. The military coupists, having gotten rid of Prats, Sepúlveda, and Pickering, having isolated Montero and replaced the vacillating Ruiz with the fascist Leigh, now controlled the leading commands of the army, navy, and air force, as well as the garrison and other troop commands of Santiago.

Meanwhile, what was the government doing? It was valiantly trying to do what it could. As soon as he heard about the demonstration by the officers' wives at Prats's house, Allende called a meeting at the presidential residence, Tomás Moro, of generals supposedly loyal to the government to determine what to do. Allende decided to retire the generals whose wives had participated in the demonstration, and since this might provoke a military revolt, it was agreed to take other measures as well—to reinforce the Santiago garrison of the Carabineros, the service with the most favorable social composition, and to prepare a defense based on the collaboration of loyal troops and the trade unions. Later that night Allende called together the leaders of the UP parties and the CUT to inform them of the plan of action, and to have them get started on the necessary preparations. Agents of the government were charged with advising the non-coupist elements of the Christian Democrats.[40]

But the plan did not work. For it to work required that the generals whom Allende wished to retire be outnumbered. Prats's meeting with the Generals' Council showed that it was the government that was outnumbered—so much so that it was he, Sepúlveda, and Pickering who resigned. Allende's plan now depended even more heavily than earlier on Pinochet—the leader of the supposedly loyal generals who had met with Allende at Tomás Moro.

Allende asked Pinochet to reinstate Sepúlveda and Pickering in their commands—that is, not accept their resignations. Pinochet told him that this was impossible, and would run counter to regulations because these generals had committed a breach of discipline by abandoning their responsibilities before having properly handed in their resignations. Allende pressed Pinochet to retire the generals he suspected of complicity in coup preparations. Pinochet stalled, saying that to do so immediately could cause uncontrollable reactions in the army, and that it was necessary to wait for the next meeting of the Qualifications Committee, scheduled for the second half of September.

The situation was now far gone. Against the coordinated opposition of the Congress, the courts, the controller general, and now increasingly in the open, the armed forces, the government couldn't maintain public order, couldn't end the truckers' stoppage, couldn't stop the arms searches, and couldn't counter the maneuverings within the officer corps, which was obviously preparing for a coup.

One day in late August Jaime reviewed the situation for me. The correlation of forces is now overwhelmingly against us, he said. We can't prevent a coup and we don't have the strength to win a civil war. But the president won't surrender; they'll have to take him by force from the Moneda; we have to think of the future struggle—*y para eso tenemos que mantener las banderas en alto*—and for this we have to keep the banners high.

The coupists had now only to put the finishing touches on their preparations. In early September *El Mercurio* carried the headline "Allende's Resignation Requested." The story told of petitions demanding resignation being circulated in various parts of the country. In the following days *El Mercurio* worked away at the campaign with stories and pictures of people collecting signatures. The director of the opposition-controlled Channel 13 broadcast an editorial urging Allende to resign. My wife and I picked up Patria y Libertad leaflets on the streets. "Resign or commit suicide," read one; "resign or we'll kill you," read another.

On September 4 the UP held a demonstration to celebrate Allende's election victory three years earlier. The turnout was gigantic, the streets and avenues of central Santiago were jammed. We met friends; several noted that there was a touch of unreality in the demonstration. My wife and I overheard people comment that after such a manifestation of strength "they" would think twice before trying anything.

I spent the afternoon of Friday, September 7 with Jaime in his office at the Moneda. He had arranged, he told me, an office near his for me and I would be able to move in two weeks. Jaime then gave me an assignment: The president had decided to call a plebiscite I was to make an analysis of the different issues that could be presented to the people in a plebiscite and the advantages and disadvantages, from the UP point of view, of each one. He would also make an analysis and next week we would meet and put together a joint one.

When I got home, I couldn't resist phoning Jaime to say something that I knew he understood as well as I. "Jaime," I said, "things are moving fast; the announcement of the plebiscite should be made quickly; otherwise the other side may act first." Jaime chuckled, and said "I agree with you, Eddie, and the others are also convinced of the need for speed."

I never saw Jaime again. Four days later the coup struck. Like President Allende and many others, Jaime fought in the Moneda and died to keep the banners high for the future struggle.

14

Some Conclusions

When the UP took over the presidency, the correlation of forces favored its doing just that and then governing legally, not doing anything it pleased or taking full power. A majority of the people, including many who had voted against Allende, favored his being allowed to take office because he had won the election; among the officers of the armed forces there were many constitutionalists, some in leading commands, who, though they had no sympathy for the UP or socialism, felt the same.

Allende was therefore on strong ground when he threatened civil war against any attempt to keep him from taking office. Illegal action by the other side would have united both the Left and Center against it. But illegal action by the UP, even more so an attempt by it to take state power, would have united the Right and Center the other way; and with only 36 percent of the population and almost no revolutionary officers in the armed forces, the UP was not strong enough to fight this combination.

The basic problem of the UP was, in the course of the struggle, to change the correlation of forces in its favor—to build up its strength to where the enemy could not carry out a successful coup, where rather the UP itself would be able to win full power, eliminate the bourgeois state, and carry out the building of socialism to the end.

But so long as the UP had not succeeded—and it never did—in revolutionizing the bulk of the people and achieving a favorable correlation of forces, its strategy of acting within the law and trying not to provoke an armed struggle was correct. It is one thing to discard bourgeois law when the people are revolutionized enough to accept, even demand, such action; it is another to do so when it would mean creating additional enemies whom one cannot afford.

The unfavorable correlation of forces explains other aspects of the UP strategy, for example, its failure to arm the people and its attitude toward the various organs of people's power that sprang up. Some critics of the UP talk as though all that one had to do to arm the people was to drive some trucks through the streets and distribute weapons like Good Humor ice cream. But winning a government through an election does not automatically put one in a position to arm the people. Arming the people requires the appropriate circumstances and the force to be able to face the consequences of such action. Under the circumstances which held throughout the UP government's tenure, any serious attempt at arming the people would have immediately brought the armed forces into action against it.

The various organs of people's power that sprang up— *cordones,* Communal Commands, etc.—were instruments of direct mass struggle, created, somewhat like the Soviets of the Russian revolutions of 1905 and 1917, in defiance of existing law. Lenin described the role of Soviets in revolution as follows: "All the experience of both revolutions, that of 1905 and that of 1917 . . . may be reduced to the concept that the Soviet of Workers' and Soldiers' Deputies is a reality only as an instrument of insurrection. . . . Apart from this the Soviets are a meaningless plaything. . . ."[1]

The Mensheviks saw the Soviets differently, namely, as organs of local self-government, as democratized municipal governments. For Lenin, state power, to be won by insurrection, was the goal; unless the old government was overthrown the Soviets were bound to collapse. Despite the differences in circumstances, points analogous to Lenin's can be made for Chile. People's power could be significant to the extent that it could help in the winning of state power or in keeping the government from being overthrown. Winning local, partial power was not in itself sufficiently significant. Unless state power could be won, people's power would be limited in what it could do; and if the government fell, people's power would fall with it.

The people's power movement in Chile had a mixed character. On the one hand, the *cordones* and Communal Commands helped keep the economy going during the stoppages and took potentially important measures for defense against a coup. On the other, many of their leaders and members, though their rhetoric was super radical, were oriented in their practical thinking and action to the winning of bits of local or partial power, or to the solution of immediate problems. Some felt that people's power should act independently of the government, in disregard of its policies and problems, and often the *cordones* and commands undertook actions which injured the government by helping to create the climate desired by the coupists.

Often they would demand that the government do something that the correlation of forces made it inadvisable to do. So the government had to adopt an ambivalent attitude toward people's power, trying to make use of it wherever possible, but also trying to keep it acting within the strategy fixed by itself, within bounds fixed by the strength of the Left.

Many people on the Left did not see the problem of revolution in its totality. Some seemed to think that to move faster and further—to nationalize not only the monopolies, but smaller enterprises, or to move quickly to a radical-sounding educational reform—was *inherently* better, more revolutionary, regardless of political circumstances, than moving slowly and cautiously. Specialists wrote learned articles on the land reform, noting what was obvious—that it had many weaknesses; few addressed themselves to the real problem—how to achieve the political circumstances that would permit a better reform to be made.

"Advance Without Compromise" sounded revolutionary to some. But what if you don't have the force to do so? Every time Allende spoke of dialogue with the Christian Democrats there was an automatic outcry from some that this was the wrong policy, or even the prelude to a "betrayal." But what if your position is weak and a dialogue offers a possible way of improving it without betrayal?

A young professor studied a factory whose workers were militant and came back with the pronouncement, "The workers are ready. What is Allende waiting for? Why doesn't he suspend the Congress?" But one group of workers being ready doesn't mean everything is ready. In Petrograd on July 3, 1917, there was a huge armed demonstration of workers and soldiers demanding the transfer of power to the Soviets—many Petrograd workers and soldiers were "ready," but those of the provinces were not, and Lenin and the Bolshevik Party opposed an uprising.

Allende, leading not one party, but a coalition of parties, first six, then more, against stronger enemies, faced an unenviable task. He had to lead amidst constant contradictory pulls from the different parties, and even factions within parties, of the UP. For the last two years, he had to lead in the face of a clear weakening of the UP position which exacerbated the difficulties. Handling the disunity and lack of discipline with inexhaustible patience, sticking to his own realistic tactics, unafraid in the face of doctrinaire criticism to be flexible, to do the unusual, he led a defensive action with consummate tactical skill. With decades of experience in Chile's parliamentary system, he knew how to exhaust all its possibilities for twists and maneuvers. No matter how frequent or prolonged, how difficult or dangerous the crises—impeachment of ministers, truckers' stoppages, the Souper uprising, the looming final coup—he worked away coolly to find a solution. He remained calm and courageous to the end.

It is a commonplace, however, that one cannot win wars or revolutions with defensive actions alone. It is legitimate to be on the defensive occasionally, to gain time or to hold in one area while attacking in another. But to stay only on the defensive is to give the enemy the initiative, to leave the enemy with the power to decide when, where, and how to fight. To a great extent, this is what happened in Chile. And the enemy, which was stronger to begin with, bided its time, laid its preparations, explored different possible types of attack, and then struck.

It is essential to have a realistic respect for the correlation of forces and not unnecessarily provoke powerful enemies such as the Chilean armed forces or U.S. imperialism. But it is not the same to be dealing with an enemy who, if you don't provoke him, won't attack, as with one who, no matter what you do, unless you surrender, will sooner or later attack anyway.

Paradoxically, the very weakness of the UP government should have enforced on it not only sober caution, but also intelligent boldness. It started out weaker than the enemy, and unless it changed this relationship, it would sooner or later be overthrown. *Somehow, no matter what the difficulty, it had to find ways of increasing its force, of making itself the stronger.* To do this it should have been prepared to run risks. For the UP, also, was applicable the famous saying of the great French revolutionary, Danton, quoted by both Engels and Lenin: *"de l'audace, encore de l'audace, toujours de l'audace."**

The UP did not have a comprehensive, integrated strategy for gaining a superiority of force, for defending itself against a coup, or for winning full state power. It had a collection of half-coordinated separate strategies for gaining various pieces of power, but not for winning the central state power on which all else depended. It had a program for gaining additional economic power by the takeover of monopolies and the elimination of large estates, and it hoped by reducing the economic power of the bourgeoisie to weaken its political power.

The UP had something of a strategy for attaining a People's Assembly; but even assuming that such an assembly could have been attained without first solving the problem of the armed forces, a government with a People's Assembly would still not be immune from a coup. The various separate strategies could have been part of an overall strategy for defense against a coup and winning state power, but they did not by themselves constitute such a strategy. Crucial to the UP's problem of gaining a superiority of force were *the people* and *the armed forces;* and the UP strategy toward both suffered from weaknesses.

The UP did aim at winning over a majority of the people, feeling that such a majority would do many things for it—provide additional support for carrying out its program, enable it to call a plebiscite and establish a People's Assembly, and reduce the likelihood of a coup. But besides—perhaps inevitably given the undeveloped state of the revolutionary process—lacking a clear

* Translation, "Audacity, again audacity, always audacity."

vision of just how the winning of a majority would lead to the achievement of state power, the UP did not have a fully rounded strategy for winning a majority. It did not have a sufficiently strong conception of the necessity, methods, and goals of ideological struggle.

Many leaders of the UP seemed to feel that the mere carrying out of the program and the benefits this would bring would by themselves win over a majority of the people. They were far from altogether wrong in their emphasis on the program and its effects; people judge by action and results, not just by talk. But given the power of the UP's enemies to sabotage and the difficulties that inevitably accompany revolutionary transformation, it could not be expected that all would go well indefinitely, or that the results of the UP's actions could simply be allowed to speak for themselves. It was up to the UP leaders to explain the revolutionary struggle to the people, in simple, clear, concrete language and systematically, regularly, at every turn of events—to explain who the enemies of the revolution were, what they were up to, why problems and difficulties were arising, and what dangers loomed.

The UP missed a crucial opportunity in failing to boldly attack the U.S. government for what it was doing in Chile, in failing to counter the U.S. policy of "low profile"—of doing its dirty work as quietly as possible—with a policy of showing the people of Chile and the world exactly what the United States was up to.

The UP did not of course ignore the issue of imperialism. Allende spoke of the transnational corporations or explained that "foreign experts" were behind some rash of bombings. But usually he shied away from mentioning the U.S. government or explaining what it was doing. The UP took advantage of windfalls like the ITT papers and carried out a propaganda offensive for a few weeks; but then the opposition press succeeded in switching the discussion to other things. The UP never mounted a systematic, continuing anti-imperialist campaign, which could have explained not just the past villainy of the ITT, but the whole strategy of the U.S. government, what it was up to at each turn, and what it was likely to do in the future.

What did the UP gain by not attacking boldly? Did the U.S. government act any better than it would have otherwise? The issue of anti-imperialism was one of the UP's best issues: After all, that the U.S. government was working to overthrow it was no more than the truth. The UP could have hammered away with this truth, trying to stir up support in the United States and other foreign countries and—above all—to mobilize additional masses of Chileans to its side.

The UP also hampered itself by failing to attack Frei relentlessly, and the other Christian Democratic leaders who followed his line. What did the UP gain by not so attacking, except to leave Frei and his henchmen free to attack it, to help create conditions for the coup?

The UP aimed to win away Christian Democratic followers from their leaders—but the true goal was to win them away fully, not just to gain their support and the agreement of the party for some specific measure such as the nationalization of copper. The UP did gain Christian Democratic agreement to the nationalization of copper—how much did this help in the basic struggle? Even taking account of the need for negotiations with the Christian Democratic leaders, it was not necessary to refrain from attacking them; they attacked UP leaders, and yet the UP saw itself forced by its weakness to negotiate with them. The best way of getting the Christian Democratic leaders to negotiate and agree was not by being gentlemanly to them, but by creating a threat that if they didn't negotiate and agree, they would lose followers. A key means for winning over Christian Democratic followers was to tell the truth about their leaders.

The UP never provided the people with a coherent, overall understanding of the revolutionary struggle. When the UP leaders were faced with economism among the workers—a short-sighted emphasis on immediate demands at the expense of the struggle as a whole—they seemed unable to do more than exhort the workers to behave better, unable to explain to them why it was in their own interest to make some immediate sacrifices in exchange for the new future that a successful revolution would bring. Although the UP leaders often used the word fascism, they did not present a convincing explanation of how close it was or what it would mean concretely in the life of most Chileans.

The UP strategy toward the armed forces was also defensive. I was obviously correct to be careful with the officers, to try not to provoke them, meet their grievances about salaries, and involve them in economic tasks; it was correct to work to strengthen the position of the constitutionalists. But these policies did not come to grips with the fundamental problem of reducing and eventually eliminating the power of the officer caste. That caste was left with the power, provided it acted unitedly, to overthrow the government. They left the fate of the government dependent on the strength and devotion to legality of the constitutionalist officers. But given the class origins, training, and outlook of the officer caste, and the strains on constitutionalism that a revolutionary struggle was bound to produce, how far could one rely on the coupists not being able to win over enough wavering and constitutionalist colleagues to swing the bulk of the officer corps behind themselves? A revolution has to include a struggle for the armed forces. The UP government carried out this struggle on the too narrow front of trying to preserve the support of constitutionalist officers; it failed to make a determined effort to win over the men.

The effort to win over the men by the MIR and Altamirano came late and when circumstances were unfavorable; it was improvised and the resources behind it were minuscule. The effort could have begun with Allende's inauguration, when the coupists in the military were disconcerted by the assassination of Schneider and the accession of the UP to the Government. A well thought out plan, backed with appropriate resources, might have been put into effect.

Many types of action could have been considered for such a plan. Allende and the other leaders of the UP might have cultivated not just the officers, but also the men—referred in speeches not just to the "professionalism" of the officers, but also to the constitutionalism of the men, to their unwillingness to participate in a coup. It was important to start as soon as possible implanting the idea that coupist orders should not be obeyed, that true loyalty and discipline lay not in obeying them, but in disobeying them. Allende and the UP parties could have made themselves the champions of solving the many grievances of the men. And the UP might have done what the coupist officers and the opposition were afraid it would do—infiltrate the armed forces, spread democratic, anti-coupist, anti-fascist propaganda and create anti-coupist organizations among the men.

The task of winning over the men would have been delicate and risky. There are few things the coupist officers, and many other officers, would have reacted to as strongly as action attempting to reduce their control over the men. Improperly handled, such action might have caused difficulties with parts of the middle classes. Allende and the UP would have had to act with subtlety and a sense of timing, stressing the right issues, taking advantage of the right opportunities. But the issues were there: the prevention of a coup and fascism, and the democratization of the armed forces. So also were the opportunities: whenever a coup plot was discovered, when the ITT papers were published, and when Finch and Klein announced that the UP government did not have long to live.

Engels wrote that "in revolution, as in war, it is of the highest necessity to stake everything on the decisive moment, whatever the odds may be."[2] A similar logic applies to a decisive issue. For an issue as decisive as winning over the rank-and-file of the armed forces, the UP needed to have staked a great deal. To fail to act out of fear of the risks was to let the officer corps become the final arbiter of the struggle, was not really to avoid the risks, but to postpone them, to let them grow.

The ideological struggle and the struggle for the armed forces were related. Had the UP succeeded in winning over more of the people, and in creating among its followers more of a revolutionary consciousness and fervor, the task of winning over the men of the armed forces would have been easier. As it was, the political struggle had its repercussions in the barracks. A heightened revolutionary ferment among the people would have had still greater effects.

Another crucial element in the Chilean struggle was the economy. It was no accident that the UP gained votes during the first year when the economy improved, and then lost some afterwards when inflation accelerated and shortages spread. Inflation and shortages cost the UP potential support, and helped radicalize the wavering middle opposition against it. They weakened the UP in the armed forces. Although the basic causes of the economic difficulties lay outside the UP's control, there were also errors—

both in the management of the economy and in how the economic difficulties were presented to the people.

With its great dependence on one unstable export, its enormous foreign debt, its deep-rooted inflation combined with high unemployment and a low rate of growth, the economy inherited by the UP was particularly weak and vulnerable. The UP had to run this economy with only a minority in the Congress and in the face of savage opposition and sabotage. Yet the UP might have done more than it did, especially in the first year before inflation had gathered the momentum that kept making it ever harder to control.

The government's lack of revolutionary élan weakened its economic actions—for example, keeping it from taking advantage of its high prestige and morale during its early months to mount a revolutionary campaign against tax evasion. Those in the UP who held that financial problems were not real helped prevent it from shifting policy with promptness and decision when the danger of inflation became apparent. In the main, the government did all that could be done to meet the balance of payments problem, but it still was slow to control two or three categories of outlays. In the face of projections showing a widening deficit, it waited a year before suspending payments on the foreign debt and two and one half years before cutting outflows for foreign travel to the bone.

The government had to find ways of making the Congress either desist from sabotaging the economy, or bear the blame for the results. Here again the UP was weak in the ideological struggle. It sporadically called attention to the failure of Congress to provide adequate financing. But it did not mount a systematic campaign to explain the enemy's strategy of deliberately provoking inflation, to tell the people what would happen to the economy if the enemy's strategy were not stopped.

Actually, the government shied away from talking about coming economic problems, acting as though it would somehow manage to make things come out all right. This left it to opposition figures like Frei to predict future difficulties and then have events prove the predictions right; it made the government seem responsible for the difficulties. The government might have taken another course—enough confidence in the people to speak to them frankly of what lay ahead and try to derive political benefits from the very difficulties, by dramatizing the greatness of the people in their struggle with these problems.

Another failure of the UP was not getting all its elements to adhere to a clear conception of the best issues on which to do battle. Its best issues were those which could unite the great mass of Chileans against the main enemy—the fight against imperialism, the need to socialize the monopolies, the economic sabotage of the opposition, and the threat of a coup and fascism. Some elements of the UP, lacking a sense that a revolution is a process in which first things must come first, involved it unnecessarily in acutely divisive issues like the National Unified School, which presented the enemy with an excellent terrain on which to fight.

Finally, the UP made specific political errors, a key one being the failure to dissolve the Congress and call a plebiscite for a People's Assembly early in the UP regime when its prestige was high. This failure was not the result of just a simple mistake in judgment, but reflected many things—the difficulties of obtaining bold, decisive action from a coalition, a general failure to be ready to seize transient opportunities, and over-optimism about the future course of the economy.

Allende knew well that the UP government had committed errors. In a talk to the workers of a former Sumar textile plant on January 18, 1973, he summarized them:

"Not having renegotiated the Chilean foreign debt the day following his installation as president instead of in late 1971. . . .

"Not having explained at the proper time the imperialist reaction to Chile's sovereign action in nationalizing the big copper mines.

"Not having been aware that the Chilean process is much more difficult than those revolutionary processes which reached power after confrontation and armed struggle.

"Not having made an internal inventory of the critical economic situation which the popular government inherited in 1970.

"Not having submitted a bill immediately to dissolve the Congress . . . and if the bill had been rejected, to submit it to a plebiscite which the UP would have won.

"Not having sufficiently explained that the revolution is not a process of advantages for those who participate in it, nor a process which excludes sectors not on the UP side.

"Not having demanded more emphatically that the Chilean people and workers have a spirit of sacrifice."[3]

To note weaknesses in the UP strategy is not to say that the MIR, or any of the parties within the UP, had a better one—they didn't. The MIR and its allies within the UP were occasionally correct in a specific criticism of the government. But these critics did not have an alternative strategy that could come near matching that of the UP in appreciation of the possibilities and problems faced by an elected socialist movement—in realism, in flexibility, and in understanding of the need for mass support and unity.

The leftist encouragement of the illegal seizure of farms, or of the blocking of roads and the takeover of public buildings to enforce demands, helped create hostility to the UP among the middle classes, while it offered no promise of solving any of the basic questions of the revolutionary struggle. Such actions were sometimes defended on the ground that they helped mobilize the people and gave them a revolutionary consciousness. But these actions mobilized only a fraction of the people at the expense of winning over a majority, and what they instilled was not a true revolutionary consciousness but a spirit of indiscipline and anarchy and the delusion that revolutions can be carried out by vanguards alone. True revolutionary consciousness is not a matter of presenting absolute demands without regard to whether the time is right for them or not; it requires an understanding of the problems of the revolution and a sense of discipline.

The attempt of the leftists to create an alternative to the UP—made in the midst of the deadly revolutionary struggle—was a profoundly erroneous tactic. Aside from other reasons for not trying to set up such an alternative, there was, given the circumstances and the size and strength of the traditional left parties, no chance of doing so. Only harm could result from the attempt.

One of the great lessons of the Chilean struggle is an old one—the need for unity. The UP suffered from the multiple leadership, from a tendency for multiple strategies to spring up. The diversity was partly the result of Chilean history—one of multiple working class and people's parties. The weaknesses in the UP strategy contributed to disunity; different groups sensed them, saw the decline in the UP position, and looked for ways to improve the strategy. Alas, it proved to be easier to sense weaknesses in a strategy than to produce a better one. Contributing to disunity was a proliferation, among some sectors of the UP, of disgustingly pedantic, verbalistic "Marxist" analyses; people engaged in interminable disputations about words, while the enemy oiled its guns.

Yet there is another side. Just the establishment of the UP coalition was a great achievement. The UP parties strove to work together, and on the whole they did. They worked together under the terrible strains and dangers of a life or death struggle.

What would have happened if the UP had had a stronger strategy and had not committed the errors it did? I find this impossible to say. Actions have consequences that ripple out and cumulate. How can one tell all that would have happened if the UP had fought the ideological struggle more strongly, had begun early a determined effort to win over the troops, and had pressed for a People's Assembly in 1971? The main certainty is that the ruling class would still not have abandoned power voluntarily.

Was the Chilean struggle foredoomed, not worth even starting? One must try to answer not just by hindsight, which can give a misleading illusion of knowledge. Anyone who enters any struggle, including revolutionary struggle, runs the risk of losing. The Chilean Revolution is not the first to have momentarily lost. As Marx pointed out in a comment on the Paris Commune: "World history would indeed be very easy to make if the struggle were taken up only on condition of infallibly favorable chances."[4]

WAR, said Clausewitz,* is the continuation of politics by other means. Imperialist-sponsored coups, like those in Chile, Thailand, Uruguay, Brazil, Indonesia, and many other countries, are a continuation of ordinary, day-in, day-out intervention.

Great efforts are made to keep the people in the United States from learning about imperialist intervention, especially about the imperialist part in coups. For example, both before and after the coup in Chile, denials of U.S. intervention flowed freely:

- Edward M. Korry, U.S. ambassador to Chile from October

---

* Karl von Clausewitz, 1780–1831, Prussian general and writer on military strategy, of Polish descent.

1967 through October 1971: "The United States did not seek to pressure, subvert, influence a single member of the Chilean Congress at any time in the entire four years of my stay."[5]

• Charles A. Meyer, former assistant secretary of state for inter-American affairs: "We bought no votes, we funded no candidates, we promoted no coups."[6]

• Jack Kubisch, assistant secretary of state for inter-American affairs: "It is untrue to say that the U.S. Government was responsible either directly or indirectly for the overthrow of the Allende regime."[7]

• Henry Kissinger: "The CIA had nothing to do with the coup, to the best of my knowledge and belief, and I only put in that qualification in case some madman appears down there who without instruction talked to somebody."[8]

• *The New York Times* editorial: "In light of the disclosure last year of schemes by the Central Intelligence Agency and the International Telephone and Telegraph Corporation to block Dr. Allende's election in 1970 or to bring down his Government, Washington's denials of involvement in last weeks coup inevitably have encountered worldwide skepticism. . . . However, nothing so far uncovered indicates that the Nixon Administration seriously considered the bizarre C.I.A. and I.T.T. proposals; and there is no evidence of American complicity in the coup."[9]

• Paul E. Sigmund, director of graduate studies at Princeton, in an article in *Foreign Affairs:* "There appears to be no substantial evidence in the ITT papers or hearings of an effort by the government or by private companies or banks to create an economic crisis to prevent Allende from coming to power in 1970. . . . The term 'invisible blockade' appears something of an exaggeration when applied to the policies adopted by the U.S. Government in the last half of 1971. Pipeline credits and aid from multilateral lenders were not cut off; only new projects were 'deferred.' "[10]

Then, portions of the true story began to leak out:

• *The New York Times,* September 8, 1974: "The director of the Central Intelligence Agency has told Congress that the Nixon Administration authorized more than $8 million for covert activities by the agency in Chile between 1970 and 1973 in an effort to make it impossible for Salvador Allende . . . to govern. The goal . . . was to 'destabilize' the Marxist Government. . . . The testimony of Mr. Colby indicated that high officials in the State Department and White House repeatedly and deliberately misled the public and the Congress about the extent of United States involvement in the internal affairs of Chile. . . ."

- *The New York Times,* September 15, 1974: "Secretary of State Kissinger personally directed a far-reaching Nixon Administration program designed to curtail economic aid and credits to Chile after the election of Salvador Allende . . . , well-informed government sources said today. . . . After the election of Dr. Allende, Mr. Kissinger . . . took charge of a series of weekly interagency meetings at which Administration officials worked out a policy of economic sanctions . . . against Chile. . . . The sources emphasized that Mr. Kissinger's economic activities against the Allende Government were distinct from his involvement in clandestine CIA operations, although both programs were controlled by him with great secrecy. . . . Over the next two years, the Chilean Government was denied dozens of loans by the World Bank, a multinational loan agency over whose activities the United States has virtual veto power, and by the Export-Import Bank, a United States Government agency. In addition, Chile's short-term line of credit with private banks fell from $220 million in 1971 to less than $40 million a year later."

- President Ford, press conference, September 16, 1974:
"Q. Mr. President, recent Congressional testimony has indicated that the CIA, under the direction of a committee headed by Dr. Kissinger, attempted to destabilize the government of Chile under former President Allende. Is it the policy of your Administration to attempt to destabilize the governments of other democracies?
A. Our government, like other governments, does take certain actions in the intelligence field to help implement foreign policy and protect national security. . . . The effort that was made in this case was to help and assist the preservation of opposition newspapers and electronic media and to preserve opposition political parties."[11]

- *The New York Times,* September 20, 1974: Intelligence sources revealed today that "the majority of more than $8 million authorized for clandestine CIA activities in Chile was used in

1972 and 1973 to provide strike benefits and other means of
support for anti-Allende strikers and workers. . . . Among those
heavily subsidized . . . were the organizers of a nationwide truck
strike in 1972. . . . Direct subsidies . . . also were provided for a
strike of middle-class shopkeepers and a taxi strike among others,
that disrupted the capital city of Santiago in the summer* of 1973,
shortly before Mr. Allende was overthrown by a military coup. At
its [sic] peak the 1973 strikes involved more than 250,000 truck
drivers, shopkeepers, and professionals who banded together in a
middle-class movement that, many analysts have concluded,
made a violent overthrow inevitable."

The Senate Intelligence Committee has made public further
details, some of which have been mentioned earlier:[12]

• On September 15, 1970, "the CIA was instructed by President Nixon to play a direct role in organizing a military coup
d'etat in Chile to prevent Allende's accession to the Presidency."
(Ambassador Korry was separately instructed to encourage the
Chilean military to make a coup.[13])

• After Allende's inauguration: "Broadly speaking, U.S. policy sought to maximize pressures on the Allende government to
prevent its consolidation. . . . Other governments were encouraged to adopt similar policies. . . ."

• "The policy of economic pressure—articulated in NSDM
[National Security Decision Memorandum] 93 of November
1970—was to be implemented through several means. All new
bilateral foreign assistance was to be stopped, although disbursements would continue under loans made previously. The United
States would use its predominant position in international financial institutions to dry up the flow of new multilateral credit or
other financial assistance. To the extent possible, financial assistance or guarantees to U.S. private investment in Chile would be
ended, and U.S. businesses would be made aware of the government's concern and its restrictive policies."

• "The 40 Committee authorized nearly $4 million for opposition political parties in Chile. Most of this money went to the
Christian Democratic Party (PDC), but a substantial portion was
earmarked for the National Party (PN)."

* In Santiago, it was winter.

- The CIA spent $1.5 million in support of *El Mercurio;* its "propaganda project" produced magazines, books, and special studies, and developed material for placement in newspapers, and on radio stations and television shows; it financially supported an opposition research organization.

- "The CIA occasionally provided [Patria y Libertad] small sums through third parties for demonstrations or specific propaganda activity. . . . It is possible that CIA funds given to political parties reached Patria y Libertad. . . . Patria y Libertad forces marched at opposition rallies dressed in full riot gear. During the October 1972 national truckers strike, Patria y Libertad was reported to strew 'miguelitos' . . . on highways. . . ."

- "Throughout the Allende years, the United States maintained close contact with the Chilean armed forces, both through the CIA and through U.S. military attachés." The CIA engaged in a "deception operation" to arouse the military against "Allende's involvement with the Cubans;" and in a "short-lived effort to subsidize a small anti-government news pamphlet directed at the armed services. . . ."

- "During 1970–73, the Station collected operational intelligence necessary in the event of a coup—arrest lists, key civilian installations and personnel that needed protection, key government installations which need[ed] to be taken over, and government contingency plans which would be used in case of a military uprising. According to the CIA, the data was collected only against the contingency of future Headquarters requests and was never passed to the Chilean military."

- In October 1971 the "group which might mount a successful coup" came to the CIA Station's attention, and "by January 1972 the Station had successfully penetrated it and was in contact through an intermediary with its leader. . . . It is clear that the CIA received intelligence reports on the coup planning of the group which carried out the successful September 11 coup throughout the months of July, August, and September 1973."

- "The CIA's information gathering efforts with regard to the Chilean military included activity which went beyond the mere collection of information. More generally, those efforts must be viewed in the context of United States opposition, overt and covert, to the Allende government. They put the United States Government in contact with those Chileans who sought a military alternative to the Allende presidency."

A final question and answer from the Senate Intelligence Committee has found no evidence that it was." Before taking up this point it is well to remind ourselves that the committee, Committee has found no evidence that is was." Before taking up this point it is well to remind ourselves that the committee, notwithstanding the information it has made public, is part of the imperialist establishment and contains reactionary members like Senators John Towers and Barry Goldwater. The committee did not reveal information on its own. Its reports, including that on Chile, were "all carefully considered *by the committee and the executive branch working together* to determine what information could be declassified and revealed without damaging national security."[14]

The committee's apparent candor didn't spring from the blue, but was a reaction to already existing worldwide knowledge concerning U.S. intervention in Chile and other countries. We must not let this apparent candor so bedazzle us that we docilely follow the committee to whatever conclusions it chooses to lead us. The committee's conclusions—concerning U.S. actions in the Congo, Santo Domingo, Cuba, South Vietnam, and Chile—fall into a pattern: They absolve the United States and the CIA of the worst. For example, the CIA may have planned assassinations or may have been involved in kidnapping plots; it may have passed weapons to the plotters; but somehow the U.S. plans and plots were never successfully consummated, and when a target was killed, it was not "as a result of assassination plots initiated by officials of the United States."[15]

Why did the committee ask, "Was the United States *directly* involved?" instead of some other question such as "Did the United States conspire to make a coup?" Obviously, because the first question lends itself to seemingly meaningful denial. What does the word *directly* mean here? How far into the process of preparing conditions for a coup does the United States have to go before the committee considers that it is directly involved? How would the United States fare if it were judged according to its own criminal code which holds that "whoever commits an offense against the United States or aids, abets, counsels, commands, induces or procures its commission is punishable as a principal?"[16]

Even if, for the sake of argument, we go along with the committee's artificially narrow use of the term "direct involvement," we can still ask, what are the chances of its finding the evidence, and of its publishing the conclusions if it did so? It helps to understand the problem of evidence of "direct involvement" to have an idea of how the imperialists go about making coups. We can obtain such an idea from the coup against Ngo Dinh Diem of South Vietnam in 1963, which because of the publication of the Pentagon Papers is well-documented.

Making it difficult to find the evidence of imperialist complicity is part of the art of imperialist coup-making; great attention is devoted to this from the earliest planning. Months before the actual coup in South Vietnam, Ambassador Henry Cabot Lodge, who managed it, decided that the "American official hand should not show."[17] Later the White House cabled Lodge: "Essential that this effort be totally secure and fully deniable. . . . In order to provide plausibility to denial suggest you and no one else in Embassy issue . . . instructions orally to Acting [CIA] Station Chief and hold him responsible to you alone for making appropriate contacts and reporting to you alone. . . ." Also: "We should avoid being drawn into reviewing or advising on operational plans or any other act which might tend to identify U.S. too closely with change in government." Still later Lodge cabled the White House: "We are . . . considering the feasibility of a plan for the introduction of an additional officer as a cutout [intermediary] between Conein and a designee of General Don. . . . I believe that our involvement to date through Conein is still within the realm of plausible denial. CAS [Code for CIA] is perfectly prepared to have me disavow Conein at any time it may serve the national interest."

The Pentagon Papers' account is also of interest for what it tells us about how the coup was made. The U.S. government arranged the coup. As the Pentagon historian puts it: "We variously authorized, sanctioned, and encouraged the coup efforts of the Vietnamese generals and offered full support for a successor government. . . . We cut off aid to Diem in a direct rebuff. . . ."[18]

But the actual carrying out of the coup was done by the Vietnamese generals. The United States did no more than it needed to.

Just as after the coup in Chile, U.S. complicity was denied. Lodge gave a press interview denying U.S. involvement. Arthur M. Schlesinger, Jr., special assistant to President Kennedy at the time of the coup, wrote: "It is important to state clearly that the coup of November 1, 1963 was entirely planned and carried out by the Vietnamese. Neither the American Embassy nor the CIA were involved in instigation or execution."[19]

In the light of this background, read the following denial by Assistant Secretary of State, Jack Kubisch, before a House subcommittee on U.S. complicity in the Chilean coup, remembering that according to the Senate Intelligence Committee, the CIA station in Santiago had by January 1972 "penetrated" the group which "might mount a successful coup" and was "in contact through an intermediary with its leader."

"Mr. Fascell (Dante B., Chairman, Dem. Florida). If the United States did not participate directly or indirectly, what assurances or committments were given to the Chilean military . . . ? Were any indirect or direct assurances given to the organizers and leaders of the coup by this government?

Mr. Kubisch. By U.S. officials?

Mr. Fascell. By the U.S. government.

Mr. Kubisch. To the best of my knowledge and belief, Mr. Chairman, no assurances of any kind were given because there was no direct contact by the organizers and leaders of the coup with U.S. officials. This is not to say that there may not have been speculation and lower-level contacts, such as, what do you think, Mr. U.S. official—whoever he was—would be the attitude of the U.S. government, and the people of the United States, and the Congress of the United States, and the press of the United States, if there were a coup, if the military intervened. That kind of speculation may have taken place but, as far as any official contact by the leaders and organizers of the coup . . . with U.S. officials and any kind of assurances, I know of none and I believe absolutely that there was none."[20]

Note the weaseling. There were no "direct" contacts by "organizers and leaders" with "U.S. officials." Lower-level

American officials may have talked about the "attitude of the U.S. government . . . if there were a coup" but this would not be "official," just "speculation." (Remember Lodge's care to work through intermediaries, his readiness to disavow Conein.)

In Chile, as in South Vietnam, the United States did no more than it needed to do; and regardless of how much or how little it entered into operational planning of the military aspect of the overthrow of the Allende government, it was not only involved in that overthrow—*it was the principal force behind it.* The overthrow consisted of much more than the final military action. It was a long, complicated operation involving mobilization of anti-UP forces, and economic, political, and psychological as well as military warfare.

The U.S. government was the first organized force to press for a coup—right after Allende's election; and for a while after the collapse of the Viaux plot when the Chilean enemies of the UP were in disarray, it was the only organized anti-UP force. With its power and experience, its worldwide organization, its network of secret agents, and its broad influence in Chile, the U.S. government was crucial to the elaboration and execution of a scientific strategy for keeping the UP government from succeeding.

Abroad it could suggest to other governments that they work to prevent the UP government's consolidation; to bankers, that they cut off credit; to suppliers, that they drag their feet; to copper companies, that they sue. In Chile, it could encourage, mobilize, and organize the opposition. It could give money to newspapers and plant stories in them; buy radio stations for opposition parties; promote and subsidize seditious strikes; fan divisions on the Left; and provide experts on psychological warfare and terrorism in which the Chileans lacked experience. It could use its money, prestige, and power to keep discipline and adherence to a central strategy among the internal enemies of the UP—to keep the impatient ones from making a "premature" coup when other possibilities still existed, to rally wavering elements behind a coup when that became "the only way out." The U.S. government could through "lower level," "indirect" contacts let the coupist officers know what they could expect from the United States after the coup.

What the coupists were led to expect is what they got—

support. The Senate Intelligence Committee reports: "The goal of covert action immediately following the coup was to assist the Junta in gaining a more positive image, both at home and abroad. . . . Another goal . . . was to help the new government organize and implement new policies. Project files record that CIA collaborators were involved in preparing an initial overall economic plan which has served as the basis for the Junta's most important economic decisions. . . . Two CIA collaborators assisted the Junta in preparing a *White Book of the Change of Government in Chile*. . . . The CIA renewed liaison relations with the Chilean government's security and intelligence forces. . . . Officials acknowledged that, while most of CIA's support to the various Chilean forces would be designed to assist them in controlling subversion from abroad, the support could be adaptable to the control of internal subversion as well."[21]

WHY did the imperialists and their local allies establish an open terrorist dictatorship in Chile? Because that was the only way they could maintain their rule. What happened in Chile was coup, not against a small ruling clique, but against the majority of the people of Chile. To rule against the mass of the people takes repression and terror. The need for repression and terror was cold-bloodedly understood by the imperialists, as shown by testimony before a House subcommittee by CIA head William Colby. "Throughout his testimony," wrote Tad Szulc, "Colby drew a grim picture of the junta's repression and, in effect, predicted that it would worsen because of the continued strength of the Chilean left. . . . Colby told the subcommittee that 'concern over security undoubtedly is what accounts for the junta's continued use of harsh measures to deal with dissidents. The military leaders apparently are willing to alienate some support at home and endure a bad press abroad, in order to consolidate their hold on the country and finish the job of rooting out Marxist influence.' " When Rep. Robert H. Steele stated that the junta killings have "done no one any good," Colby replied: "I think *our appreciation is that it does do them some good*. . . . The junta, their concern is whether they could take this action of taking over the government and not generate a real civil war, which was the real chance because the Allende supporters were fairly active."[22]

The problem goes beyond Chile. The rule of imperialism is being threatened throughout the third world and it has had to resort to the establishment of fascism in many countries. Several hundred million people—in Indonesia, Brazil, South Korea, and elsewhere—live under imperialist-sponsored fascist regimes. Presumably, the CIA evaluates the need for fascism—for repression, torture, and murder—the same way as it does in Chile.

The developed capitalist countries, including those with the longest democratic tradition, are not immune to the fascist plague. For thirty years after World War II these countries succeeded in containing their economic problems. But now a period of economic crisis has set in, and economic crises have political repercussions.

The United States is not immune. The case of Chile provides a glimpse of the fascism latent in a monopoly-dominated United States government. The highest U.S. officials—the president, the secretary of state, the members of the National Security Council—authorized or participated in actions which meant the replacement of democracy by fascism in a foreign country. A number of members of Congress knew what was going on; or if they didn't, it was because they didn't want to because the knowledge might prove embarrassing. If these officials react this way when peripheral interests are threatened, what will they do as the threat moves closer to vital areas?

That imperialism has had to resort more and more to fascism is a sign of its deterioration—over a growing area it can no longer maintain itself in the old way. On a world scale also, the correlation of forces is crucial; and the world correlation of forces is inclining against imperialism. Against the defeat in Chile must be placed the great people's victories, like Cuba, Vietnam, and Angola, and the eruption of difficulties for imperialism everywhere. Even where it succeeds in staving off the advance of the people by establishing fascism, its "victory" is the transitory victory of a system retreating and crumbling.

Fascism in Chile has unified the people against itself. The fascist regime is forced to struggle desperately against international isolation. What has happened in Chile gives an idea of the additional forces the imperialists will let loose against themselves throughout the world as they turn to fascism in their attempt to hold on.

DOES the Chilean experience tell us that the "electoral road to socialism" is to be rejected, that the only way for socialist revolutionaries is to proceed directly to armed struggle? The answer is no.

The problem is not whether a socialist revolution can be made by electoral means alone, but whether electoral means can play a part in the revolutionary process, whether it is possible to carry through to a successful conclusion a revolutionary process started with an election. The theory developed by Marx and Lenin that to make a socialist revolution the people must win state power and eliminate the bourgeois state machinery is profoundly true and important. But there is far more to Marx, Lenin, and revolution than just the theory of the state. There is also the problem of how the people can build the movement and gather the force that will enable them to win state power and eliminate the bourgeois state machinery.

In a struggle that takes place in many different countries, under different circumstances, and at different times, there have to be many different ways of meeting this problem. But all the different ways have one point in common: The revolutionaries must win the people because the people are the main force in revolution. Winning the people requires understanding them, fighting for and side-by-side with them in the struggles they are themselves engaged in. In countries with bourgeois democratic systems, winning the people requires working with many means, including electoral means.

Engels once wrote: "In election agitation [universal suffrage] provided us with a means, second to none, of getting in touch with the mass of the people where they still stand aloof from us. . . ."[23]

And Lenin wrote: "If you want to . . . win the sympathy and support of the 'masses,' you . . . must absolutely *work wherever the masses are to be found*." Speaking of the left Communists in Germany who held that parliamentary forms of struggle have become "historically and politically obsolete," Lenin said: "It is obvious that the 'Lefts' in Germany have mistaken *their desire,* their politico-ideological attitude for objective reality. . . . we must *not* regard what is obsolete *to us* as something obsolete *to a class, to the masses.* . . . Even if only a fairly large *minority* of the industrial workers . . . follow the lead of the Catholic clergy . . . it undoubtedly signifies that parliamentarianism in Germany has *not yet* politically outlived itself, that participation in parliamentary elections and in the struggle on the parliamentary rostrum is *obligatory* on the party of the revolutionary proletariat *specifically* for the purpose of educating the backward strata of *its own class,* and for the purpose of awakening and enlightening the undeveloped, downtrodden and ignorant rural *masses.* Whilst you lack the strength to do away with bourgeois parliaments and every other type of reactionary institution, you *must* work within them. . . ."[24]

But if revolutionary parties participate in elections and parliaments, the possibility exists that they will win the right to take over the executive arm of the government. Should they not try to win this right? Winning the right to a government by election is not the same as winning state power, but it is still a great step forward. The question is not just state power, but whether winning the right to the government advances the revolutionary process.

Winning the right to a government by election does not guarantee a revolutionary movement that it will be allowed to govern. But the Chilean experience does not warrant the conclusion that an elected revolutionary government must inevitably be overthrown. What it does illustrate is that it must be prepared to back with force its right to govern.

The "electoral road" may open up in another country under circumstances different from those in Chile. Instead of winning with only 36 percent of the vote, a revolutionary party or coalition might win with 55 or 60 percent. The revolutionaries might control not only the executive arm of the government, but also the parliament. No armed forces are above classes, but the situation in some other country's armed forces might be different; for example, a portion of its troops and officers might have been radicalized by a colonial war or a sharp economic crisis. These different circumstances could enhance the possibility of victory.

A word on the economy. For a socialist government without state power to run the economy is simply not the same as for one that possesses state power; and it is devilishly difficult. Yet it would be a mistake to conclude that it must always be as difficult as in Chile, and that the results must be similar. The many variations in power short of state power can affect the ability of the government to manage the economy. The economic circumstances faced by another elected socialist government might be different. The economy might be less dependent on external factors, less vulnerable to economic warfare from abroad.

As Goethe said:

> Gray, dear friend, is all theory
> And green life's golden tree.

The Chilean experience must be interpreted not pedantically, but creatively. We have now had socialist revolutions in a large number of countries under different circumstances. Each new socialist revolution broadens our vision of how such revolutions can occur. They have arisen in the midst of world war as in Czarist Russia, or in peacetime out of the struggle against a bloody dictator as in Cuba; they have taken the form of short urban insurrection as in Russia or protracted guerilla warfare as in China and Vietnam. But so far there has been no successful socialist revolution among the great bourgeois democracies. How will the socialist revolutions be made in these countries? The crisis of capitalism is many-sided, and there are many possible ways. One is the "electoral road," a way that would flow from the democratic tradition and system of a number of countries, from the actual political life of their peoples. Chile was a first. Its road will probably be taken by other countries regardless of the tut-tutting of pedants.

To the leaders and members of the UP belongs a great historic honor—they broke new ground. Only by pondering how difficult and significant breaking new ground is, can one truly understand the Chilean experience.

The Chilean Revolution is part of a long historic process with both a past and a future. The immortal Neruda, in his poem "Recabarren," written years before the coup, talks of Chile's experience since the time of its first socialist revolutionary leader:

> How much has happened since then.
> How much blood on top of blood,
> how many struggles on the earth.
> Hours of splendid conquest,
> triumphs won drop by drop,
> periods of bitterness, defeats,
> times as dark as tunnels,
> betrayals which seemed
> to cut life short with their knife edge,
> repressions armed with hatred,
> crowned militarily.
> The earth seemed to sink.
> But the struggle remains.*

For the future struggle, the Chilean Revolution leaves a vision of a government that fought for the people and socialism, of the great revolutionary president who never buckled, of leaders and members of all parties of the Left who resisted fascism at the cost of death or imprisonment and torture.

The struggle Chile faces against fascism is arduous and bitter. But the Chilean people will no more accept fascism than the indomitable Araucanians accepted the rule of the Spanish intruder. And the junta cannot, despite the foaming of its General Leigh, "extirpate" Marxism in Chile; Marxism is too firmly rooted there. Marxism can do something the imperialists for all their resources, cunning, and experience with coups can never do—solve the problems of the people.

Allende's last political actions were directed to the future struggle. He knew that fascism would call forth resistance, would unite the great majority of the people against it. He sent several companions out of the besieged Moneda on missions in behalf of resistance; he emphasized the need to work for a united political

* Author's translation

leadership for that resistance. His last words to the Chilean people will prove to be prophetic:

I have faith in Chile and its destiny. Others will surmount this gray, bitter moment in which treason seeks to impose itself. You must go on, knowing that sooner rather than later the grand avenues will open along which free men will pass to build a better society.

Reference Notes

Preface

1. Volodia Teitelboim, "Prelude to Future Victories," *World Marxist Review,* March 1974, p. 83.
2. Ibid., p. 83.

1 A Personal Introduction

1. *Fidel in Chile,* International Publishers, New York, 1972, p. 207.
2. K. Marx and V.I. Lenin, *Civil War in France: The Paris Commune,* International Publishers, New York, 1940.

2 Bits of Background

1. Francisco A. Encina, *Resumen de la historia de Chile,* 3 volume edition edited by Leopoldo Castedo, Zig Zag, Santiago, 1959, Vol. 1, p. 33.
2. Luis Galdames, *A History of Chile,* Russel and Russel, New York, 1969, p. 91.
3. Ibid., pp. 58–59.
4. Encina-Castedo, op. cit., Vol. 1, p. 75.
5. Frederick B. Pike, *Chile and the United States, 1880–1962,* University of Notre Dame Press, Notre Dame, Indiana, 1963, pp. 290–91.
6. George M. McBride, *Chile: Land and Society,* American Geographical Society, New York, 1936, p. 110.
7. Ibid., p. 83.
8. Miguel Cruchaga, "Estudio sobre la organización económica y la Hacienda Pública de Chile, 1878" as quoted in Aníbal Pinto, *Chile, un caso de desarrollo frustrado,* Editorial Universitaria, Santiago, 1962, p. 14.
9. McBride, op. cit., p. 121.

10. U.S. Department of Commerce, *Investment in Chile*, U.S. Government Printing Office, Washington, D.C., 1960, pp. 56–57.
11. Ibid., p. 58.
12. Claude G. Bowers, *Chile Through Embassy Windows: 1939–1953*, Simon and Schuster, 1958, p. 25.
13. Elisabeth Reiman and Fernando Rivas, *La lucha por la tierra*, Empresa Editora Nacional Quimantú, Santiago, 1971, pp. 15–16.
14. Frank W. Fetter, *Monetary Inflation in Chile*, Princeton University Press, Princeton, 1931, p. vii.
15. Francisco A. Encina, *Historia de Chile*, 20 volume edition, Editorial Nascimiento, Santiago, 1945, Vol. 5, p. 264.
16. Hernán Ramírez Necochea, *Historia del imperialismo en Chile*, Editora Austral, Santiago, 1969, p. 46.
17. Ibid., p. 58.
18. Ibid., p. 103.
19. Sociedad de Fomento Fabril, quoted in Hernán Ramírez Necochea, *Balmaceda y la contrarrevolución de 1891*, Editorial Universitaria, Santiago, 1958, p. 109.
20. Julio Cesar Jobet, *Ensayo crítico del desarrollo economico-social de Chile*, Editorial Universitaria, Santiago, 1955, p. 87.
21. Ramírez, *Balmaceda y la contrarrevolucion de 1891*, p. 195.
22. Ibid., p. 198.
23. Ramírez, *Historia del imperialismo en Chile*, pp. 238–42.
24. Eduardo Novoa Monreal, *La batalla por el cobre*, Empresa Editora Nacional Quimantú, Santiago, 1972, p. 17.

3 From González Videla to Allende

1. Bowers, op. cit., pp. 161–62.
2. Edwin Lieuwen, *Arms and Politics in Latin America* (Revised edition), Frederick A. Praeger, New York, 1961, p. 222.
3. *Covert Action in Chile, 1963–1973*, Staff Report to the Select Committee to Study Governmental Operations with Respect to Intelligence Activities, United States Senate, U.S. Government Printing Office, Washington, D.C., 1975, p. 18.
4. Sergio Ramos Cordova, *Chile: ¿una economia de transicion?*, Casa de las Américas, La Habana, 1972, pp. 97–99.
5. Francisco A. Encina, *Nuestra inferioridad económica*, Editorial Universitaria, Santiago, 1955, pp. 76–77.
6. Dale Johnson, editor, *The Chilean Road to Socialism*, Anchor Books, New York, 1973, pp. 19, 399–400.
7. Eduardo Labarca Goddard, *Chile invadido*, Editora Austral, Santiago, 1968, pp. 54–56.
8. *Covert Action in Chile, 1963–1973*, op. cit., p. 16.
9. Ibid., pp. 9, 15–16.
10. Ibid., p. 17.
11. Michael T. Klare, *War Without End*, Vintage Books, New York, 1972, p. 308.
12. *New Chile*, North American Congress on Latin America, New York and Berkeley, 1973, pp. 57–58.
13. *Covert Action in Chile, 1963–1973*, op. cit., p. 17.
14. Ibid., p. 19.

15. Ibid., p. 9.
16. Giles Wayland Smith, *The Christian Democratic Party in Chile*, Sondeos, no. 39, Gentro Intercultural de Documentación, Cuernavaca, Mexico, 1969, p. 2/7.
17. Quoted in Ernst Halperin, *Nationalism and Communism in Chile*, M.I.T. Press, Cambridge, Massachusetts, 1965, p. 196.
18. *Primer mensaje del Presidente de la Republica de Chile, don Eduardo Frei Montalva, al inaugurar el periodo de Sesiones Ordinarias del Congreso Nacional, 21 mayo 1965*, p. 6.
19. Ibid., pp. 8–10, 21–26, 61, 65–66.
20. Gonzalo Martner, editor, *El pensamiento económico del Gobierno de Allende*, Editorial Universitaria, Santiago, 1971, pp. 187–89.
21. Eduardo Novoa Monreal, op. cit., pp. 50–51.
22. Ibid., pp. 67–68.
23. Ibid., pp. 75–84.
24. *Primer mensaje del Presidente de la Republica de Chile*, op. cit., p. 50.
25. Ley no. 16,640, Reforma Agraria 1967 (official text), Mario Barrientos Contreras, distributor, Santiago, 1967, Articles 3 and 4.
26. Ibid., Articles 16 and 30.
27. Wilson Cantoni, "Poder popular en el agro chileno," *Cuadernos de la Realidad Nacional*, Santiago, enero 1972, p. 81.
28. Organization of American States, Inter-American Committee on the Alliance for Progress (CIAP), OAS/Official Records/Ser. H/XIV CIAP 468, "Report on the Economy of Chile," Washington, D.C., Feb. 16, 1971, p. 11.
29. Oficina de Planificación Nacional (ODEPLAN), *Informe económico anual 1970*, Editorial Universitaria, Santiago, 1971, p. 10.
30. *Covert Action in Chile, 1963–1973*, op. cit., p. 17.
31. Patricio Manns, *Las Grandes Masacres*, Empresa Editora Nacional Quimantú, Santiago, 1972, pp. 71–79.
32. Alain Labrousse, *L'Expérience Chilienne: Réformisme ou Révolution?*, Editions du Seuil, Paris, 1971, pp. 145–46.
33. Quoted in Eduardo Novoa Monreal, op. cit., p. 111.

4 Constitutionality—Myth and Reality

1. Edwin Lieuwen, op. cit., pp. 168–69.
2. V.I. Lenin, *State and Revolution*, International Publishers, New York, 1943, pp. 8–9. (Emphasis in the original.)
3. Encina-Castedo, op. cit., Vol. 2, p. 837.
4. Quoted in Julio César Jobet, op. cit., p. 33.
5. Frederick B. Pike, op. cit., p. xxv.
6. Hernán Ramírez Necochea, *Historia del movimiento obrero en Chile*, Editora Austral, Santiago, no date given, p. 214.
7. Ricardo Donoso, *Alessandri, agitador y demoledor, Cincuenta años de historia política de Chile*, Fondo de Cultura Económica, Mexico-Buenos Aires, 1952, p. 156.
8. Hernán Ramírez Necochea, *Origen y formación del Partido Comunista de Chile*, Editora Austral, Santiago, 1965, pp. 186–238, passim.
9. Fernando Casanueva Valencia y Manuel Fernández Canque, *El Partido Socialista y la lucha de clases en Chile*, Empresa Editora Nacional Quimantú, Santiago, 1973, pp. 101–02.
10. Ibid., p. 112.

11. John Reese Stevenson, *The Chilean Popular Front,* University of Pennsylvania Press, Philadelphia, 1942, p. 72.
12. Sergio Guilisasti Tagle, *Partidos políticos chilenos,* Editorial Nascimiento, Santiago, 1964, p. 314.
13. Documentos del XIII Congreso del Partido Comunista de Chile, 1965, Folleto no. 2, *La unidad socialista comunista, cimiento del movimiento popular,* pp. 10, 25, 27.
14. *El Programa de la Unidad Popular.*

5 Between Election and Inauguration

1. *Covert Action in Chile, 1963–1973,* op. cit., pp. 19, 20, 22.
2. Ibid., p. 13.
3. Victor Marchetti and John Marks, *The CIA and the Cult of Intelligence,* Dell Publishing Co., New York, 1974, p. 39.
4. Dirección del Registro Electoral, as given in Dieter Nohlen, *Chile, Das Sozialistische Experiment,* Hoffman und Campe Verlag, Hamburg, 1973, p. 132.
5. *El Mercurio,* Sept. 7, 1970.
6. Ibid., Sept. 9, 1970.
7. Quoted in Luis Vitale, *¿Y después del 4, qué?,* Editorial Prensa Latinoamericana, Santiago, 1970, pp. 55–57.
8. Senate Committee Hearings on *The International Telephone and Telegraph Company and Chile, 1970–1971,* U.S. Government Printing Office, Washington, D.C., 1973, Part 1, pp. 582–86.
9. Ibid., Part 1, p. 102.
10. Ibid., Part 2, pp. 542–43.
11. *Alleged Assassination Plots Involving Foreign Leaders,* Interim Report of the Senate Intelligence Committee, U.S. Government Printing Office, Washington, D.C., 1975, p. 227.
12. *Covert Action in Chile,* op. cit., p. 23.
13. ITT Hearings, op. cit., Part 2, p. 608.
14. *Covert Action in Chile, 1963–1973,* op. cit., p. 26.
15. ITT Hearings, op. cit., Part 2, p. 610. (Emphasis in the original.)
16. Ibid., p. 611. (Emphasis in the original.)
17. *Alleged Assassination Plots Involving Foreign Leaders,* op. cit., p. 228.
18. ITT Hearings, op. cit., Part 2, pp. 626–27. (Emphasis in the original.)
19. Ibid., p. 622. (Emphasis in the original.)
20. Speech to the Plenum of the Central Committee of the Socialist Party on Oct. 11, 1970. *Prensa Latina* dispatch, Oct. 12, 1970.
21. Michael J. Harrington, "The CIA in Chile: A Question of Responsibility," *The New York Times,* Jan. 2, 1976.
22. *Alleged Assassination Plots Involving Foreign Leaders,* op. cit., p. 233.
23. Ibid., pp. 239–40.
24. Florencia Varas, *Conversaciones con Viaux,* 1972 (no publisher given) and Patricio García, editor, *El caso Schneider,* Editora Nacional Quimantú, Santiago, 1972.
25. Florencia Varas, op. cit., pp. 126, 128.
26. Patricio García, op. cit., p. 172.
27. Florencia Varas, op. cit., pp. 127, 132–133.
28. Ibid., p. 135.

29. Allende's Victory Speech, *Prensa Latina* dispatch, Sept. 5, 1970.
30. *El Mercurio*, Sept. 15, 1970.
31. *El Mercurio*, Sept. 14, 1970.
32. Press conference, *Prensa Latina* dispatch, Sept. 6, 1970.
33. Ibid.
34. ITT Hearings, Part 2, p. 660.
35. *El Mercurio*, Oct. 9, 1970.
36. "The Dual Power" from V.I. Lenin, Collected Works, Vol. 24, Progress Publishers, Moscow, 1964, p. 38.
37. *El Mercurio*, Oct. 9, 1970.
38. Ibid.
39. Florencia Varas, op. cit., p. 139.
40. *The New York Times*, July 24, 1975.
41. *El Mercurio*, Nov. 4, 1970.

6 Tactics and Strategy

1. Sergio Ramos Córdova, op. cit., pp. 287–88.
2. Alain Labrousse, op. cit., p. 215.
3. "Left-Wing Childishness and Petty-Bourgeois Mentality" from V.I. Lenin, *Selected Works in One Volume*, International Publishers, New York, p. 434.
4. Augusto Pinochet, *Síntesis geográfica de Chile*, 1955, (no publisher given), p. 9.
5. *Covert Action in Chile*, op. cit., p. 36.
6. Quoted in Pío García, *Las Fuerzas Armadas y el golpe de estado en Chile*, Siglo Veintiuno Editores, Mexico, 1974, pp. 458–59.
7. Quoted in Alain Labrousse, op. cit., pp. 213–14.
8. Claudio Orrego, *El paro nacional, Vía chilena contra el totalitarismo*, Editorial del Pacífico, Santiago, 1972, pp. 47–49.
9. ITT Hearings, op. cit., Part 1, p. 44.
10. Ibid., Part 2, p. 794.
11. Ibid., Part 1, p. 268.
12. *The New York Times*, Jan. 5, 1971.
13. Ibid., Jan. 6, 1971.
14. Hearings before the Subcommittee on Inter-American Affairs of the Committee on Foreign Affairs, House of Representatives, *United States and Chile During the Allende Years, 1970–1973*, U.S. Government Printing Office, Washington, D.C., 1975, p. 5.

7 The Chilean Commercial Agencies in the United States

1. *The New York Times*, Sept. 8, 1972; also *The Wall Street Journal*, Sept. 13, 1972.
2. Quoted in a pamphlet, *The Kennecott Case, the unfinished story of an embargo*, Quimantú, no date given, p. 9.
3. *The Wall Street Journal*, Sept. 13, 1972.

8 Running the Economy—November 1970 to Mid-1972

1. ODEPLAN, *Informe económico anual*, op. cit. 1970, p. 79.
2. "La política de transformación y el corto plazo," extracto de la exposicion del Ministro de Economía, Pedro Vuscovic ante el Ciap, Washington, 22 de

febrero 1971, as published in Gonzalo Martner, editor, *El pensamiento económico del Gobierno de Allende*, Editorial Universitaria, Santiago, 1971, p. 105.

3. J. Ann Zammitt, editor, *The Chilean Road to Socialism*, University of Texas Press, Austin, 1973, p. 50.

4. "Renegotiation of Chile's Foreign Debt," *Chile Economic Notes*, issued by Corporación de Fomento de la Producción (CORFO), New York, Nov. 23, 1971.

5. "Chile—Survey of Economic Development and Prospects," IMF Staff Paper, Washington, D.C., Feb. 25, 1972, p. 3.

6. Oficina de Planificación Nacional, *Informe económico anual 1971*, Editorial Universitaria, Santiago, p. 49. Also Banco Central, *Boletín Mensual*, 1971, p. 157.

7. IMF Staff Paper, op. cit., pp. 11–12.

8. J. Ann Zammitt, op. cit., pp. 85–86.

9. Banco Central, *Boletín Mensual*, 1972, passim.

10. "Why Allende Failed," *Challenge*, The Magazine of Economic Affairs, May-June 1974, p. 8.

11. J. Ann Zammitt, op. cit., p. 86.

12. "En pie de guerra para defender nuestra revolución y seguir avanzando," Informe al Pleno, in *El Partido Comunista de Chile en el Gobierno de la Unidad Popular*, Información Documental de América Latina, Caracas, 1974, pp. 143–45.

13. Report on article in *El Mercurio* in Rubén Corvalán Vera, *Economic and Financial Survey*, Carta Semanal, Santiago, May 14, 1972, pp. 3–4.

9 Structural Economic Transformation

1. *El Programa de la Unidad Popular*.

2. Eduardo Novoa Monreal, op. cit., pp. 96–98.

3. Ibid., p. 109.

4. Ibid., p. 52.

5. Ibid., p. 144.

6. Ibid., pp. 281, 445–46.

7. *The New York Times*, July 19, 1971.

8. *The Wall Street Journal*, Oct. 14, 1971.

9. "Resumen del informe soviético sobre la Gran Minería del Cobre," *El Mercurio*, July 23, 1971.

10. ODEPLAN, *Informe económico anual*, 1971, op. cit., p. 32.

11. Quoted by Reinaldo Ruiz Valdés, "El area de propriedad social," *Gestión Económic*, November-December 1972, University of Chile, Valparaiso, p. 16.

12. Herbert E. Meyer, "Dow Picks Up the Pieces in Chile," *Fortune*, April 1974, p. 148.

13. Instituto de Economía, Universidad de Chile, *La economía chilena en 1971*, 1972, pp. 574–76.

14. "The Constitutional and Legal Aspects of the Popular Government's Policy," by Eduardo Novoa Monreal in J. Ann Zammitt, op. cit., pp. 29–30.

15. "La clase obrera en las condiciones del Gobierno Popular," *El Siglo*, June 5, 1972.

16. Quoted in Rubén Corvalán Vera, *Economic and Financial Survey*, Enfoques Políticos, Santiago, May 15, 1972.

10 Land Reform

1. "The Agrarian Policy of the Popular Government" by Jacques Chonchol in J. Ann Zammitt, op. cit., p. 107.
2. ODEPLAN, *Informe económico anual 1971,* op. cit., p. 94.
3. Solon Barraclough and J.A. Fernández (Coordinators of study), *Diagnóstico de la reforma agraria chilena,* Siglo veintiuno editores, s.a., Mexico City, 1971, pp. 37–38, 71–75.
4. Ibid., p. 196–97.
5. *The New York Times,* May 9, 1972.
6. *The London Economist,* March 11, 1972, pp. 29–30.
7. *La economía chilena en 1971,* op. cit., p. 513.
8. Figures from President Allende's *Third Message to the Full Congress,* quoted in Stefan de Vylder, *Chile 1970–1973, The Political Economy of the Rise and Fall of the Unidad Popular,* Unga Filosofers Förlag, Stockholm, 1974, p. 195.
9. "Diagnóstico de la reforma agraria chilena (noviembre 1970-junio 1972)," *Cuadernos de la Realidad Nacional—CEREN,* abril 1973, p. 75.
10. Solon Barraclough and J.A. Fernández, op. cit., p. 38.
11. J. Ann Zammitt, op. cit., p. 134.
12. Solon Barraclough and J.A. Fernández, op. cit., p. 179–80.
13. Ibid., pp. 124–25, 160–63.

11 Political Developments—November 1970 to Mid-1972

1. *Covert Action in Chile, 1963–1973,* op. cit., p. 36.
2. *El Mercurio,* Dec. 15, 1970.
3. Ibid., Dec. 16, 1970.
4. *The New York Times,* Sept. 20, 1974.
5. *Covert Action in Chile, 1963–1973,* op. cit., p. 59.
6. *El Mercurio,* Dec. 13, 1970.
7. Ibid., Dec. 15, 1970.
8. Article in *Clarín,* quoted in Luis Maira, *Chile: dos años de la Unidad Popular,* Empresa Editora Nacional Quimantú, Santiago, 1973, p. 104.
9. *El Mercurio,* Jan. 13, 1971.
10. *Covert Action in Chile, 1963–1973,* op. cit., p. 29.
11. Quoted from *Ercilla* in David Morris, *We Must Make Haste Slowly,* Vintage Books, New York, 1973, p. 145.
12. *El Mercurio,* Jan. 14, 1971.
13. Quoted in David Morris, op. cit., p. 147.
14. *El Mercurio,* Jan. 13, 1971.
15. *Covert Action in Chile, 1963–1973,* op. cit., p. 28.
16. *El Mercurio,* Jan. 7, 1971.
17. *Reuters* dispatch, March 22, 1971.
18. *ANSA* (Italian News Agency) dispatch, April 15, 1971.
19. *Agence France Press* dispatch, May 6, 1971.
20. Ibid., May 14, 1971.
21. Speech of June 16, 1971, from extract in Gonzalo Martner, editor, *El pensamiento económico del Gobierno de Allende,* op. cit., p. 94.
22. *Covert Action in Chile, 1963–1973,* op. cit., pp. 27, 59.
23. *El Mercurio,* June 10, 1971.
24. Ibid., June 25, 1971.

25. Quoted in Mario Toer, *La "Vía Chilena," un balance necesario*, Editorial Tiempo Contemporaneo, Buenos Aires, 1974, pp. 144–45.
^6. *Covert Action in Chile, 1963–1973*, op. cit., pp. 29–30, 60.
27. Ibid., pp. 37–39.
28. *The New York Times*, Sept. 24, 1974.
29. *Cuba-Chile, Encuentro simbólico entre dos procesos históricos*, Ediciones Políticas, La Habana, 1972, p. 265. (Also, *Fidel in Chile*, International Publishers, New York, 1972.)
30. Ibid., pp. 133, 268–69, 278–79, 345–48.
31. *The New York Times*, Sept. 24, 1974.
32. Ibid., Dec. 1, 1971.
33. *Compañero Presidente, Ideario Político de Salvador Allende*, Editorial Samoc, Mexico, 1973, pp. 155–157.
34. All quotes of Fidel Castro from *Cuba-Chile, Encuentro simbólico entre dos procesos históricos*, op. cit., 439, 474–77, 480–81, 486, 499, 510–11, 517.
35. *Covert Action in Chile, 1963–1973*, op. cit., p. 38.
36. Ibid., pp. 28, 38.
37. Ibid., p. 39.
38. *¿Como llegaron las Fuerzas Armadas a la accion del 11 de septiembre 1973?*, special supplement published by *El Mercurio*, Sept. 11, 1974, giving a quasi-official account of the background of the coup.
39. Comité Nacional de la Unidad Popular, "Nuevas tareas para el Gobierno Popular y el pueblo chileno," *El Siglo*, Feb. 10, 1972.
40. *Covert Action in Chile, 1963–1973*, op. cit., p. 60.
41. "General Pinochet, El hombre del 'Dia D,' Diálogo con *Ercilla*," from undated photostat of clippings. Contents indicate that the story appeared approximately six months after the coup.
42. *¿Como llegaron las Fuerzas Armadas a la acción del 11 de septiembre 1973?*, op. cit., p. 5.

12 Running the Economy—July 1972 to September 1973

1. Rubén Corvalán Vera, *Economic and Financial Survey*, Chile News, Aug. 14, 1972, p. 5.
2. *El Mercurio*, Sept. 2, 1972.
3. "Exposición del Ministro de Hacienda, don Orlando Millas, a la Comisión Mixta del Presupuesto, 15 Noviembre 1972," Boletín Mensual del Banco Central, 1972, p. 1423.
4. Ibid., pp. 1423–1424.
5. *The New York Times*, Sept, 20, 1974.

13 Political Developments—July 1972 to the Coup

1. *El Siglo*, August 1, 1972.
2. "El Partido Nacional y la situación politica actual de Chile," Texto del Informe de Fernando Maturana, given in Rubén Corvalán Vera, *Economic and Financial Survey*, Enfoques Politicos, July 10, 1972.
3. *¿Como llegaron las Fuerzas Armadas a la acción del 11 septiembre 1973?*, op. cit., p. 5.

4. Pío García, editor, *La Fuerzas Armadas y el golpe de estado en Chile*, Siglo Veintiuno, Mexico, Buenos Aires and Madrid, 1974, pp. 15–16.
5. Philip Agee, *Inside The Company: CIA Diary*, Penguin Books, Great Britain, 1975, p. 309.
6. Claudio Orrego, op. cit., p. 12.
7. Ibid., p. 21.
8. *El Mercurio*, Oct. 23, 1972.
9. See text of law, *El Mercurio*, Oct. 22, 1972.
10. Pío García, op. cit., p. 91.
11. *Covert Action in Chile, 1963–1973*, op. cit., p. 60.
12. Declaration of Nov. 8, 1972, quoted in Mario Toer, op. cit., p. 181.
13. Quoted from *Ercilla*, November 1972, in Robert Moss, *Chile's Marxist Experiment*, David & Charles, Newton Abbot, England, 1973, p. 167.
14. Texto de la Constitución Política de la Re · ´ ʰlic· de Chile, Article 72, 5a.
15. Dieter Nohlen, op. cit., p. 285.
16. Ibid., p. 268.
17. Address by Pinochet on the first anniversary of his becoming Commander-in-chief of the Army, *El Mercurio*, Aug. 24, 1974.
18. *¿Como llegaron las Fuerzas Armadas a la acción del 11 septiembre 1973?*, op. cit., p. 6.
19. *Covert Action in Chile, 1963–1973*, op. cit., p. 60.
20. Jorge Insunza, "Informe a la asamblea del Partido Comunista de Chile," *El Siglo*, 25 April, 1973.
21. *The New York Times*, Sept. 27, 1973.
22. Insunza, op. cit., *El Siglo*, 25 April, 1973.
23. *El Mercurio*, Edición Internacional, 9–15 abril, 1973.
24. *El Mercurio*, Edición Internacional, 28 mayo–3 junio, 1973.
25. *Chile Hoy*, No. 64, Aug. 31, 1973.
26. *El Mercurio*, Edición Internacional, 25 junio–1 julio, 1973.
27. *¿Como llegaron las Fuerzas Armadas a la acción del 11 septiembre 1973?*, op. cit., pp. 9–10.
28. V.I. Lenin, *Collected Works*, Vol. 11, 1962, Progress Publishers, Moscow, p. 174.
29. *¿Como llegaron las Fuerzas Armadas a la acción del 11 de septiembre 1973?*, op. cit., p. 12.
30. *El Rebelde*, No. 97, Aug. 23–Sept. 3, 1973.
31. *El Mercurio*, Edición Internacional, 6–12 agosto, 1973.
32. Pío García, op. cit., pp. 267–83.
33. *El Mercurio*, Edición Internacional, 23–29 julio and 6–12 agosto, 1973.
34. *¿Como llegaron las Fuerzas Armadas a la acción del 11 de septiembre 1973?*, op. cit., pp. 11–14.
35. *El Mercurio*, Edición Internacional, 6–12 agosto, 1973.
36. Ibid., 13–19 agosto, 1973.
37. *¿Como llegaron las Fuerzas Armadas a la acción del 11 de septiembre 1973?*, op. cit., pp. 10, 15.
38. *El Mercurio*, Aug. 24, 1974.
39. Supplement to *El Mercurio*, September 1973.
40. Joan Garcés, *El estado y los problemas tácticos en la Gobierno de Allende*, Siglo Veintiuno, Buenos Aires, 1973, pp. 48–49. (Joan Garcés worked in the office of the presidency.)

14 Some Conclusions

 1. V.I. Lenin, "Theses For A Report At The October Conference of the Petrograd Organization, etc.," *Collected Works,* Progress Publishers, Moscow, 1964, Vol. 26, p. 143.
 2. *Revolution and Counter Revolution in Germany,* in Karl Marx and Frederick Engels, *Selected Works,* Progress Publishers, Moscow, 1973, Vol. 1, p. 361.
 3. *Prensa Latina* dispatch, Jan. 18, 1973.
 4. "Letter to L. Kugelmann, April 17, 1871, in K. Marx and F. Engels, *Selected Works,* International Publishers, New York, 1968, p. 681.
 5. Testimony before Senate Committee, quoted in *The New York Times,* Sept. 16, 1974.
 6. Testimony March 29, 1973, at *Hearings Before the Senate Subcommittee on Multinational Corporations,* op. cit., p. 406.
 7. Testimony Sept. 20, 1973, at hearings before the Subcommittee on Inter-American Affairs of the House of Representatives, *United States and Chile During the Allende Years, 1970–1973,* U.S. Government Printing Office, Washington, D.C., 1975, p. 96.
 8 Testimony before Senate Foreign Relations Committee, quoted in *The New York Times,* Sept. 8, 1974.
 9. *The New York Times,* Sept. 16, 1973.
10. *Foreign Affairs,* January 1974, pp. 324, 332.
 1. *The New York Times,* Sept. 17, 1974.
12. *Covert Action in Chile, 1963–1973,* op. cit., pp. 10–39.
13. *Alleged Assassination Plots Involving Foreign Leaders,* op. cit., pp. 225, 232.
14. Excerpts from the final report of the U.S. Senate Intelligence Committee, *The New York Times,* April 27, 1976. (My italics—E.B.)
15. *Alleged Assassination Plots Involving Foreign Leaders,* op. cit., p. 256.
16. 18 U.S.C.§2.
17. *The Pentagon Papers,* as published by *The New York Times,* Bantam Books, New York, 1971, p. 195.
18. Ibid., pp. 162, 216, 217–18.
19. Arthur M. Schesinger, Jr., *A Thousand Days: John F. Kennedy in the White House,* Houghton & Mifflin Company, Boston, 1965, p. 997.
20. *United States and Chile During the Allende Years, 1970–1973,* op. cit., p. 97.
 1. *Covert Action in Chile, 1963–1973,* op. cit., p. 40.
 2. "The View from Langley," *The End of Chilean Democracy,* Seabury Press, New York, 1973, pp. 162–64. (My italics—E.B.)
23. Introduction by F. Engels to Karl Marx's *The Class Struggle in France, 1848–1850,* International Publishers, New York, 1964, p. 21.
24. *Left-Wing Communism—An Infantile Disorder,* V.I. Lenin, *Selected Works* in one volume, International Publishers, New York, 1971, p. 545.

Index